About the Author

CARL SFERRAZZA ANTHONY is the author of the two-volume *First Ladies* and provides frequent media commentary on the subject. His work has appeared in the *New York Times, Los Angeles Times, American Heritage, Details, Town & Country, Cigar Aficionado, Smithsonian,* and *Vanity Fair.* His other books include a biography of Florence Harding and books about America's First Families.

ALSO BY CARL SFERRAZZA ANTHONY

First Ladies: The Saga of the Presidents' Wives and Their Power

As We Remember Her

Jacqueline Kennedy Onassis
in the Words of Her
Family and Friends

CARL SFERRAZZA ANTHONY

Perennial

An Imprint of HarperCollins*Publishers*

For Sully

A hardcover edition of this book was published in 1997 by HarperCollins Publishers.

First Perennial edition published 2003.

Designed by Ruth Lee

The Library of Congress has catalogued the hardcover edition as follows:

Anthony, Carl Sferrazza.
    As we remember her: Jacqueline Kennedy Onassis in the words of her family and friends / by Carl Sferrazza Anthony. — 1st ed.
      p.   cm.
    ISBN 0-06-017690-3
    1. Onassis, Jacqueline Kennedy, 1929–1994—Quotations. 2. Celebrities—United States—Quotations. 3. Presidents' spouses—United States—Quotations. I. Title.
    CT275.0552A68 1997
    973.922'092—dc21   96-47518

ISBN 0-06-054857-6 (pbk.)

03 04 05 06 07 RRD 10 9 8 7 6 5 4 3 2 1

CONTENTS

ACKNOWLEDGMENTS

I WOULD LIKE TO THANK RICHARD SULLIVAN, WHO WORKED INTENSELY FROM April to August 1995 as my sole research assistant for data and photographs, painstakingly transcribed over two hundred hours of taped interviews, and finally read the entire manuscript for corrections and improvements. Melody Miller was also helpful in providing her own analysis of material I discussed with her and was personally quite supportive throughout. Lisa Drew, my friend and past editor, also assisted in providing her analysis and perspective.

My thanks to editors Suzanne Oaks and Leigh Ann Sackrider, assistants Ashok Chaudhari and Janet Dery, and attorney Bob Lasky.

At the Kennedy Library, I would like to thank Brad Gerratt, director; Charles Daly, director of the JFKL Foundation; Will Johnson, head archivist; and most especially the dynamic duo of the research room—Maura Porter and June Payne. In Audiovisual, Alan Goodrich, chief, and Donna Cotterell gave incredible support and guidance as I went through some forty thousand images. Thanks also to Jim Cedroni and Jim Hill. Alan's knowledge was absolutely invaluable.

I would also like to personally thank: James Harden, who assisted by researching obscure and difficult-to-find materials; Raul Escuza, who provided computer expertise and programming; Ellen McDougall of the Senate historian's office, who provided resources and friendship; John Cantrell, deputy editor of *Town and Country*, for source guidance; Kathy O'Callaghan of the Municipal Arts Society; Addison Mullen, my host in Boston; Evan Smoak, my host in New York; John McGuire, my host in Los Angeles; Ann Garside of the Peabody Institute; Kathleen Bouvier; Eric Rauscher of Archive Photos; Maria Danielle Sferrazza, who provided research in Paris; Marc Sferrazza, who provided clipping materials from New York; Angelina Martirano; Mr. and Mrs. Carl Sferrazza, for their support; Gail Fleshman, for providing access to the letters to her uncle Zeke Hearin from over the years; Bob and Donnie Radcliffe, for their hospitality at their Eastern Shore home while I researched; Shirley Langhauser and Andrea Harris at the Miss Porter's School archives, for their thorough research efforts; L. C. Chapman, cabdriver extraordinaire; Paul Shure, who provided memorabilia from the 1960 election; Byron Kennard, Meredith Burch, Ed Purcell, and David MacKay, for their levity and general chumminess.

Finally, without the trust, cooperation, and efforts of those individuals who provided their reminiscences, this book quite literally would not exist. I thank them (and one individual who requested anonymity) together, and individually in the Sources, under Author Interviews.

INTRODUCTION

Person versus Persona

Jackie would have preferred to be just herself, but the world insisted that she be a legend too. She never wanted public notice, in part I think because it brought back painful memories of an unbearable sorrow, endured in the glare of a million lights.

—SENATOR EDWARD M. KENNEDY, BROTHER-IN-LAW

SOME PEOPLE WILL ALWAYS INSIST ON THINKING OF HER AS SAINT JACKIE THE Mysterious, Wonder of the World. Eighteen months after her death, a magazine noted with hyperbolic enchantment, "Few lives are better documented, yet remain so elusive. With Jackie's death and the passage of time, the question is still unanswered: Who is the real woman behind the myth?" The curious article is incongruously titled, "The Private Jackie."

That every notable person should be expected to reveal every feeling about everything that has happened to him or her is unrealistic: such a reaction would be contradictory to human nature. Every person is a mystery. Not just Jacqueline Onassis. Nobody ever knows everything about someone. None of us reveal our every thought and reaction to every encounter. Perhaps the difference is that so many people for so long seemed to want to know everything about her. If so, then the mystery is not with Jackie.

What seemed like a complicated character to the outside world was someone quite basic in what she liked and did, and the manner in which she portrayed herself. She kept to her values easily. Her simplicities were her elegance. She never curried favor. She knew what she liked and how she felt about things. She had no exaggerations.

—PAMELA HARRIMAN, FRIEND

Jackie Kennedy on the presidential yacht, Newport, 1962.

With the highly publicized sale of her effects, the international press went into a frenzy, somehow shocked that this icon had personal items, piles of baskets, a living room with old books and magazines—a real life. She had already been installed in the modern pantheon, but owning something that she used or touched seemed to make her real, prove that she was a person. The media had managed to continue to make her—even posthumously—its best cottage industry. And yet, the public certainly had a need for placing her on that pedestal.

For herself, it was at times flattering and encouraging to be placed on that pedestal, but it was a place where only a statue, not a person, could exist. When a friend remarked that her 1968 remarriage would in fact "knock you off your pedestal," Jackie Kennedy replied, "It's better than freezing there."

Jackie herself understood the human need for the process of mystifying mortals. If she was to be remembered at the time of her death not as a person but as a mythological figure, then it was appropriate that the icon of her at John F. Kennedy's funeral was the one most persistently recalled. One book project that quite absorbed her was *The Power of Myth*, a transcribed interview of Joseph Campbell by Bill Moyers, Jackie being "the prime mover in the publication," said editor Betty Sue Flowers. In the book's introduction, Jackie's own historical destiny is revealed in her organizing the funeral, "a ritualized occasion of the greatest social necessity," said Campbell, which reestablished "the sense of solidarity. Here was an enormous nation, made those four days into a unanimous community, all of us participating in the same way, simultaneously, in a single symbolic event." Moyers felt that such orchestrated images, like the persona of Jackie at that event, would forever "line the walls of our interior system of belief like shards of broken pottery in an archeological site."

The irony was that Jackie was as human as they come, truly a good person but far from a saint. She irritated her friends, angered her family, confounded her colleagues, and fell prey to all the common vanities, selfishnesses, and insecurities. At a basic level, apart from the wealth and privilege she was born into and the glamour and fame bestowed on her, Jackie was not unlike the millions of other women of her generation who emulated her: influenced by parents and husbands on what was the "right" course for a college graduate and wife of the 1950s and limiting her choices, despite her talents. The incredible material comfort provided by her second marriage proved to her not only that money did not equate with happiness but that it also couldn't substitute for pride of family and satisfaction of accomplishment. The conscious efforts she made in raising her children, nurturing her friendships, developing relationships with her grandchildren, and avidly pursuing a late-blooming career belatedly brought her the full range of life's genuine joys.

Jackie had physical courage and the courage of her convictions. She had determination combined with natural self-discipline, a sense of purpose with a desire for perfection and capacity for concentration. The object of her caring always could depend on her, and knew where she stood. She instinctively gave credit to others, including the horses she rode. There was generosity, both materially and of her time, and if she hinted she would do something, she did.
—YUSHA AUCHINCLOSS, STEPBROTHER

Perhaps what was at the core of the public fascination about her was the unspoken recognition that while she was obviously just another person coping with crises like parental divorce, murder, moments of marital discord, even cancer, she was also remarkable and unusual, not by virtue of fame, wealth, or glamour but because of her own very real, hard-earned efforts. Perhaps she became a public figure worthy of emulation because people, by acknowledging her simultaneous commonality and unusualness, recognized possibilities within themselves.

> She was unique in that she was the role model for two generations simultaneously. Both mothers and daughters watched her every move to try to emulate her grace at entertaining, her elegance of dress, her commitment to our culture and history, and her devotion to her family.
>
> —MELODY MILLER, KENNEDY SPOKESPERSON,
> WHO WORKED IN JACKIE KENNEDY'S OFFICE

Perhaps she was ultimately more useful to the American people as a symbol, for what she represented, than as a person like everyone else, who through nothing short of hard work had been successful at her career. In the aftermath of recollections following her death in 1994, it seemed that the person was being usurped by the persona. There was surprise when some friends revealed that—beyond looking great in clothes—she was a highly intelligent woman who through intensive reading and thought had developed her own historical, artistic, literary, and political sensibilities.

After having researched and written about those accomplishments in tandem with her in 1987 and 1989, it became clear to me that some effort should be made to at least leave an informal record of who she was as a person and what she did. I, for one, had been intrigued by her own struggles with writing and ultimately her decision that she would rather edit. I was not a friend of hers but rather someone she knew. I did know some of her friends and family, and it was to them that I turned in this effort, to record her as she was, in combination with her own words, written and spoken, reflecting on herself and the changing worlds around her.

Although the general effort was to follow the format of the book *As We Remember Him*, about President Kennedy, compiled after his death, two great differences about Jackie's life made that impossible. First, her life was twenty years longer than his own and filled with a wider variety of change, and second, she and those who were closest to her rigidly saw her as a genuinely private citizen. Many of those friends and family members, torn by the question of the human being versus the historical figure, were ambivalent about speaking of her. Ultimately, then, this book is an attempt not to record every fact and detail, or address every rumor and speculation about Jackie, but to try and capture some of the more important things about her as a person, and how that person managed to use the status she both accepted through marriage and then earned on her own, to create a public legacy. In trying to present her as closely as possible to the way she saw herself, this book does not intend to portray an icon. And, since it is told through her own recollections, and the voices of those who loved and protected her, it is an affectionate view.

> I loved her very much. Extremely intelligent, helpful to those she knew. There was a quality about her that was winning. She drew people to her. I felt almost as if she could absorb my life. She was not selfish or demanding. She gave as good as she got, but she was so strong a personality and had such charisma about her, that one felt compelled and drawn to her, one did it to oneself. She never demanded—you brought it to her. It was that aura, it was that moment.
> —Kitty Carlisle Hart, friend

That she was "the world's most famous woman" is secondary in this work to the simple fact that she never laid claim to being an icon untouched by the experiences of every other mortal. In fact, she constantly laid claim to being just a person. For Jacqueline Bouvier Kennedy Onassis, however, fate, outside circumstances, events, made her a public figure, eventually a global one; fate forced her into people's minds, the pages of history, and then people's imaginations. In that final process, speculation was dragged along. While understanding the human need for myth, she also quickly understood that it was her very own life which people insisted on mythologizing, but which *she* had to live, and had the right to choose how to live it, as was best for her. In so understanding that, she kept her sense of self in perspective and proportion to the routine of her own everyday life. She went about her business not as an historical figure but as a person. In doing that, she generally did as most people would attempt to do: she kept her own counsel.

One night in Hyannis Port, around the large family dinner table at the big house, Jack Kennedy was troubled because Jackie had fallen silent after some political argument. He turned to her and said, "Penny for your thoughts?"

She turned back with a smile. "But they're my thoughts, Jack, and they wouldn't be my thoughts anymore if I told them. Now would they?"

ONE

The Young Woman
1929–1942

I only care for the lonely sea,
And I always will, I know,
For the love of the sea is born in me
It will never let me go.

—Jacqueline Lee Bouvier, 1942

SHE WAS SUPPOSED TO BE BORN IN THE MIDDLE OF JUNE, BUT SHE WAS BORN IN late July. She was supposed to be born in the city, but she was born by the sea. It seemed as if she came into the world precisely when and where she wanted to.

Jacqueline Lee Bouvier was born in the small and newly constructed Southampton Hospital, near the south shore of Long Island, New York. Twenty-one-year-old Mrs. Bouvier, the former Janet Norton Lee, was spending the summer weekend in nearby East Hampton as a short break from the past six weeks at home waiting for the baby to arrive. Finally, on the afternoon of July 28, 1929, the small but sturdy woman was rushed to the hospital, where her eight-pound daughter was born.

Everyone was excited, waiting for word from the hospital. When the baby came home, the family rushed over and surrounded her.

—JOHN DAVIS, COUSIN

Jackie Bouvier, sister Lee, and Ryan cousins, circa 1930s.

It had been a hot Sunday; "record throngs at local beaches," reported the *New York Times*. That same day, a St. Louis pilot won an airplane race—flying five hundred hours, refueling only thirty-five times; Aristide Briand became the new premier of France; and plans were finally developed to have a lower reservoir in Central Park converted into a children's playing field, while retaining the larger reservoir uptown. The Coolidge administration had just ended five months before, but prosperity was continuing under the new president, Herbert Hoover. More American families of all classes now owned radios to keep up with the news. Model T Fords were already congesting the bridges and avenues of Manhattan, and although blacktop now stretched all the way out to East Hampton from the city, on Montauk Highway, many of the roads in the social hamlet were still unpaved dirt roads, winding under bowers of wisteria and banked by overgrown beach rosebushes and honeysuckle, swarming with bumblebees.

It was Jackie's first summer at the shore.

PARENTS

*J*ACK BOUVIER WAS A WALL STREET STOCKBROKER, BUT HE STILL RACED ABOUT in a black Lincoln convertible as he had since graduating from Yale. He was nicknamed "Black Jack" because of his jet-black hair and dark, perpetual tan. Others called him "The Sheik" because his exaggerated manner resembled that of Rudolph Valentino. "A most devastating figure," his daughter Jackie recalled. His twin sisters, Maude and Michelle, were close friends of the strong-willed Janet Lee, a noted equestrian, educated at Sweet Briar College and Barnard. Jack was sixteen years her senior.

> He was powerful, wealthy, exotic and undeniably, darkly attractive. . . . He was always rushing off. To some meeting of importance, or the Yale game, or the Dempsey fight, or the horse show at the Garden. Most of the time, he was just dropping off some stunning young lady, or about to pick one up. If the twins' friend [Janet Norton Lee] was particularly lucky, he would pause in the doorway, flash his heart-melting smile, and whisper the word, "Hullo." Then he would vanish. He was dashing out of the house one day when he stopped dead in his tracks. However long it had been since he had last seen Janet, it had been time enough for biological magic to have turned her into full and deliciously admirable womanhood. There, across the room she stood, in all

her glory. Frozen, Jack eyed her, then leapt into the breach of courtship without another moment's hesitation. As he proceeded along familiar lines with his usual earnestness, the twins looked at one another in bewilderment. It must have been overwhelming for the girl as well. . . . It didn't take long before they became engaged.

—KATHLEEN BOUVIER, NIECE-IN-LAW OF JACK BOUVIER

Janet married Jack on July 7, 1928, at the Bouvier family's East Hampton church, St. Philomena. The wedding was quintessential high society in the Jazz Age, a page out of F. Scott Fitzgerald, with bridesmaids in yellow chiffon dresses and green straw hats. An afternoon reception for five hundred followed at the Lily Pond Lane estate that Janet's parents had rented for the summer. Dance music was provided by the popular Meyer Davis orchestra. After a wedding night at the Plaza Hotel in New York, the Bouviers set off on a European honeymoon, crossing the Atlantic on the SS *Aquitania*—the luxury liner the Joseph P. Kennedys sailed on two months later. Upon their return the newlyweds initially set up house in Jack Bouvier's former bachelor apartment at 375 Park Avenue. At East Hampton, they hosted their first party at the Devon Yacht Club, turning it into a speakeasy of sorts. To attend, one had to give the passwords "Jack and Janet," a whimsical reference to the speakeasy "Jack and Charlie's," later to be known more famously as the 21 Club.

THE BOUVIERS AND LASATA

THE FIRST OF JACKIE'S PATERNAL ANCESTORS TO SETTLE IN AMERICA WAS Michel Bouvier, who arrived from France in 1815. He was a descendant of tradesmen from Pont Saint-Esprit in the Provence region of southern France, near Marseilles, on the Rhone River. Bouvier immigrated to Philadelphia, where he earned his fortune as a master carpenter and cabinetmaker. Later, he dealt in real estate. The family were listed in the first edition of the Social Register published before the century's end, but by then they had turned to law and investment. Jackie's father, great-grandson of Michel, was born and raised in Nutley, New Jersey, but came of age in New York, where he eventually bought a seat on the stock exchange. By the time Jackie was christened, three days before Christmas at New York's St. Ignatius Loyola Church, Jack's brother, Bud, had died. His son, Michel, known as "Mish," was shortly thereafter adopted in name by his uncle Jack. In turn, Mish became Jackie's godfather.

Besides Jack and his twin sisters, there was also Edith, married to Phelan Beale. Aunt Edie Beale would remain an alluring and delightfully hilarious character to her nieces and nephews, "a genteely subversive influence," Jackie recalled. A theatrical singer, given to Bohemian costumes and melodramatic exaggerations, Aunt Edie was the one who first exposed young Jackie to the colorful world of artists, actors, and performers. With her droll wit, Aunt Edie was the one Jackie made a beeline for at family gatherings.

My mother was so different—she didn't want to marry—she wanted a career in singing and the stage, which was not encouraged by the Bouviers. But to the children she was beloved for her singing.

—EDITH "LITTLE EDIE" BEALE, FIRST COUSIN

The Bouviers gathered in the summers, at the family estate on Further Lane in East Hampton, called Lasata, which meant "place of peace" in Native American. Jackie lived with her parents nearby, at their rented summer cottage, Rowdy Hall at 111 Egypt Lane and later Wildmoor, on Appaquogue Road, owned by the Bouviers.

Ancient elms, old Dutch windmills, and foursquare wood houses dating back to the 1600s were and are the landmarks of East Hampton. As a little girl, Jackie loved exploring the village, always fascinated by the Lily Pond grave of Lion Gardiner, born in 1599, upon which lay a carving showing his effigy in full European military regalia.

Back at Lasata, the expansive grounds were managed by Jackie's maternal grandmother, the former Maude Frances Sergeant, daughter of a Kent, England, immigrant. There were fifteen acres of manicured lawn, privet hedges, vegetable fields, fruit orchards, a sunken Italian garden, a decorative fountain filled with goldfish, tennis courts, a stable, and a riding ring. It was at the stable that Jackie was happiest, grooming her horse and putting it through various paces. Athletic like her mother, at Lasata Jackie played tennis and baseball. Among her favorite pastimes was wandering alone through the wild blueberry bushes that stretched along the brush between Lasata and the ocean.

Jackie was always somebody I wanted to become, because she was so wonderful. There was a calmness, a serenity. She was never riled, never irritated, never raised her voice. And she was kind.

—BARBARA JOHNSON, CHILDHOOD FRIEND

Her sense of personal style—not just how to wear clothing, but her posture, movement, and manners—were ingrained early on by the Bouvier clan, but it was those childhood summers at Lasata—that place where the air was filled with the sound of seagulls and the musty scent of the nearby beach roses, running riot just beyond the hedge—that gave her a lifelong passion. Jackie would always be drawn to the seaside, to the ocean community, to life at the shore.

THE LEES AND PARK AVENUE

JACKIE'S MATERNAL GREAT-GRANDPARENTS JAMES LEE AND MARY NORTON emigrated from County Cork, Ireland, to America during the famous potato famine in the 1840s. While working as superintendent of New York City's public school system, Lee began attending medical school and eventually became a doctor. His son, James Thomas, born in 1877, in New York's Lower East Side Irish neighborhood, was another success story. Educated in the public schools and City College, "Jim" Lee then worked his way through law school, receiving his degree at Columbia University. He began working in the legal department of Chase National Bank, went on to serve as vice president, and later became president and board chairman of New York Central Bank for Savings. He earned $2 million before turning thirty and eventually befriended President Hoover.

My grandfather was the family patriarch. He was the family brain who was into education. He and Jackie were close and really had a good relationship with one another through the years. Grandpa Lee and Jackie corresponded frequently with each other—Jackie was good about that—and from him she got a strong sense of the importance of striving for excellence.

—MARY LEE (MIMI) RYAN CECIL, FIRST COUSIN

He had five sisters, and they were all fiercely devoted to him. He had three daughters, all vying for his attention. Being strong, being tough, setting his mind with determination to accomplish things—that was his greatest influence on Jackie. In fact, one of the few times he didn't get what he wanted was after he told his friend Joe Kennedy that he was planning to buy the Chicago Merchandising Mart, and spoke of it as a good investment. Joe Kennedy took the tip and bought it before James Lee could.

—JAMIE AUCHINCLOSS, HALF BROTHER

Besides Janet, Jackie's unassuming maternal grandmother, Margaret Ann Merritt Lee, had two other daughters, Winifred and Mary. Margaret Lee was remembered as having arms full of toys for her grandchildren—and loving the horse races and playing the track.

> Our grandparents were separated, but they decided not to divorce until their children were married. There had been no divorce in our family, it was unheard of then. Well, my mother married at about twenty. Janet at about all of nineteen. So then my grandparents went to Win and asked when she was getting married. And she said, "Not until I'm good and ready!" She got married at twenty-seven. By then my grandparents never divorced, they just stayed separated.
>
> —MIMI CECIL

From law and banking, James Lee went into real estate, eventually constructing the city's most famous and prestigious apartment building, 740 Park Avenue. Jackie grew up there with her parents and sister, Caroline Lee, called Lee, who was born on March 3, 1933. Their home was an eleven-room apartment, with a nursery for the two girls and a gymnasium for their father. Living at 740 meant Jackie could explore daily one of the world's most eminent parks: just two blocks west lay Central Park. For her, its winding paths, open fields, and trees to climb made it a paradise.

Jackie Bouvier, uncle and aunt Fred and Win D'Olier, aunt Mary Ryan, and grandmother Margaret Merritt Lee, Belmont Racetrack, Nassau County, New York.

HORSES, DOGS, AND PUBLICITY

By JULY 1931 THE BROWN-EYED TWO-YEAR-OLD ALREADY HAD HER NAME IN the public press. That month the *East Hampton Star* carried a report of her birthday party of games, pony rides, and Jack Horner pie. A month later, little Miss Bouvier was again in the headlines, this time for her poised promenade with Hootchie, a Scottish terrier, her first pet, in the 1931 East Hampton dog show. In fact, during her childhood she would often attract attention because of her love of animals, a characteristic she acquired from Janet, who first put Jackie on a horse at the age of one.

Described by a friend as "smart, aggressive as hell, a daredevil rider who believed in self-reliance," Janet's equestrienne passion certainly rubbed off on her daughter. It was not just a matter of grooming a horse the right way, or saddling it correctly. It was a subtle process, requiring a balance between a gentle and strong hand in controlling the horse, maneuvering it carefully, and teaching it who is in charge. By 1940, it was the *New York Times* that reported:

> Jacqueline Bouvier, an eleven year old equestrienne from East Hampton, Long Island, scored a double victory in the horsemanship competition. Miss Bouvier achieved a rare distinction. The occasions are few when a young rider wins both contests in the same show.

Her mother's prize chestnut mare, Danseuse, became Jackie's constant companion. In the mid-1930s, they were a familiar duo at the East Hampton stables, and at Durland's stables in New York during the winter. By the time she was seven, Jackie had won two national championships, but she didn't need a show horse to prove her talent.

> One day we were riding and Jackie got up on one of these massive workhorses, with the large feet like Clydesdales. He had never been ridden before, and tried to buck her. She stayed on, with her feet straight out, and she jumped rolls of hay on this workhorse.
>
> —MIMI CECIL

Just as she was never far from horses, she also was never far from dogs. Most adults in East Hampton were frightened of King Phar, her father's huge

Jackie Bouvier in riding outfit, East Hampton, 1932.

Harlequin Great Dane, but Jackie had a strange fearlessness in the presence of all animals. Besides the Great Dane and Scottish terrier, the family menagerie included a white rabbit kept in the bathtub, a white bull terrier, a dachshund, a Dalmatian, and a Bouvier des Flandres.

> She loved animals, and they had one of those huge black Bouvier des Flandres dogs in their apartment. One Sunday, Janet took them out to church, and when they came back this dog had destroyed everything, jumped from one table to the sofa to desks, all over and made a mess on the carpet as well. I don't think there was a lamp left standing.
>
> —MIMI CECIL

Jackie's love for animals even led her, as a child, to express her first opinion on a public issue. When her father read to her a newspaper article about the practice of vivisection, it enraged her, and together they drafted a telegram of protest against the use of animals for research to the *New York Journal-American*, which was acting as a clearinghouse for protest letters.

> I like to use the world *original* in describing Jacqueline. She was brilliant. . . gifted artistically and always good in her studies. . . . She was very intense and felt strongly about things. She had enormous individuality and sensitivity and a marvelous self-control that perhaps concealed inner tensions. I wouldn't dream of telling Jacqueline what to do. I never have.
>
> —JANET LEE AUCHINCLOSS, MOTHER

From early on, Jackie had a sense of the ridiculous, giving great potence to small things and routine occurrences, and describing important or large events in trifling ways. It was a humor often tinged with sarcasm and delivered with a poker face. She was always fascinated by somewhat eccentric people like "Beach Mary," the red-haired Irish woman who was a well-known character and who took care of the towels and blankets at the Maidstone Club, and "Fingers," the widow who wore white gloves and a bathing suit while reading her newspaper.

Once, when she was four years old, Jackie, deep in thought, meandered away from her nurse in Central Park. Spotting a policeman, she came resolutely up to him with a direct gaze, remarking offhandedly, "My nurse is lost."

BOOKS AND BALLET

*A*FTER HER FIRST YEAR OF SCHOOL AT MISS YATES'S KINDERGARTEN, JACKIE WAS enrolled in Miss Chapin's School on East End Avenue. She wore the school's green linen uniform every day—though she balked at it initially. At Chapin, described in an information booklet at the time as providing "a liberal education as well as training in the social graces," it was immediately evident that she was intelligent. Once, recalled classmate Nancy Tuckerman, all the students were sent home with the assignment of memorizing a stanza of a lengthy Tennyson poem. Jackie returned the next day and surprised her teachers by reciting from memory the *entire* ballad. A self-confessed "tomboy," she frequently found herself sent to the office of Ethel Stringfellow, the headmistress. Miss Stringfellow finally persuaded the young student to change her behavior by drawing a comparison to a willful and skilled thoroughbred: without self-discipline and training, the horse's abilities would serve no use. She was, said Jackie, "my first great moral influence."

I mightn't have kept Jacqueline, except that she has the most inquiring mind we'd had in the school in thirty-five years.

—ETHEL STRINGFELLOW

She was someone you'd never forget. She was very lively and full of mischief. She had great green eyes and wonderful hair. . . . She was one of the most interesting persons we ever had. I had to work hard to keep ahead of her.

—MARION EATON, ART TEACHER

She was the prettiest little girl, very clever, very artistic and full of the devil. She was efficient and finished her work on time and then had nothing to do until her classmates finished theirs. . . . Jacqueline Bouvier was a great mischief as a young thing, with a wonderful sense of humor, . . . sharp wit and a keen perception that sometimes poked fun at the snobbishness of her school and sheltered environment.

—MISS AFFLECK, HOMEROOM TEACHER

As a birthday present one year, Janet gave her daughter a bookcase, which Jackie quickly filled with children's books given to her by her grandparents. She was able to read before she began her formal grammar school education, and after she had read all the children's books on her shelves several times she would surreptitiously venture into the guest bedroom to find adult fiction to try and get through. She also became expert at reciting poetry. "Mummy always asked us to memorize a poem for each holiday or birthday," Jackie recalled. As a seven-year-old, for Mother's Day, she learned James Russell Lowell's "Vision of Sir Launfal," remarking in retrospect, "I must have said it in a racing monologue." In a later autobiographical account, she recalled:

> I lived in New York City until I was thirteen and spent the summers in the country. I hated dolls, loved horses and dogs, and had skinned knees and braces on my teeth for what must have seemed an interminable length of time to my family.
>
> I read a lot when I was little, much of which was too old for me. There were Chekhov and Shaw in the room where I had to take naps and I never slept but sat on the windowsill reading, then scrubbed the soles of my feet so the nurse would not see I had been out of bed. My heroes were Byron, Mowgli, Robin Hood, Little Lord Fauntleroy's grandfather, and Scarlett O'Hara.

Like many New York children of her background, each week Jackie went to Miss Hubbell's dancing class, which was held in the Colony Club's ballroom, but it was the classical ballet lessons at Miss O'Neill's in the old Metropolitan Opera House that captured her genuine fascination. Weekly, in her black leotards Jackie learned the strict movements and eventually performed in her first ballet, "Golliwog Cakewalk."

> Jacqueline accepted the life that fate offered her and did all the things that were expected of her. . . . Her outward conformity to the conventions of her class, however, belied a fiercely independent inner life. . . . From an early age Jackie displayed an originality, a perspicacity, that set her apart from her other cousins. . . . She often said things that were wise beyond her years.
>
> —JOHN DAVIS

Jackie learned the basics of French both at school and at home, where it was spoken at the dining room table. She recalled:

> When we were children our mother used to make us play a game. We sat at the table and every child had in front of them ten matches. Each time you said an English word, you'd throw a match away. [The winner held the last match.]

Without her mother's knowledge, however, Jackie had been taking some lessons in another language from her Swiss governess.

> Jackie perversely wanted to speak German. Maybe we pushed her too far [with the French], and she went the other way. I always thought she had the temperament and talent of a writer, that perhaps she could write novels, poetry, or fairy tales.
>
> —JANET LEE AUCHINCLOSS

GRAMPY JACK AND POETRY

PERHAPS THE GREATEST CHALLENGE TO JACKIE'S ABILITIES WAS HER PATERNAL grandfather, John Bouvier. Most called him "Major," because of a World War I commission, but to Jackie, he was "Grampy Jack." She visited him regularly at his apartment at 765 Park Avenue, and in the summer she would walk around the golf course with him and her father, caddying for them and running after lost golf balls. She and "Grampy" spent intensive time alone discussing his editorials, which appeared in the *East Hampton Star* on subjects ranging from aging to the Constitution.

Bouvier was not only the first in his family to go to college; he also earned a master's in political science and a law degree from Columbia, becoming one of New York's most renowned trial lawyers. He eloquently orated a patriotic address before a crowd of thousands at the Colorado state capitol, and at the dedication of the George Washington Bridge he made a speech that was carried over the radio to millions of listeners. Every Fourth of July, Jackie listened to him recite the Declaration of Independence from memory. With his walking cane, waxed mustache, pince-nez, and booming voice, Grampy made an indelible impression on Jackie, and their shared interest in writing, history, the classics, and poetry helped stimulate her intellectual curiosity. It was Grampy who wrote Jackie poetry and short stories and encouraged her to do the same. They corresponded—even though they lived in close proximity—and he critiqued her literary efforts. To her 1941 Easter poem, for example, he responded:

> Holy Writ informs me that it was a futile labor to paint the lily white, and it is equally fatuous for me to attempt the perfecting of the perfect, in any suggested emendations to your delightful lines. On the other hand, I am a bold technician, and have been impelled to suggest a few inconsequential verbal

alterations that perhaps do not add a d—n to your verses, but may, never-the-less tend to bring them within some textbook of rules of scansion. Your idea is extremely clever, and you have developed it admirably.

For Jackie's fourteenth birthday, Grampy wrote her a poem that clearly showed his love. He compared her to a youthful version of the goddess Artemis and declared that the goddess Diana, "has since crowned a modern Queen . . . bestowed on Jacqueline." She responded with her own poem "Sailing," which he sent to the *East Hampton Star*, where it was published in 1943:

When the breakers are long off Sandy Point
And angry clouds are dark'ning the sky
I could sail like that forever and ever
As I head for the open sea
With the wind in my hair and a laugh in my heart
And spray flying up at me.

Although the teenage Jackie was developing into a person who already rigidly guarded her privacy, and often preferred to be alone, she revealed herself in the cryptic short stories she wrote about animals—assigning them human characteristics, thoughts, and feelings. Her first "book" was *The Adventures of George Woofty, Esquire,* about her pet terrier's doomed romance with the "Bouvier des Flandres" dog, doomed because they came from different backgrounds. She also expressed her emotions in poetry. While her poem "Thoughts," for example, was the obvious work of a teenager, it already evidenced a strong tactility to the subtleties of nature:

I love the Autumn,
And yet I cannot say
All the thoughts and things
That make one feel this way.
I love walking on the angry shore,
To watch the angry sea;
Where summer people were before,
But now there's only me.

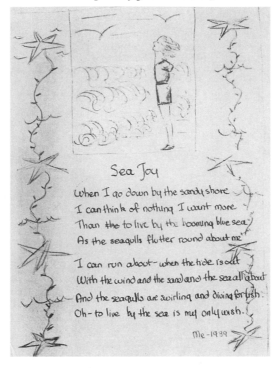

Sea Joy

When I go down by the sandy shore
I can think of nothing I want more
Than the to live by the booming blue sea
As the seagulls flutter round about me

I can run about - when the tide is out
With the wind and the sand and the sea all about
And the seagulls are swirling and diving for fish
Oh - to live by the sea is my only wish.

Me - 1939

I love wood fires at night
That have a ruddy glow.
I stare at the flames
And think of long ago.
I love the feeling down inside me
That says to run away
To come and be a gypsy
And laugh the gypsy way.
Turtle neck sweaters, autumn fires,
Swirling leaves and the sky,
Riding my horse along the hills,
To say a last good-bye.
Undressing in the cold at night,
And getting warm in bed,
Star-gazing out the window
At the cold sky overhead.
The tangy taste of apples,
The snowy mist at morn,

The wanderlust inside you
When you hear the huntsman's horn.
Nostalgia—that's Autumn,
Dreaming through September
Just a million lovely things
I always will remember.

———◆———

Grampy Jack was Jackie's first true adult friend, an affectionate figure of authority who commanded her respect. His death on January 14, 1948, was a great loss to her, and the event affected her deeply. Three years later, she wrote a short story about his funeral for a writing contest. Set in the family living room, it opened:

> I was sitting beside my grandfather's coffin looking at him as he lay in his dark blue suit with his hands folded. I had never seen death before and was ashamed that it made no more of an impression on me.

The story went on to tell of how her aunts and father argued over their inheritance; and she tartly added, "I was glad he couldn't see how his children behaved once he was dead." When a working-class man came by to pay his humble respects to Grampy with a simple handful of violets, a haughty aunt snapped them up and shoved them behind "a sheaf of gladioli," then tells Jackie to leave the room as the casket is about to be closed. Jackie concluded her story:

> I knelt on the bench beside the coffin and put the violets down inside, beneath my grandfather's elbow, where the people who came to close the coffin could not see them.

Among the personal papers that Jackie long saved were letters sent to her by Grampy Jack. One of them illustrated just how much he influenced her growing sense of herself:

> The capacity to adapt oneself to his or her environment not only marks evolutionary progress, but discloses a practical philosophy which is more wise to cultivate.

With you, happily, this process of adaptation has not been in the remotest degree difficult. . . . I discern in you more than passing evidence of leadership, but before leading others we must guide and direct ourselves. . . . Don't be pretentious or labor under false impression of indispensability. To do so spells the prig, either male or female.

A QUICK TRIP TO WASHINGTON

At Easter 1941 Janet Bouvier took her two daughters to the nation's capital for the first time. Although Jackie had traveled to Aiken, South Carolina, on vacations as a child, she recalled, in 1961, that the Washington trip was her first venture into a new world:

> The twentieth birthday of the National Gallery of Art seems almost like a birthday to me too because my love of art was born there. I remember as a young girl my first visit there. . . . We had lunch with . . . the chief curator [then] looked at the paintings and sculpture together. It was then that I first discovered one of my greatest delights—the deep pleasure experienced in looking at masterpieces of painting and sculpture. This was the first of countless visits I made to the National Gallery through the years. . . . After all, a child of any age gets his own message, his very own important emotional response from looking at a work of art. He should be encouraged to have that opportunity often, by his parents and by his teachers.

She enjoyed Mount Vernon, and going through the FBI headquarters, "because they fingerprinted me," and when the Bouvier trio arrived at 1600 Pennsylvania Avenue, Jackie recalled waiting anxiously in the long line of tourists. Once inside, however, she was crestfallen:

> I felt strangely let down by the White House. It seemed rather bleak. There was nothing in the way of a booklet to take away, nothing to teach one more about that great house and the presidents who lived there.

Later that year, she returned to Washington with Janet to visit her friend Hugh D. Auchincloss, a Standard Oil heir. His son Hugh, known as Yusha, took his new friend to the familiar monuments and to a site she would become personally associated with, in perpetuity.

Jackie Bouvier, grandfather John Bouvier, and father, Jack Bouvier, Maidstone Club, East Hampton, circa late 1930s.

We went to Arlington National Cemetery. Row after row, she went to see the generals' graves, the soldiers' graves. She was impressed with the guards at the Tomb of the Unknown Soldier and their precision. Then we stood high on the hill below the Custis-Lee Mansion. That was the first full vista she had of Washington. How impressed she was with the sweeping view.

—Yusha Auchincloss

TWO

~

Student

1942–1950

All my greatest interests—in literature and art,
Shakespeare and poetry—were formed because I was for-
tunate enough to find superb teachers in these fields.
—Jacqueline Lee Bouvier

Jackie Bouvier in the French countryside, summer 1950.

A NEW LIFE

BY THE TIME JACKIE WAS SIX YEARS OLD, JACK AND JANET BOUVIER'S MARRIAGE had begun to fall apart. Like many wealthy families, they were not able to recoup their losses from the Great Crash to maintain their accepted lifestyle. While this was a cause of friction between the couple, it was Jack Bouvier's rakish behavior that most deeply affected his wife. On October 1, 1935, the Bouviers had separated with no hope of a reconciliation. While her father moved into the residential Westbury Hotel, eventually settling permanently at 125 East Seventy-fourth Street, she and her sister and mother went to live at 1 Gracie Square. In 1940, the Bouviers divorced.

Janet Bouvier continued to raise her daughters as Catholic, taking them to church at St. Ignatius Loyola on Park Avenue, where Jackie was confirmed. Divorce among Catholics, at that time, was rare, and families were morally ostracized for it by the stricter elements of the church. Although it can only be speculated that, like many children of divorce, Jackie felt a sense of personal responsibility for her parents' breakup, it is known that after the divorce she became more subdued and introspective.

She was much more private than any other person I've ever known. She was always standing back watching the scene and, sort of, recording it in her mind.

Looking at people, seeing how they acted toward one another. She was a born observer.

—AILEEN BOWDOIN TRAIN, FAMILY FRIEND

Years later, she reflected on how fleeting her memories were of happiness between her parents, as well as the effect on her of the divorce in a Catholic family. In talking to the son of bandleader Eddy Duchin, her friend Peter Duchin, who is half Jewish, Jackie recalled:

I'll never forget the night my mother and father both came into my bedroom all dressed up to go out. I can still smell the scent my mother wore and feel the softness of her fur coat as she leaned over to kiss me good night. In such an excited voice she said, "Darling, your father and I are going dancing tonight at the Central Park Casino to hear Eddy Duchin." I don't know why the moment has stayed with me all these years. Perhaps because it was one of the few times I remember seeing my parents together. It was so romantic. So hopeful.

You know, Peter, we both live and do very well in this world of Wasps and old money and society. It's all supposed to be so safe and continuous. But you and I are not really of it. Maybe because I'm Catholic and because my parents were divorced when I was young—a terribly radical thing at the time—I've always felt an outsider in that world.

After the divorce, both parents did attempt to provide for their children's well-being. Jackie later told a close family friend that her parents tried their best to make her "feel securely loved." Certainly, the new arrangement was a relief for the children from the tension and acrimony that had previously existed between their parents. In the summer, Janet took a house in Bellport with her daughters, about forty miles from East Hampton, enabling them to see their father. In the winter, Jack would spend Sundays and holidays with his daughters, taking them to the floor of the stock exchange, jaunts to Schrafft's for sundaes, on excursions to the Fulton Fish Market, to Baker's Field, and to Radio City Music Hall matinees. He even took Jackie to a prizefight, and she sometimes joined him on his daily runs through Central Park.

Jack's love for Jacqueline and Lee was a kind more common in Latin countries than in America and reflected the predominately Latin tinge in his makeup. . . .[He] influenced his daughters profoundly . . . transmitting certain qualities to them that they would one day project to the entire world. One of these was a sense of style; . . . elusive individualism was another.

—John Davis

After the divorce my grandfather [James Lee] wouldn't speak to Uncle Jack and he forbade us to speak with him, saying, "He isn't your uncle anymore." But we used to see him at the beach and just run into his arms. You couldn't help it with Uncle Jack. He was wonderful to his daughters in giving them treats that they didn't get at home with their mother. He was much older than Aunt Janet. After the divorce, he realized he wasn't the marrying type.

—Mimi Cecil

Janet married Hugh Auchincloss in June of 1942, and Jackie and Lee thereby acquired two stepbrothers, Yusha and Tommy, and a stepsister, Nina. In time, there would be two children born to Janet and Hugh, Janet in 1945 and James in 1947.

She did have a tremendous sense of family. After Tante Janet married Uncle Hughdie and they were all together—his children from other marriages, her children—Jackie never once spoke of step-this or half-that. To Jackie they were all her brothers and sisters. There was a great mothering quality about her. She looked after Janet and Jamie when they were babies and when they were young. She was concerned with the welfare of Tommy and Nina when they went through bad times and needed help.

—Mimi Cecil

Jackie and Lee moved from New York City to the Auchincloss house, Merrywood, in McLean, Virginia, in a cool forested area with the sound of the Potomac River within earshot of Jackie's upstairs room. Summers were spent at Auchincloss's Newport estate, Hammersmith Farm. Jackie's bedroom there was painted pale yellow, with a handpainted flower frieze, and filled with white cane furniture. Both estates provided a permanent sense of belonging for her in young adulthood, as she wrote in a letter to Yusha:

I always love it so at Merrywood—so peaceful—with the river and the dogs—and listening to the Victrola. I will never know which I love best—

Hammersmith with its green fields and summer winds—or Merrywood in the snow—with the river and those great steep hills. I love them both—whichever I'm at—just as passionately as I loved the one behind.

I began to feel terribly homesick as I was driving—just like a dream—I started thinking of things like the path leading to the stables at Merrywood with the stones slipping as you ran up it—and Hammersmith with the foghorns blowing at night—all the places and feelings and happiness that bind you to a family you love—something you take with you no matter how far you go.

On the tenth anniversary of her mother's marriage to "Uncle Hughdie," as she called her stepfather, Jackie put together an anthology of limericks representing different aspects of her new life. In the introduction to the booklet, she revealed just how vital family stability was to her:

At the start, in 1942, we all had other lives and we were seven people thrown together, so many little separate units that could have stayed that way. Now we are nine—and what you've given us and what we've shared has bound us all to each other for the rest of our lives.

In September 1942, Jackie was enrolled in the seventh grade at Holton-Arms, a private girls' school in Washington, D.C., not far from Merrywood. There she followed Uncle Hughdie's advice to "take the course given by the best teacher, even if you're not interested in the subject," and with Helen Shearman, began studying Spanish and Latin—which "though I hated to admit it," she later said, "I adored." Soon she was building a collection of conversational Spanish, French, and German record albums to sharpen her linguistic skills.

Jackie had wanted her mother to remarry. When Janet arrived in Washington for a brief visit just before Auchincloss left on a War Department assignment to Jamaica, he had impulsively asked her to marry him. Jackie telephoned her mother, then called Yusha Auchincloss.

Jackie was trying to influence her mother to get married. The day before they did marry, she called me very excited. "Won't this be fun? I've always wanted a brother and now I'll get one."

—YUSHA AUCHINCLOSS

Within her new family, Jackie found an instant comradery and deep affection for Yusha. They soon developed the lifelong habit of writing each other whenever they were separated, particularly during boarding school years, and her letters were filled with comic melodrama. In one letter, Jackie wrote of a rabies quarantine and "being pursued by mad dogs." In another, she compared a house flood to "the one in the Bible," excited at the sight of familiar, valuable items "swimming aimlessly in the basement." She also wrote plenty about her rebellions as a teenager, sardonically recording Janet's "Downward Path and Sins of Tobacco" lecture. When she experimented with smoking, Jackie feared her mother's well-known temper. One time when she heard Janet's footsteps on the staircase, Jackie quickly threw her cigarette into a cushion. Janet came in and began talking to Jackie—until she smelled something burning. It was the sofa.

WORLD WAR II

DESPITE THE PRIVILEGES OF WEALTH, WITH THE ONSET OF WORLD WAR II there was no way life could be preserved as it was for any American family. For the men in Jackie's life, this often meant a career move: briefly, her stepfather served in the planning unit of the Office of Naval Intelligence in Kingston, Jamaica, and later at the War Department. Yusha joined the marines toward the end of the war. Her godfather and beloved cousin, Mish Bouvier, volunteered as a private in the army and graduated from officers' candidate school as a second lieutenant.

With the shortage of men and economy measures in effect, every stratum of American society was expected to make do. What this meant for a family as rich as the Auchinclosses was fewer gardeners and servants to run Hammersmith Farm, and fewer hands to care for the farm. Mrs. Auchincloss put the children to work and remembered that she "was always asking Jackie to come down and weed." The last working farm in Newport, Hammersmith Farm supplied the nearby naval base with tomatoes and other vegetables, fresh chickens, dairy products, and eggs during the war. Jackie was given the assignment of feeding over two thousand chickens every morning, tending to a little bull calf, collecting eggs, milking cows, picking basket after basket of apples, tilling the soil, and mowing the unending lawn. She least liked feeding the chickens because, she noted, "they were so mean to each other." The only phone for the entire farm was in the basement, and someone always had to be there to answer it. With magazines and newspapers at her side, Jackie often served on telephone duty:

She read a great deal in the newspapers, and had a lot of background history on why the Japanese really attacked Pearl Harbor and why Hitler went into Poland. She wanted to understand all the reasons, completely. She had a tremendous fascination with World War II and the French Resistance fighters. Jackie had kind of a hero worship for all the great leaders—General Eisenhower, MacArthur, Patton, de Gaulle. Even in history, her heroes were often military leaders—Alexander the Great, Charlemagne, Napoleon, George Washington, and Robert E. Lee. MacArthur became her great hero. I remember her thinking that MacArthur should be president and began a collection of presidential campaign buttons. That was just after he had returned from the Philippines. She felt he walked on water.

She liked to go down to the bay and sit by herself, and watch the battleships coming in, the destroyers, and the aircraft carriers. During the war, we even had submarine nets that came into Hammersmith Farm. Because of the naval base here, Newport was full of sailors, and all kinds of navy people. They were always streaming down through all the streets in town. We knew about a little bar in the red-light district, and we'd sneak off down there together. We were teenagers! I wouldn't let Jackie go by herself. Her sense of mischief really came out. She was very careful, of course, but she was always interested in knowing what the sailors were practicing, and she'd naturally just get into a conversation with them, putting on her very low sultry voice. Needless to say, they were quite impressed by her! I always liked to have steaks. Jackie would go and take the chickens out to the sailors, flirt innocently just a very little bit—then exchange the chickens and bring back steaks!

At sixteen, I wanted to quit school and join the marines. Jackie wrote to me that, "The marines only want men who won't give up. Your father is counting on you to continue your education, and graduate, so don't cover up feeling sorry for yourself, and expect our government to take care of you. Up or down, work hard. Brains are better than brawn. If you try your best, you'll succeed, and when you do graduate, and finally join the marines, always remember you'll have a proud sister behind you." I did as she advised.

—YUSHA AUCHINCLOSS

Raised in a Republican family, Jackie was nevertheless shaken by the news of President Franklin D. Roosevelt's death in April 1945. As she wrote her brother two days later:

I'm still so dazed. I don't know what to do. Isn't it awful about the president? I'm so worried about what will happen now that Roosevelt is dead. I think he was really great, and I know the only reason I didn't like him was because Daddy was always moaning about what he did to the stock exchange. Did you have a memorial service or something like that for him at school? Do write me and tell me that everything won't be so bad. . . I feel sorry for poor Mrs. Roosevelt. It will be awfully hard to leave the White House after all those years.

FARMINGTON

IN THE FALL OF 1944, JACKIE ENTERED MISS PORTER'S SCHOOL, A GIRL'S boarding school in Farmington, Connecticut. She was to remain there for three years. Living in the town of Farmington were Jackie's step aunt and uncle Wilmarth S. Lewis and Annie Burr Auchincloss. Lewis was an authority on Horace Walpole, the English man of belles lettres and history, and he devoted a good part of his life to collecting Walpole letters and developing a library of his works. Jackie liked to browse through "Uncle Lefty's" library, and it was he who introduced her to the works of Thomas Jefferson and Benjamin Franklin, whom, along with Diderot, he considered to be the three great geniuses of the eighteenth century.

> If you were a "Farmington" girl, you were trained not only in the classics and all kinds of literature, language, and so forth, but it was also a training for life. You were bred with deportment and elocution—how to move, how to speak, how to behave. The girls were good, they behaved, but were not particularly encouraged to pursue a college education. But what woman was back then?
> —EDITH BEALE, COUSIN AND MISS PORTER'S STUDENT

Jackie was well liked at Farmington, but the one person she spent the most time with was Nancy Tuckerman, who she had known from Chapin School days and with whom she roomed for her second and third years. In essence, Jackie was a loner. She was perfectly happy spending time in her room reading, writing poetry, and drawing. She was in the dramatic club and the riding club, and an editor of *Salmagundy*, the school newspaper. Jackie's imagination and love of adventure often got her into trouble with the headmistress: stealing cookies from the kitchen, stuffing the dormitory fire bell before a drill, dumping a pie on the lap of a teacher while clearing plates from the dining room, poking the fencing teacher during class, and instructing Yusha on how he was to get calls through to her by impersonating his father on the phone. During the winter of 1945, she trained her horse Danseuse to pull a sleigh, a teacher remembering that "she used to hitch up the old sleigh to her own horse and ask the girls to ride through the town's snow-covered Main Street." All told, Jackie and her friends were quintessential teenage girls, as illustrated in a letter to Sue Norton, her first-year roommate, then in the infirmary:

There's not much news today. Ballet was pretty good except I just watched. In prayers this morning Mr. J gave us the worst lecture on "getting our friends in the infirmary to come to the window thereby making a common cold turn into pneumonia!!!!" Tucky and I were bright red and felt so guilty. Thank heavens he didn't know it was us. If it ever happens again we will be murdered—but we might do it tonight so don't make a lot of noise if we do.

Pete says she has an offer to make you of $3.00 for your Hotchkiss [boys' preparatory school] banner—what do you think?

Miss Bond found out that Yusha called and gave me IIE— but nothing worse will happen. I wrote Clare about it so if you want the details see her note! I have a Latin test tomorrow and am petrified. I sat next to Nancy Ewing during ballet and she told me all about Sammy Robinson—WOW! B. Weld—the study head—suspects I'm writing a note so so long. . .

Jackie Bouvier, Nancy Tuckerman, and friend, with her horse Danseuse, Miss Porter's School, Farmington, Connecticut, 1945.

Jackie focused a great deal of attention at school on writing short stories and poetry for *Salmagundy*. The first stanzas of one poem, "Song of the Night Watchman," illustrate her love of solitude:

———◆———

I walk the city in the rain
Up and down my lonesome beat.
The street lamps make the puddles shine
And I hear echoes of my feet.

Through the mist the buildings blur,
Strung on strands of neon light
I smell the Cohans' Irish Stew
But cannot stop to have a bite.

Along the waterfront I go
And hear the steamers' empty sighs
The river laps against the docks
And in the fog a seagull cries.

Far away a clock is chiming.
Soon I'll hear the midnight train.
At home the family sleeps,
but I Must walk the city in the rain.

———◆———

One of Jackie's regular contributions to the newspaper was a cartoon series following a character, "Frenzied Frieda," she created. It was based on the trials and tribulations of a frenetic young woman who always found herself in trouble, imagined or real. Many of her other cartoons took on a humorously ghoulish quality, reminiscent of the famous Edward Gorey illustrations, and more frequently than not, Jackie made herself the victim of her own irreverence.

At Farmington, there was a student group known as Little Meeting, consisting of girls with qualities of strong leadership. About six times a year, Little Meeting required a senior to publicly deliver her thesis on a philosophical idea. Jackie was so honored in 1947. In what became her first of many public speeches, Jackie addressed the theme of "Be Kind and Do Your Share." She stated in part:

"Be Kind and do your share, that's all there is to it." These were the words of a great humanitarian and in them lies a whole philosophy of life. Nothing more could be asked of us than to be kind and to stick to our share of the bargain and if we could do those two things throughout our lives, we would have a great deal to be proud of.

A person can be kind in such little ways; just by stopping to think of how others feel. Doing something for a girl when she is lonely and discouraged, congratulating her on some achievement and not being bitter because you wanted the same thing—those all add up to real kindness.

To be kind one must live outside oneself—and care about the happiness of others. Kind people are givers. A lot of us are takers and we cannot help it, but if we want to change enough, we can. Where some give instinctively, takers will have to give consciously—and only by working at it can they make themselves into kinder people. And of all the qualities in man, kindness is perhaps the most desirable.

Doing our share is just as important as being kind. It means doing what we are expected to do and not disappointing those who put their trust in us. It means being honest and dependable so that someone can give us a job to do and know we'll get it done. We are not to be praised for doing our share; we are only to be blamed for not doing it.

Our whole lives will be spent with people, many of them strangers. The best time to learn how to get along with them is now—here at boarding school among our friends. If we can just live up to those few words, "Be Kind and do your share," then we should have full and contented lives. And we will be happy, because we will be making other people happy too.

Throughout high school, literature had continued to most engross Jackie, and at her graduation in June of 1947, she was presented with the Maria McKinney Memorial Award in Literature. The prize was a book of poetry by Edna St. Vincent Millay. Her last contribution to *Salmagundy* was a final salute to her school, in which she thought of "being on our own in the world from now on. . . ."

In an autobiographical account she later wrote, Jackie reminisced about her transition to adulthood:

It happened gradually over the three years I spent at boarding school trying to imitate girls who had callers every Saturday. I passed the finish line when

I learned to smoke, in the balcony of the Normandie theater in New York from a girl who pressed a Longfellow upon me then led me from the theater when the usher told her that other people could not hear the film with so much coughing going on. Growing up was not so hard.

POUGHKEEPSIE

*I*N SEPTEMBER 1947 JACKIE, HAVING SCORED IN THE HIGHEST PERCENTILE ON her college board exams, enrolled as a freshman at Vassar College in Poughkeepsie, New York. Working toward a degree in literature, Jackie befriended other young women who enjoyed writing, including Charlotte Curtis, later a *New York Times* columnist, and Selwa Showker Roosevelt, who would later become a journalist and chief of protocol in the Reagan administration.

> Her thoughtfulness of others was prominent. That might not be expected from someone coming from that background. Yet there was nothing about her that was in the least bit snobbish. She was discriminating in her tastes, but not discriminatory toward people. In fact, she was always open to new ideas, new people and new ways of thinking. For some reason, she was fascinated by my own family background and the story of my parents, Lebanese immigrants who settled in Tennessee. She would sit at the edge of the bed and ask me all kinds of questions.
>
> —SELWA SHOWKER ROOSEVELT,
> VASSAR CLASSMATE AND FRIEND

Jackie earned A+ in some of the college's most difficult courses—the history of religion and a Shakespeare class, for which she recited from memory an entire work, *Antony and Cleopatra*. The two courses gave her "the greatest intellectual pleasure," she said, but the latter was "the greatest course I have ever had," and the instructor, Helen Sandison, "the most inspired teacher." Jackie also pursued the fine arts, taking two years of studio art, learning the techniques of charcoal and pastel drawing, watercolor, gouache, and oil painting. She carried over her passion for the arts in her free time as well and joined the Dance Group, the college newspaper, and the art club and designed costumes for the Dramatic Club.

Jackie enjoyed weekend jaunts to football games and parties along the eastern seaboard, and she used the strangers she met on the train as models for characters in her short stories and letters. After one trip, she wrote of a slick

Hollywood agent who ominously regaled her with tales of "blonde dame" actresses and the "wolves" who plagued them as a lesson to her on the dangers of young women traveling alone in the presence of men—exactly the situation she had been in. In a 1948 letter, in jittery script, written on a bumpy train car, she recalled a "tall thin young congressman with very long reddish hair, the son of a [former] ambassador" on his way north from Washington who heavily flirted with her. It was a brief meeting, which she soon forgot, but not before recording the unnamed man's insistent ardency.

Later she would recall that she had "hated" the "isolated but safe little world" of small, upstate Vassar College and wished she had gone to Radcliffe, where at least she would have had access to the cultural opportunities of Boston. After her freshman year, however, Jackie broke from her corner of the East. That summer she went to Europe.

A NEW WORLD

THE SIX WEEKS JACKIE SPENT VISITING FRANCE, SWITZERLAND, ITALY, BELGIUM, and England in July and August of 1948 opened her sheltered world. Traveling with three friends—Julia Bissell and Helen and Judy Bowdoin—and chaperone Helen Shearman, she sailed to England on the *Queen Mary*, attended a Buckingham Palace garden party where they glimpsed the queen, and shook hands with Winston Churchill.

Jackie had taken her education very seriously. She had learned and memorized her European history beforehand, and read more than guidebooks. She polished her language skills, so that when she went on this trip, she was really prepared to speak in the native tongue and see everything she had studied. She knew much more than anyone about which paintings were in the Louvre. Young, educated, and interested, but it was more than preparing because while we were there, she wanted to know even more.

We landed in Southampton, and took the train to London. We could all see that they hadn't built the city back again, but were trying. It was very emotional, to see great buildings like St. Paul's Cathedral half-destroyed and just standing there. I think it was England that left the greatest impression on us because clearly they had not recovered—the food was terrible. We visited Shakespeare's home and many of the great English country houses.

In Paris, we saw every cathedral and museum. We went thoroughly through the Louvre and the Rodin museum. Jackie was particularly fascinated by the beautiful palace Versailles. We spent a lot of time at Versailles because she loved it. I remember it was wonderful weather, and we spent a lot of time walking around the palace grounds, looking at everything, and our guide and Jackie spoke French, and she was so into French history.

—HELEN BOWDOIN SPAULDING

Jackie brought back gifts from Europe—an illustrated journal of the trip for her family, a rosary blessed by the pope for a Catholic maid, and a British horse racing form for a butler who played the track. Shortly after her return, she also attended a wedding with Charles Bartlett, a friend who was the brother of the groom. Bartlett, however, had an ulterior motive for making sure she was there.

My brother got married in 1948 and I can really remember at that wedding in Long Island trying to get Jackie Bouvier across this great crowd over to meet [him]. I got her about halfway across, but then she got involved in a conversation—I introduced her to Gene Tunney who was a friend of my father, who was there. And by the time I got her across, why, he'd left.

—CHARLES BARTLETT, FRIEND

In her second year at Vassar, Jackie grew visibly bored with the constraints of campus life, calling herself a "schoolgirl among schoolgirls." She wanted to live in the city. At one point she shocked her father by telling him she was considering taking time off from college to work as a fashion model in New York. She did not quit school, but she was drawn back to the cultural life of postwar Paris—experimental theater, modern dance, jazz clubs. By the spring of her sophomore year, she was determined not just to visit Europe, but to *live* there.

LIVING IN PARIS

SEEING A NOTICE ON A COLLEGE BULLETIN BOARD ABOUT A JUNIOR YEAR exchange program for Smith College students with the Sorbonne in Paris, Jackie arranged for her credits to be transferred and applied to the program. She was accepted on the condition that she take an intensive six-week summer language course at the University of Grenoble. Arriving there in August 1949, she lived with a French family, and assiduously wrote her observations home:

I just can't tell you what it is like to come down from the mountains of Grenoble to this flat, blazing plain where seven-eighths of all you see is hot blue sky—and there are rows of poplars at the edge of every field to protect the crops from the mistral and spiky short palm trees with blazing red flowers growing at their feet. The people here speak with the lovely twang of the "accent du Midi." They are always happy as they live in the sun and love to laugh. It was heartbreaking to only get such a short glimpse of it all—I want to go back and soak it all up. The part I want to see is La Camargue—a land in the Rhone delta which is flooded by the sea every year and they have a ceremony where they all wade in on horses and bless it—La Bénédiction de la Mer—gypsies live there and bands of little Arab horses and they raise wild bulls.

Last Sunday we all went to Sassenage, a village on the plain near Grenoble. We visited the grottoes and waded in underground rivers—and explored the town and sang songs and danced in a lovely little restaurant under rustling trees by a brook with a waterfall—the magic broken only by two "pièces de résistance" of the restaurant—"Bongo, Bongo, Bongo" and "Chattanooga Choo-choo." We missed the last tram and had to walk back to Grenoble (all the way back)—about five miles!

In October, Jackie enrolled at the Sorbonne, part of the University of Paris system and chose to live in the city with a French family. Along with two other American girls, Jackie took up residence at 76 Avenue Mozart in the apartment of Countess Guyot de Renty. Madame de Renty's two daughters, Claude and Ghislaine, were living at home at the time, as was the latter's four-year-old son, Christian. Madame de Renty did the cooking for the household. In 1949, food was still not as abundantly available as it had been before the war, and in addition, energy costs were high. Consequently, Jackie said she was often "swaddled in sweaters and woolen stockings, doing homework in graph-paper *cahiers*." Once while trying to regulate the bath temperature, she exploded the water heater, shattering the bathroom window. She chronicled to Yusha:

It is so different, the feeling you get in a city when you live there. I remember last summer when we were here—I thought Paris was all glamour and glitter and rush—but of course it isn't—I was so goggle-eyed at that night-club you took me to [he had been in Paris at that time]. I went there the other night and it just seemed too garish. I really have two lives—flying from here [the de Renty apartment] to the Sorbonne and Reid Hall, in a lovely quiet, rainy world—or, like the maid on her day out, putting on a fur coat and going to the middle of town and being swanky, at the Ritz. But I really like the first part best. I have an absolute mania now about learning to speak French perfectly. We never speak a word of English in this apartment and I don't see many Americans.

The most wonderful thing here is all the operas and theaters and ballets and how easy they are to get to and how cheap—you could go out every night all winter and still not have seen everything that's playing.

I do love Paris and am so happy here but it is not the dazzled adoration for it I had the first time I saw it—a much more easygoing and healthy affection this time.

Although she described herself as "a chubby little thing eating pastries and studying with inky fingers half the night," she also began serious dating regularly but claimed that "mostly the boys I knew were beetle-browed intellectual types who'd discuss very serious things with me. Nothing romantic at all." Jackie added her own agenda to the Sorbonne curriculum. She took an art course at the École de Louvre and one in diplomatic history at the École de Science Politique. She considered these courses "essential" to her education and said studying abroad was "an excellent way to perfect yourself in a language."

When she arrived, she spoke fairly good French. I took her to have a drink in the Latin Quarter, on the Boulevard Saint-Michel, then we walked around the Sorbonne, just to give her the feeling. My mother gave her a distinct and ironic understanding of everything and everyone. I think this is what attracted Jackie to her and made them close. I think my mother wanted to show that although she had had troubled times and changes, and financial difficulty, she kept her dignity. Jackie got that and liked it. She always called my mother the Countess.

The mood of the Parisians at that time was joyous. We were meeting friends and going around everywhere. The attitude was that we should enjoy life. We had gone through troubled times. We needed to enjoy ourselves. Go to big parties, go out, have fun. We did that.

As she began to explore Paris in depth, she discovered that, for her, French culture meant mostly French art. She had been in Washington and New York and could see museums and become familiar with European paintings and sculpture. Once she was in Paris, however, she realized that nothing was comparable to what she would see there, in French museums, or French homes. She realized that France was the place where she could see the best of the arts she loved—even of Italian, and German, and Dutch. And some French homes were like museums, where you could find the best quality of things. France did not mean just French culture but the best of European art and culture. I think she took the best from everywhere. Good paintings, good architecture, good wallpaper, good furnishings.

It was her first time abroad alone. She discovered what it was to be alone, but she was also now free to do what she wanted. The great part of that was a deeper pursuit of culture.

—CLAUDE DE RENTY DU GRANRUT

Jackie herself later wrote of her year in Europe:

I loved it more than any year of my life. Being away from home gave me a chance to look at myself with a jaundiced eye. I learned not to be ashamed of a real hunger for knowledge, something I had always tried to hide, and I came home glad to start in here again but with a love for Europe that I am afraid will never leave me.

Enthralled as she was by Paris, Jackie took pride in her own nationality, reflecting in 1987:

I was galled at the patronizing attitude toward America, annoyed by the compliment "but no one would think you were American," if one showed a knowledge of literature or history.

DACHAU

DURING A BRIEF WINTER BREAK AT THE SORBONNE, IN FEBRUARY 1950, THE Auchinclosses visited Jackie in Paris. They took her on a brief tour of Austria and Germany. It was only four years after the end of World War II, and traveling conditions were not up to prewar standards. She wrote:

It's so much more fun traveling second and third class and sitting up all night in trains, as you really get to know people and hear their stories. When I traveled before it was all too luxurious and we didn't see anything.

Jackie outlined her itinerary:

I had the most terrific vacation in Austria and Germany. We really saw what it was like with the Russians with tommy guns in Vienna. We saw Vienna and Salzburg and Berchtesgaden where Hitler lived: Munich and the Dachau concentration camp.

Little is known about the details of Jackie's trip to Dachau, since she never further documented her visit there. Others recall from talking to her afterward, however, that she was deeply affected by what she saw there and never forgot it.

She was drawn to Dachau by her sense of history. She was appalled and outraged at what the Nazis did, but she did not condemn the Germans as a race. She was a very emotional person, but she would try to repress her emotions, and after seeing the camp, she managed still to never speak of all the Germans in a derogatory way. She always saw the Nazis as distinct from the German people. She was able to have a great appreciation for German culture, and remained interested in Bismarck and went to touch his grave. But . . . she never forgot what she saw.

—YUSHA AUCHINCLOSS

Jackie attested to the fact that she often was "too emotional." She said of herself that she could be "sensitive to pain and unfairness toward people I don't know from a hole in the wall." Seeing Dachau was perhaps one of the more shocking experiences of her early life.

During the war, Monsieur and Madame de Renty had worked as part of the French Resistance underground. They were captured and placed in separate German concentration camps. Guyot de Renty survived; her husband did not. As their daughter recalled, "Jackie knew what had happened to my parents, but did not ask any questions. At that time, nobody talked about it."

She came to see me and my husband and stayed with us in Rome. It must have been right after she had been through Dachau because she was talking to me about it. She had wanted to see it. She wanted to know. She was so appalled. I had been there with my Italian husband, who thought it was awful. He wondered, Why would she want to see something like this? History. She wanted to know about these things. I remember what it was like, all those ashes beneath you as you walked through.

—VIVIAN CRESPI, FRIEND

EXPLORING HER ROOTS

IN LATE MAY, AFTER HER YEAR AT THE SORBONNE ENDED, JACKIE REMAINED IN France. Having visited Pont Saint-Esprit, the Bouvier ancestral village, and other French towns, she wanted to see more of the country. With Claude, and later Ghislaine, Jackie drove through France, headed toward Saint-Jean-de-Luz, on the west coastal Bay of Biscay, near the Spanish border. They made stops in Toulouse and Montauban, and Bordeaux, La Rochelle, and Nantes.

We both realized that it was a time of freedom, a discovery of landscapes and the châteaus and small towns, and museums that were small and perhaps not well known. It was an exploration of "deep France." Also, it was a real freedom, on our own, doing exactly what we wanted to do. We could stay where we wanted to stay, and see what we wanted to see. We had no special itinerary.

Everybody in France has a cousin somewhere and everybody is a cousin of someone else, so we would stay with cousins for a day or two, go away and return. We also stayed in small hotels. We would picnic in the woods, swim in a river, go fishing, wash clothing in the open water.

—CLAUDE DE RENTY DE GRANRUT

After touring France, Jackie joined Yusha for a tour of Ireland and Scotland.

We spent a joyful three weeks traveling in northern Scotland from John o' Groat's, where she climbed onto the sharp rocks, overlooking the sea, to southern Ireland and Dublin—Blarney, Limerick, Cork. She tilted over backward and kissed the Blarney Stone, as her feet were held for good luck. To save money, we often shared a bathroom or a suite. The concierge would raise an eyebrow when an Auchincloss and a Bouvier claimed to be brother and sister. Jackie's sense of humor never bothered to explain our "steps"! And she joked that my loud pajamas must have been "stolen from Cab Calloway." She was always studying the complicated history of the kings of Ireland.

She was sort of a royalist, from an historical perspective. She loved these old castles and the battles. She knew all about the legends of Ashley Court, and the Crusades, and Henry IV, but she was really crazy about the Irish kings. She knew that her grandfather's [Lee] family came from Ireland. She was always very proud of her European roots, the French but also the Irish. The more she traveled in Ireland, the more she wanted to be Irish, and also Scottish [which she had a little of on the Bouvier side]. The pubs and the village people caught her imagination. She bought kilts and a Royal Stewart dress for herself, and in Inverness, we went to the Edinburgh Festival and the Dublin Horse Show. Her knowledge of art and architecture and of military history all combined on that trip because the castles and paintings matched the history she knew.

—YUSHA AUCHINCLOSS

Jackie Bouvier, Claude de Renty in French countryside, summer 1950.

Jackie Bouvier in the Scottish highlands, summer 1950.

THREE

The Writer
1950–1953

I want above all to become a working girl who earns her own living.

—JACKIE BOUVIER

Jackie Bouvier typing at her desk with coworkers at the Washington Times-Herald newspaper office, 1952.

G. W. U.

Upon her return from Europe, Jackie chose not to return to Vassar but to take her senior year of college at George Washington University, in Washington, D.C., switching her major to French literature and enrolling in intensive classes. In her French literature class with Merle Protzman, students read French texts but wrote assignments in English; Jackie, however, insisted on doing her writing in French. She also took creative writing and journalism courses because, "I wanted to know people better. I thought studying journalism would be a great chance."

I taught her in advanced composition class. She always sat in the back of the classroom next to another student, Joe Metivier. He was a Maine man who had lived on the Canadian border, so he spoke French. And that was certainly a reason she enjoyed speaking with him—always in French. They were quiet about it so I never scolded them. She was an extremely intelligent young woman, but she also possessed a brilliant imagination. This was coupled with a genuine talent for the craft of writing. She had a gift as a writer and might have become prominent in her own right as a writer had she followed another path. She covered many different subjects—the beauty and peace of her family's home in Virginia, the night of faint romance in Florence, a festival in Italy, the purpose and excitement of art to the soul. She was beautiful, and she could write like a million. She didn't need to take my class.

—MURIEL McCLANAHAN,
PROFESSOR EMERITUS OF ENGLISH, G.W.U.

Jackie's February 1951 story, "In Florence," immediately evidenced that gift. It was later read publicly by McClanahan at a ceremony at the University, and broadcasted:

The summer crowd drifted out of the open-air opera, down the colonnade past the cold statues of Lorenzo El Magnifico, staring out of his empty marble eyes.

"Don't try and push," said Monty. "It will make you hotter."

And so we let ourselves be shoved around with girls in swinging skirts and perspiring young men in seersucker jackets. It smelled of hot, summer bodies and perfume. Someone was singing Pagliacci's aria, the three notes with the sob in the voice.

I loved it. He looked like Watteau's *Gilles,* standing before the tent in his fat Pierrot costume, his hands hanging stupidly at his sides.

We were out in the Piazzo Vecchio, now. The black shadow of the clock tower flattened itself over people bickering with the horse and buggy drivers.

"Come on," said Monty, steering me by the elbow. "Let's go this way."

We walked down the middle of a narrow street towards the Arno. I could feel the cobblestones through my sandals, and as I stepped to avoid a smoking pile of horse manure, I tripped and scraped my toes. Monty walked out in long strides. His heels struck the stones, and echoed off the sleeping walls of houses.

We passed the little restaurant where we'd had dinner, spaghetti and red wine in a straw bottle at a table right in the street. At the foot of the street, it was light. The right side crumbled into an empty, bombed lot, and the street light shed patches of yellow light over it.

A melon vendor, bare-footed, his shirt open down to his hairy chest, was laughing with a bunch of ragged Italians. Monty asked him the price of two slices of watermelon, and laughed good-naturedly when the man told him a dollar.

"Look," he said in Italian. "I'm poor, too." And they haggled happily for a few minutes.

Monty's mother was half Italian, and he spoke almost more beautifully than a native; slower and carefully turning each word into a golden bell that pealed against the next and turned the whole sentence into a tune. We got our watermelon, deep green slices streaked with yellow, and a sweet juice spurted out as you bit into the red-pink pulp with the slippery seeds.

"Teach me something to say in Italian, Monty," I said as we walked toward the river.

He wiped the juice from his face with the back of his hand. "What do you want to say?"

"Something different. Not 'thank you' or 'good morning,' but something really Italian."

"I'll tell you what you can say," he told me. "'*Come bello fare l'amore quando piove.*' It's a proverb which means 'how beautiful it is to make love in the rain.'"

I said it slowly. "'*Come bello fare l'amore quando piove.*'" And then faster.

What a lovely Italian thought! I didn't think it would be very beautiful to make love in the rain, but it was so pretty to say so.

We came to the river, and across the still, black water was the old town, stacked in ocher slabs of houses on the banks, and rising dark against the paler eastern sky. We crossed the Ponte Vecchio, dark and silent at night, and walked up the river on the far side, along a dusty path, passed old coils of barbed wire. The path led down to the river at its widest. Flat rocks like stepping stones were dull patches in the oily blackness of the water.

"Look," I said. "We can wade across on those rocks. Oh, take off your shoes." I removed the slippery thongs of my sandals.

"No," said Monty, "I'll carry you, then you can tell your grandchildren that you were carried across the Arno on a summer night."

"Please don't carry me. I'm much too heavy, and you'll just slip and it won't be half as romantic when we're sitting in the dirty water."

But he picked me up, and we started in. His bare feet making silver splashes, looked white in the water, like dead martyr's feet in paintings. I clutched his neck, and hoped that when he fell, it would be backward, not forward, so he'd get wet and I would just be sitting on him.

We teetered across, wading between stepping-stones, and he put me down on the scrambled rocks on the other side of the base of a looming, dark wall that rose to the end in the Lungarno street.

"I'll climb it," said Monty, "and lean over and pull you up."

He started up, clawing for footholds. I looked at the riverbed. The rocks were slimy beneath my dripping toes, and the water trickling between them, unpleasantly warm. Something moved a few yards away, and I saw the black shadow of a water rat, trailing its tubular tail.

"Monty," I called. "Please, hurry. There's a rat, here."

"Watch out! He'll bite you," he laughed as he grunted over the wall.

He leaned down to reach my hands, and I got a foothold in the wall, lost it, and scraped my knees. My hair was in my eyes, and all I could feel was my arms being pulled out of their sockets, and my bare feet slipping off the rocks. He dragged me over the top, and we sat on the wall, out of breath, drying our feet on his handkerchief, and laughing as we put on our shoes.

Dimly, far away, a church bell gonged one o'clock, and it vibrated in the hot, cotton wool of the summer night.

Although she lived with Janet and Hughdie in suburban Virginia, Jackie made a lasting impression on campus during the day:

> She was so striking. She had such a spirit, even then as a very, very young person, such a dignity, and a bearing, and a feeling, that while none of us would come up and speak to her, we all knew who she was. The very fact that the campus and the school were part of the city, rather than being isolated in an ivory tower, made it a special experience for all of us who went there during the heyday, following World War II. Sometimes at a mutual friend's home I used to play music that Jacqueline enjoyed hearing. Music from another part of the world, from the Khyber Pass where Pakistan and Afghanistan meet. She always had that "world view."
>
> —DAVID AMRAM, MUSICIAN, COMPOSER,
> CLASSMATE, AND FRIEND

In many respects, Jackie was mature beyond her years, enjoying the company of people older than she, such as Lorraine Cooper, who would marry a sena-

tor and invited her to intimate Georgetown dinner parties she gave. Another friend, Martha Buck, was now married to her friend Charles Bartlett, who once again tried to persuade the college senior to make time to come to dinner and meet this unusual friend of his whom he was sure she would like. "He got to be quite a bore about it," Jackie recalled. Finally, she relented. Jackie agreed to go to dinner.

VOGUE

WHILE JACKIE WAS TRAVELING ABROAD IN THE SUMMER OF 1950, SHE WROTE to her mother, telling her how much she would like to live abroad. Janet, having read in *Vogue* magazine about its annual Prix de Paris contest, tore out the article and sent it to Jackie.

That fall, as Jackie prepared for her last year of college, she made the decision to pursue some form of a writing career. The *Vogue* article described its contest as a chance to "dissolve the 'no experience' barrier that exists between the young and the professional world." The winner of the prize would get to work as a staff writer in their New York and Paris offices, six months in each city. At this point, Jackie entered. During her senior year, she worked on the required eight essays and a final thesis. This is how she perceived herself at the time:

A self-portrait written from the author's viewpoint is liable to be a little biased. Written from the viewpoint of others it would probably be so derogatory that I would not care to send it in. I have no idea how to go about describing myself but perhaps with much sifting of wheat from chaff I can produce something fairly accurate.

As to physical appearance, I am tall, 5'7", with brown hair, a square face and eyes so unfortunately far apart that it takes three weeks to have a pair of glasses made with a bridge wide enough to fit over my nose. I do not have a sensational figure but can look slim if I pick the right clothes. I flatter myself on being able at times to walk out of the house looking like the poor man's Paris copy, but often my mother will run up to inform me that my left stocking seam is crooked or the right-hand top coat button about to fall off. This, I realize, is the Unforgivable Sin.

I suppose one should mention one's hobbies in a profile. I really don't have any that I work at constantly. I have studied art, here and in Paris, and I love to go to Art Exhibits and paint things that my mother doesn't put in the closet until a month after I have given them to her at Christmas. I have written a children's book for my younger brother and sister, as it amuses me to make up fairy tales and illustrate them. I love to ride and foxhunt. I drop everything any time to read a book on ballet. This winter I am trying to catch up on things I should have learned before. I am taking typing and Interior Decorating outside of college and learning to play bridge and try-ing to cook things from recipes I found in France. I am afraid I will never be very successful over a hot stove.

One of my most annoying faults is getting very enthusiastic over some-thing at the beginning and then tiring of it halfway through. I am trying to counteract this by not getting too enthusiastic over too many things at once.

Her article on "People I Wish I Had Known" was equally revealing:

Putting them in chronological order, I would say that the three men I should most like to have known were Charles Baudelaire, Oscar Wilde, and Serge Diaghilev. They followed close upon each other in the three-quarters of a century from 1850–1925. They came from three different countries and specialized in three different fields; poetry, playwrighting and ballet, yet I think a common theory runs through their work, a certain concept of the interrelation of the arts.

Baudelaire and Wilde were both rich men's sons who lived like dandies, ran through what they had and died in extreme poverty. Both were poets and idealists who could paint their sinfulness with honesty and still believe in something higher. The Frenchman, an isolated genius who could have lived at any time, used as his weapons venom and despair. Wilde, who typified the late Victorian era, could, with the flash of an epigram, bring about what serious reformers had for years been trying to accomplish.

Serge Diaghilev dealt not with the interaction of the senses but with an interaction of the arts, an interaction of the cultures of East and West. Though not an artist himself, he possessed what is rarer than artistic genius in any one field; the sensitivity to take the best of each man and incorporate it into a masterpiece all the more precious because it lives only in the minds of those who have seen it and disintegrates as soon as he is gone.

It is because I love the works of these three men that I wish I had known them. A Boswell's Knowledge of their lives would throw so much light on their works. If I could be a sort of Overall Art Director of the

Twentieth Century, watching everything from a chair landing in space, it is their theories that I would apply to my period, their poems that I would have music and paintings and ballets composed to. And they would make such good stepping-stones if we thought we could climb any higher.

In her essay on fashion, Jackie said that she found professional models to be practical but that "*Vogue* would lose an enormous amount of its appeal were it to abandon sketches and clothes photographed on personalities. . . . It is fun to come across Marlene Dietrich brooding in a great black cape." In another essay, she advised a beauty regimen on Thursdays to "avoid smudged nails daubed on the New York Central from a bottle of polish that has spilled in your pocketbook, strange unwanted waves in your hair because you have washed it at midnight and gone to bed too tired to wait for it to dry, stubbly legs with razor cuts, and a legion of other horrors." Her tactile senses emerged in Jackie's essay on how *Vogue* could best present perfume:

Perfume was just as effective in piquing the male olfactory glands before our era of adjective-laden advertisements. Why not quote some of the poetry it has inspired? It also is analogous to wine. Both are liquids that act upon the closely related senses of taste and smell to produce an intoxicating effect. Wine has had an ever stronger appeal in literature, from Omar Khayyám to Colonel Cantwell and Renata. Why not pilfer some of its drawing power and incorporate it into an article on perfume?

An analogy of wine and perfume, entitled "Intoxicating Liquids," "The Petal and the Grape," etc., would be done in much the same way. The left-hand page would show the compartments of a wine cellar. In each compartment a bottle of perfume would be standing upright. The label beneath it would say "Lentheric-Numero 6, 1950" in the same way that wines are catalogued. This layout would be most effective in black and white photography with the black depths of the compartments pointing up the reflections of the glass bottles. The right-hand page—also with black background—would show some strewn flower petals, a thin-stemmed crystal wineglass with blurred suggestion of a woman (a long neck, an earring, her hand) pouring perfume out of a Dioram bottle into the glass. Again in the right-hand corner would be a few lines of copy stressing the analogy between perfume and wine.

Using "Nostalgia" as her theme of an entire hypothetical *Vogue* issue, which contestants were asked to propose, Jackie outlined the underpinnings of her idea:

You can swish out to lunch at your new little restaurant in a jacket cut like a Directoire Dandy's; you can wrap yourself in a great Spanish shawl in your very own U.S.A. living room; you can dance as you used to in the twenties in a wisp of a flapper's sheath. It is always fun to pretend, and we think that these harking-back clothes will make you feel quite secretly mysterious. Call them nostalgic; they are really just variations on the theme of coquetry . . . romanticism of the far-off and the bygone.

Ultimately, Jackie was named as one of twelve award finalists, all of whom were invited to meet the editors. Ten days after she met with them at lunch, she received a congratulatory telegram. Out of the 1,280 entries for the prize from 225 colleges, she had won the contest.

In late May, Jackie returned to New York with trepidation and filled out her first job application. In it, she wrote that she could type but not take shorthand, disliked math and science, and had never been bonded, owned a house, had a hospitalization plan, been a Communist, or joined a group to overthrow the government. She had just read *From Here to Eternity*, and regularly read *Life*, *Time*, the *New Yorker*, *Vogue*, *Harper's Bazaar*, and the *Atlantic Monthly*.

And then, seemingly out of the blue, Jackie, pressured by her mother, turned down the Prix de Paris. Janet had encouraged her to enter the contest, but Jackie admitted to the editors that Janet felt "terrifically strong about 'keeping me in the home.'" Jackie, too, felt ambivalent about accepting, later reflecting, "I guess I was too scared to go. I felt then that if I went back I'd live there forever, I loved Paris so much." Carol Phillips of *Vogue*, reflecting on Jackie's decision, accurately sensed that she was insecure, "a sweet, darling girl with not a great deal of confidence." "Go [back] to Washington," she told her. "That's where all the boys are."

JUNE 1951

*I*N JUNE 1951 JACKIE WAS BUSY PREPARING FOR HER GRADUATION, AS WELL AS another trip to Europe. With the skill she had learned in preparing her *Vogue* fashion essay, Jackie designed her own clothes for Europe, working with Janet's seamstress:

I always thought that Jacqueline had reached her decision not to enter the fashion field for another, unvoiced reason—she hated to tell other people what to do. I noticed over and over again that, while she was always very sure of what she wanted for herself, she was very careful never to impose her opinion on others. Jackie . . . had . . . depth and understanding and sympathy for the highest and the lowest. Some of my customers treated me like a maid, stepping out of their clothes and leaving them on the floor for me to pick up while they watched. But Jackie didn't want a lady's maid and she had great respect for every individual.

I never saw Jackie excited in the slightest, except once. . . . She came hurrying in and asked quickly, "Mrs. Rhea, where can I get a pitcher of water?" I ran to the door in time to see her calmly pouring the water into her car—through the window. Smoke billowed out. "I set my car on fire with a cigarette," she said, smiling, as she passed me on her way to the kitchen again. "I think one more pitcher and I won't have to call the fire department."

—Mini Rhea

Just days before she left for Europe, Jackie finally kept her promise to accept her long-standing dinner invitation at the Bartletts' and meet the man Bartlett had tried to introduce her to at his brother's wedding. It turned out that he was the congressman she had briefly met on a train two years before, but the matchmaking didn't seem to be as successful as Bartlett had hoped. The congressman later said he "leaned across the asparagus and asked her for a date."

She said there was no asparagus served that night.

He wanted to go for a drink. She turned him down. They made no plans to see each other again. Only later did he tell her that it was during dinner that he decided someday to marry her.

"How big of you!" she would retort.

THE SPECIAL SUMMER

I was seventeen and my greatest dream was to go abroad as soon as I graduated from school. The main reason was that Jackie had [gone]. . . . Her letters to me, of which there were many, were so full of detailed descriptions of how fascinated she was by the history of the places she'd seen. . . . Also, I couldn't imagine anything that could be more fun than a trip with Jackie. . . . My mother was extremely apprehensive about letting her daughters go alone on such a venture. . . . Jackie was dutifully convincing about how well she would look after me and how wisely she would behave.

—LEE RADZIWILL, SISTER

As a gift to their mother, the Bouvier sisters kept a detailed journal of their wanderings. It was illustrated with imaginative and humorous drawings, and droll tales of their adventures.

As passport number 218793, Jackie was off to Europe again on the evening of June 7, 1951, departing with her sister aboard the *Queen Elizabeth*. On the ship they promptly abandoned their third-class room shared with a bizarre old woman, encountered a Lebanese man about whom Jackie warned Lee of the "quirks in the sex lives of Near Easterners," snuck onto the first-class deck, ignoring a PLEASE OBSERVE SOCIAL BARRIERS sign, and arrived in England, where they promptly bought their touring car. In France, after a dull chamber music concert, brightened only by the loss of Lee's petticoats, they interrupted a military ceremony and headed straight into the antitank gun and tank maneuvers of an open field, in search of their friend Paul de Ganay of the French Army. They failed in their aspiration to "kiss him on both cheeks the way they do in newsreels," but did retrieve him from duty, "off into the antitank fire, the 'Marseillaise' throbbing in our heads and thanking God for the North Atlantic Treaty." After almost being arrested and put in prison for trying to cross the Spanish border without car ownership papers—which they had left in a suitcase in Paris—they suddenly blew a tire in the dead of night in the middle of rural Spain. Jackie noted for Janet's benefit:

I know you are right about us representing our country and that we must never do anything that would call attention to us and make people shocked at Americans. We do sew on all our buttons and wear gloves and never go out in big cities except in what we would wear to church in Newport on Sundays.

Beneath the comment, to test their mother's sense of humor, Jackie pasted a photo of herself in sandals and pants and Lee in shorts. In Venice, Jackie composed a lengthy poem, creating a fictitious pastiche of a fantasy ball where the mundane aspects of their traveling gave way to mystical dances in exotic costumes that masked their identities as they encountered Molière and Watteau.

In Spain, the sisters jitterbugged beneath Flemish paintings, sat in Columbus's chair, and climbed the Pyrenees. During a visit with the American ambassador in Madrid, they ran into American senators. One of the senators asked if they were Republicans and promised "to take us to lunch in the Senate cafeteria because he always liked to bring a little pleasure into people's lives by showing them around the nation's capital."

Without question, the greatest impact of the trip on both young women was an afternoon spent with noted art critic Bernard Berenson, at his residence I Tatti outside Florence. Lee had arranged the meeting after initiating a friendship with Berenson by writing him a letter. Born in Lithuania, educated at Harvard, he was not only the world's most renowned Italian Renaissance scholar but also the first critic to focus with intense sensitivity on the visual and textural details of an artwork, and one of the first to use detail photography in that process. He conceived of the terms "ideated sensations" and "tactile values" to describe an observer's emotional connections and reactions to any given piece of art, making appreciation of the fine arts more than a pastime, but an experience that could be "life enhancing" yet utterly mysterious.

One particular biographical fact about Berenson left a lasting recollection on Jackie. "Despite all he did to help people understand the magnificence of the Italian Renaissance, he was forced to leave his beloved Italy during the war because of his background," she later recalled. Berenson was a Catholic convert, but born and raised Jewish. Mussolini's fascist regime would tolerate no Jews, a dramatic example of, as she later said, "intolerance trying to crush the spirit."

The memory of the meeting and its significance remained with Jackie. As Jackie dictated, Lee wrote down her sister's impressions of Berenson:

"The only way to exist happily, [he said], is to love your work." Anything you do, he could find a philosophy for. "Anything you want, you must make enemies for and suffer for. . . ." He sets a spark burning. It was the difference between living and existing that he had spoken of and both of us had simply been existing in our selfish ways far too long. Maybe that was why it was so upsetting but more because you longed to reap out of life what he had but knew you never could. . . . Such a pillar of strength and sensitivity, and such a lover of all things. He is a man whose life in beauty is unsurpassable.

Don't waste your life with diminishing people who aren't stimulating [he concluded].

He said, "Come back soon darlings and see me—soon." I told him he would live for years and he answered and said no—that he didn't simply want to exist, as soon as he stopped living he wanted to die and not simply exist for years.

In great part, Jackie attributed her appreciation of art to Berenson:

Because I love art, I'm sometimes asked how one can learn to appreciate painting and sculpture. I feel the best way is by using your eyes, by focusing your whole attention on a work of art, to try to understand the message the artist wants to convey. I remember this is one of the most important things I learned, from one of the most remarkable art critics, Bernard Berenson, whom I knew and from whom I learned a great deal.

In Rome, Jackie was exposed to abstract and contemporary art on "the sleepy little pink street hidden behind the taxi-tooting shopping swank of the Piazza di Spagna" in the courtyard studio of artist Pericles Fazzini. As Fazzini sculpted, the Bouvier sisters sat and smoked and talked with the artist's curious collection of friends—Vincent, an American GI working as a movie extra; his wife, Teddy, who spoke only of going home to Brooklyn; "Romeo the poet"; and "wild Carlo," the artist's assistant. After shopping and taking in museums, the odd crew would meet for espressos in a "bamboo-curtained cafeteria," then repair to the studio. Fazzini drew pictures of Jackie, which she said were "slightly more abstract than I imagined myself—but I loved them—splotches and lines . . ." She was taken aback by his spontaneously generous nature as he welcomed curious strangers who just poked into his studio, paid for all his friends' lunches, and presented her with his sketches of her. "You couldn't stop him from giving," she wrote. When the sisters learned that his wife was dying of a bone disease and had a four-year-old daughter, they bought the child a rocking horse. Jackie found that despite the language barrier, she and Fazzini could still communicate. "He couldn't speak English, nor we Italian, but we talked together incessantly."

Educated, talented, and well-traveled, upon her return to America, Jackie began to focus on work:

For a young woman of our background and time, it was still considered almost revolutionary to go to college, let alone have a career! We were supposed to do what we were told. In the 1950s, one was practically considered an old maid to marry at twenty-two, but Jackie wanted a college education, to live in Europe, and to get a job as a writer.

—VIVIAN CRESPI

"DARE TO DEVIATE"

*I*N THE FALL OF 1951, JACKIE DECIDED AGAINST PURSUING WRITING FOR THE fashion industry because "I wanted to do something useful" and felt "a career like that would be limiting me." She then asked a friend of her stepfather, Arthur Krock, bureau chief of the *New York Times*, to help her get a job in journalism. Krock found her an entry-level position as a receptionist to Frank Waldrop, the editor of the *Washington Times-Herald*. Within weeks, however, she approached her boss to convey her true ambition:

She wanted to write. So, I started her out by putting her to work on the "Inquiring Cameragirl" column. She didn't know anything about taking photographs. But she certainly knew how to get to people. She didn't come in there to me with her dukes up and say, "I demand to be a writer," but she did say, "I want to be in the newspaper business." So, I said to her "Look, do you want to make a career, or just hang around until you get married? Because I don't have time to fool around with this." This was just before Christmas. She said, "No. I really want to write. I'm serious about making a career of writing."

What I always liked was her straightforward manner in dealing with me. She was a bright young woman. She could see around corners. She had gone to Krock. She wasn't wasting time. She was just getting right into things. She had sense enough to do that.

She was always a little short on money. She always had to be careful how she spent, about paying the bills. She would always be looked after by her stepfather, but he had his own children. She certainly wasn't going to get anything substantial from her father. She worked, and she earned a living.

—FRANK C. WALDROP, EDITOR IN CHIEF,
WASHINGTON TIMES-HERALD

Jackie bent over backward to keep people from thinking she was anything other than a hard-working girl reporter who needed the salary.

—MINI RHEA

Jackie's job did a lot to heighten her self-esteem. Years later she said she was concerned by "the myth that I am just a sheltered socialite. I proved that I could support myself by holding down a newspaper job for a year and a half and by winning the *Vogue* Prix de Paris."

At the *Times-Herald* office, located at 1317 H Street, she was often pursued by the "fourth floor wolves," the single men on staff who frequently but unsuccessfully tried to get dates. ("How do you feel when you get wolf whistles?" she asked women in one of her columns.)

> She was a hard worker. The photographers all liked her, but she focused on going about her business thoroughly. She concentrated on the question of the day. She listened carefully. She treated it as a business, small, but important enough as a start in a writing career.
>
> —FRANK WALDROP

> The job did not merely provide a comment on the news but rather more insight into the way people felt. . . . This sort of question took skill and sensitivity on the part of the interviewer not to ridicule or ham up. The column's interest depended on how exactly the interview was handled and not on the photographs.
>
> —MARY VAN RENSSELAER THAYER, FRIEND AND BIOGRAPHER

Among Jackie's closest colleagues was Zeke Hearin, at various times an editor and reporter. The two frequently went out riding near his home in Chantilly, Virginia, not far from the Auchincloss house, where she continued to live. Hearin was known in the newsroom for making up little verses, his signature remark to reporters about to go out on a story being "dare to deviate." Jackie met the challenge. As she later explained:

> Being a journalist seemed the ideal way of both having a job and experiencing the world, especially for anyone with a sense of adventure. I wouldn't chose it as a profession now—journalism has variety but doesn't allow you to enter different worlds in depth . . . though I understand why so many young people are attracted to it. Being a reporter seems a ticket out of the world.

In the late afternoon Jackie could be found in her office typing the next day's copy and developing her pictures. Because she had difficulty handling her Graflex, she enrolled in a photography course. Soon she was able to develop her own black-and-white shots, and simultaneously became interested in photography as an art. When Jackie became the newspaper's "Inquiring Cameragirl" columnist, her beat was everywhere in the city: hotels, construction sites, district courts, police and fire stations, hospital emergency rooms, or the airport. She attended events ranging from spelling bees to Shakespearean readings. She asked strangers' opinions on everything from income tax to psychoanalysis.

It was remarkable to me that a young woman who had mingled only with society had chosen to attempt to make her way in the workaday world—to succeed on her own merits if possible. And it was also remarkable that she, who was basically shy, developed the courage to stop strangers of every age and walk of life on the street, how she understood their interests, and was able to blend seriousness with comedy. I noticed that she never talked down to them. And if they seemed curious about her and asked questions, she never let on. . . . I used to think Jackie must get a little kick out of startling some of the people she questioned. . . . She asked, for example, "If you were to be electrocuted tomorrow morning, what would you order for your last meal?"

—Mini Rhea

By March 26, 1952, her third month on the column, Jackie was given her own byline. There was nothing shy about her approach. She would walk up to people and beg for fourteen cents, then write down their reactions. Once, she stopped people and asked them exactly what they were thinking when she stopped them. Other questions were equally direct:

Do you consider yourself normal?
You look important. Are you?
Would you like to be famous?
What prominent person's death affected you most?

Most of her questions required people to give pause and think before they spoke:

What is the greatest need in the world today?

What are you living for?

Do you think hope ever dies?

If you could be reincarnated, who would you be?

Do the rich enjoy life more than the poor?

Do you believe there is a Dr. Jekyll and Mr. Hyde in all of us?

If you capsized at sea with your mother, husband or wife, and child and could only save one, which one would you save?

As Shaw suggests in *The Doctor's Dilemma*, would you rescue "a great artist who is a scoundrel, or a commonplace, honest family man"?

Many questions reflected popular topics of the early 1950s:

Do you think bikini bathing suits are immoral?

If you had a date with Marilyn Monroe, what would you talk about?

How do you feel about Li'l Abner's getting married?

What do you think flying saucers really are?

If you secretly found out that you had married a former Communist, what would you do?

Other questions seemed to reflect a subversive feminism:

A Boston University professor said women marry because they're too lazy to go to work. Do you agree?

Do you think a wife should let her husband think he's smarter than she is?

Chaucer said that what women most desire is power over men. What do you think women desire most?

When did you discover that women are not the weaker sex?

What do you think of wrestling as a sport for women?

Jackie often found her best material by asking a routine question of the most incongruous people. She asked a truck driver his view on fashions, a circus clown if he was really hiding a broken heart, and manual laborers, "Would you like to crash high society?" At the American Psychological Association convention, she cheekily asked "How do you think you're maladjusted?" For some columns, she "interviewed" animals, writing her own responses on why they were at the vet's or what circus life was really like. Her responses were whimsical but also threatened retaliation to humans for their cruelty. Jackie reflected, "You could make the column about anything you wanted to. So I'd find a bunch of rough, salty characters and ask them about a prizefighter just so I could capture the way they talked. . . . Often it was difficult to get anything out of them. It taught me not to expect too much and not to take things for granted."

Among those who answered the question of whether their southern charm helped them in daily life were Senator Richard Russell of Georgia, Governor John Battle of Virginia, and actress Tallulah Bankhead, who told Jackie, "My magnolia-scented southern charm has served me well, both professionally and privately. It has melted many a manager, chilled many a carpetbagger, and confused many a swain. Exercise of it in lavish doses has brought me from Huntsville, Alabama, dash—that's [Senator] Sparkman's hometown—dash, you heard me—dash—to New York, London, Hollywood, and other spots it would be indiscreet to mention."

Once Jackie showed up at Griffith Stadium for a home game of the Washington Senators against the Boston Red Sox, hoping to interview Ted Williams in the locker room after the game. She stood outside the locker room door dreaming up all sorts of reasons as to why she should be let in. But to no avail. She did manage to ask Dick Williams, an outfielder, "How do you Bums feel in this city of culture?" He cracked back at Jackie, "Get this straight. I'm no Bum. I'm from California . . . the only place in the country that's got the kind of culture I go for."

TELEVISION—AND THE WHITE HOUSE

WHILE JACKIE WORKED ON HER COLUMN ALL DAY, HER EVENINGS DURING THE spring of 1952 were spent writing in a new format, for a television documentary. Inspired to try writing a script and proposal for the latest popular form of entertainment as a way of making history more alive, she was unprompted by anything except her own ambition. Her final product was a television documentary special on the city's legendary Octagon House, which had served as the temporary residence for James and Dolley Madison following the burning of the White House during the War of 1812. In her written proposal, she set the stage:

> For fifty years, talk of ghosts, of ghastly shrieks, and thuds of falling bodies
> at midnight, of white-robed apparitions, had hovered about Octagon

House. It was Washington's haunted house. Colored folks went out of their way to walk around the block to avoid passing it. Little boys and girls dared each other to run up the front steps, then ran back to the sidewalk squealing with delight and horror. . . .

There are days when you can smell lilacs . . . no matter what time of year it is. They say those days that Dolley Madison is "around."

Sometimes she holds court at midnight, standing before the drawing room mantel "in the meridian of life and queenly beauty." A gay company assembles to dance once more to muted violins; the crystal punchbowl sparkles, and footmen call for carriages that never come.

Once the script was completed, Jackie met with public relations executive Stephen M. Walter about finding an interested television station. Unfortunately, the station that was interested in Jackie's documentary went out of business before it got produced.

The subject of the script, however, revealed an increasing and new fascination of Jackie's—the White House, presidents, and first ladies. It was frequently evident in her column. For a special Fourth of July column, she even went to the Library of Congress to research quotes of Washington, Jefferson, Adams, and Lincoln and compose the "answers" that the long-gone presidents would have given to her question on the meaning of national independence. Her regular beat became the White House gates, where she asked questions of those emerging from the mansion:

Which first lady would you like to have been?
Do you think Mamie Eisenhower's bangs will become a nationwide fashion?
What's it like, meeting Mamie?
What did you like best about the new White House?
What are your memories of presidents?
Would you like your son to grow up to be president?
What are some things most people don't know about Lincoln's assassination?

An acquaintance during 1952 and 1953 recalled of her:

Jackie was especially intrigued with everything about the White House. She was always asking the White House reporters, male and female, about their jobs and telling them they were lucky to go there. Everything about the White

House was exciting to her. "How was it there?" she'd ask them about their White House visits covering a press conference or a social visit. "Did you get to see Mrs. Truman?" She asked the reporters and photographers if they got to see other parts of the White House. "Do they let you in the family's rooms or just in the president's office? Can you wander from the press room now and then or do the guards stop you?"

—MINI RHEA

In her coverage of the 1953 Eisenhower inauguration, Jackie focused on first ladies:

Mamie's lively laughter could be heard far back in the crowd . . . while Mrs. Truman sat stolidly with her gaze glued on the blimp overhead through most of the ceremony. . . . Ike planted a kiss on Mamie's cheek right after taking the oath.

Several days after the inauguration, when writing a story on the disassembling of the reviewing stands in front of the White House, Jackie asked workers if they'd caught a glimpse of the new first lady. One man told her, "I haven't seen Mrs. Eisenhower even go out and buy a tube of toothpaste. She's a prisoner of the Secret Service for the next four years."

After tracking down Ellen and Mamie Moore, the two young nieces of the new first lady, as they left school, she asked them how the election of their uncle had changed their lives. Jackie then illustrated her story with a sketch of little Mamie with her Uncle Ike. When the story and cartoon appeared in the *Times-Herald*, the girls' mother was livid and complained through a friend to Waldrop to "do something to make that brash cameragirl, whoever she is, know her place." Jackie was mortified. The article also attracted the attention of Arthur Krock, who clipped a copy for Bess Armstrong, the *New York Times* reporter who covered first ladies. Mrs. Armstrong wrote to the young reporter, praising her story, and suggesting that she write a children's book on the history of the White House as told through the eyes of young Mamie Moore. Jackie's thank-you letter reflected her enthusiasm:

That is the most wonderful idea—the children's book. I know something like that would go over wonderfully—if I could only do it the right way. It is so funny—you try and think up all these fantastic, rather forced ideas that would make good children's books—and they never quite jell—Then something so simple like this comes along—and is the best of all. I never would have thought of that—or anything remotely like it—if you hadn't suggested it—and now poor little Mamie Moore, whom I bearded coming out of school, just might turn out to be my meal ticket! . . .

I would love to see you and ask you just how you think it should be done. This is such a lovely idea—I would hate to mangle it. . . . I would so love to meet you—if you ever have time. Mrs. Graves said you'd been a newspaperwoman all your life—I'm so in love with all that world now—I think I look up to newspaper people—the way you join movie star fan clubs when you're ten years old.

A GROWING CURIOSITY FOR POLITICS

ALTHOUGH SHE ONCE REMARKED THAT THE "TROUBLE WITH NEWPORT" IS that "everyone is Republican," Jackie had not, by the late 1940s, shown any particularly strong political ideology. Like her family members, she was clearly affiliated with the Republican side of issues. Growing up, she said that if she did something bad, one of two names would be mentioned as a threatening scare to set her straight—Bruno Hauptmann, kidnapper of the Lindbergh baby, and President Roosevelt. Working in Washington, she focused her interests more on individual political candidates rather than on a particular party. In 1952, she became a loyalist of Democratic presidential candidate Adlai Stevenson. If Stevenson became "the first political voice to whom she listened," recalled her friend Arthur Schlesinger, it was because of his personality. She remained aloof from the political process and was not registered to vote.

In the midst of the transition from Truman to Eisenhower, however, Jackie began to show her growing curiosity in politics. Throughout the campaign and election of 1952, as a one-woman pollster, she began posing political questions to her subjects on the streets:

What do you think of the nomination of Governor Stevenson?
Is Truman's whistle-stop tour helping Stevenson?
Stevenson charged we have a one-party press. Do you agree?
What do you think will be President Truman's place in history?
What do you think of General Eisenhower's winning the nomination on the first ballot?

Mamie's Namesake, 10, Glad Uncle Ike Will Be President

By JACQUELINE BOUVIER

What's in a name? Well, there's a lot in it right now for Mamie Moore. Ten-year-old Mamie Moore is Mamie Eisenhower's niece and namesake and she's just discovered she's a celebrity.

[Drawings by Jacqueline Bouvier]
"Mamie and Uncle Ike at White House Wedding"

Jackie Bouvier's cartoon of President Eisenhower and his niece, 1953.

Before leaving office, President Truman ordered the tidelands oil areas set aside as a navy reserve. Should these oil reserves be held for national defense?

What do you think about the UN in general?

Who would you like to see as members of President Eisenhower's cabinet?

Should Charles E. Wilson be confirmed as secretary of defense while holding $2,400,000 worth of General Motors stock?

Do you think Eisenhower should confer with General MacArthur before going to Korea?

Will Indochina turn into another Korea?

She displayed a rather pronounced interest in the leadership of the Soviet Union and the Cold War:

What four Americans would you name or delegate to the UN to match Russia's team of Vishinsky, Gromyko, Zorin, and Zorubin?

Would Stalin's death benefit or injure the cause of world peace?

Malenkov said all issues between the United States and Russia are solvable by peaceful means. Do you agree?

Jackie also was intrigued by the growing debate concerning women's being elected or appointed to political office:

> Would you support a woman for president of the United States?
> What do you think of women in politics?
> How has the League of Women Voters affected the political scene in your community?
> What do you think of Clare Boothe Luce being appointed ambassador to Italy?
> Do you approve of Eisenhower's naming two women to high posts in the government?

On election night, after Eisenhower's victory was declared, she infiltrated Republican headquarters as if she were Mata Hari, sneaking in her huge Graflex camera under a coat, coaxing quotes from drunk revelers wearied after celebrating the first Republican win in twenty years. She would soon interview the new vice president's wife, Pat Nixon, and ask people, "Should a candidate's wife campaign with her husband?" and "Do a candidate's looks influence your vote?"

Jackie would later coyly remark that "I was born and reared a Republican. But you have to be a Republican to realize how nice it is to be a Democrat."

If it appeared that Jackie was solely focused on a career as a Washington journalist, there was more than met the eye. In her early months at the newspaper, Jackie had suddenly became engaged to John G. Husted Jr., a New York stockbroker and part of the social milieu of the Auchinclosses. The January 21, 1952, *Times-Herald* announced that the Bouvier-Husted wedding would take place six months later, in June. His parents and sisters were friends with Janet and Hugh Auchincloss. When he met her at a Washington party, he was smitten and encouraged a relationship. Jackie, rather passively, enjoyed dating him.

Despite her affection for him and the many trips she took to New York to see him, she felt ambivalent about marriage. Having been either a student or living under her mother's thumb for so long, she was now just enjoying her independence as an adult and meeting different kinds of people on her own, outside of the narrow confines of her family's social circle. In fact, about a week before she spontaneously accepted Husted's telephone suggestion that they marry—by meeting his challenge to show up at the Polo Bar in New York in the midst of a snowstorm—Jackie had been down in Florida with some of her new friends.

The first I ever heard of Jackie was sometime during the winter of 1951. She—and her younger sister, Lee, as I recall—were vacationing with their family in Hobe Sound, up the coast from Palm Beach. Jackie worked in Washington on one of the newspapers and knew several of our children, since by that time Jack, Eunice, and Bobby were working in Washington. She was invited to spend a few days at our Palm Beach house while some of them were there. I wasn't there myself at the time; I was detained on other matters and arrived a little later that year. Soon afterward, however, I received a thank-you letter. It was signed "Jackie." I thought it was from a boy, and how extraordinary for a boy to write such a charming letter.

I wondered, who is Jackie?

—ROSE KENNEDY

THE CAT-AND-MOUSE COURTSHIP

When I was about nineteen, I knew I didn't want the rest of my life to be there [Newport]. I didn't want to marry any of the young men I grew up with—not because of them but because of their life. I didn't know what I wanted. I was still floundering.

—JACKIE BOUVIER

By March of 1952, Jackie had changed her mind and decided not to marry John Husted. She had accepted his proposal on a whim, and began postponing the planned wedding date until she finally just returned his ring. She had also by then taken a definite interest in a certain charismatic and wealthy Massachusetts congressman.

Despite her social background and connections and the increasing number of men interested in dating her, Jackie had resisted serious involvement. Her brother Yusha not only lived with her at Merrywood in 1951 and 1952 but also had become a close companion. He recalled her during this period:

She didn't like any phony social business, and always going to parties. She'd prefer to just be with a few intelligent people and have in-depth conversations. There was a group of us, we'd have dinner and they'd come out to swim in the evening. After we finished we'd talk about the questions she had asked during the day, and who'd she seen that she found particularly enlightening or interesting.

> She had no secret plan to get herself married. She never understood her own charm or her beauty. She never thought she had a good figure. She didn't know whether anybody was going to be attracted to her. She was insecure in this respect. We were very close and went around together, as companions. She said, "Do you think the two of us will be going out the rest of our lives? If you find somebody else, don't worry about dumping me."
>
> —YUSHA AUCHINCLOSS

Jackie's insecurity about her appeal to men certainly manifested itself when the Bartletts were planning another dinner party. Martha Bartlett told her that she needed "an extra man" and asked Jackie to invite the congressman. Jackie hesitated. Martha "urged her."

It had been a year since Jackie first met Jack Kennedy at the Bartletts' for dinner and six months since she had visited him in Florida, but on May 8, 1952, it was obvious that the congressman, now running for the United States Senate and voted "America's Most Eligible Bachelor" over even Rock Hudson, had not forgotten Jackie.

> My brother really was smitten with her right from the very beginning when he first met her at dinner. Members of the family knew right away that she was very special to him, and saw the developing of their relationship. I remember her coming up to Cape Cod at that time and involving herself in the life of the family. He was fascinated by her intelligence: they read together, painted together, enjoyed good conversation together and walks together.
>
> —SENATOR EDWARD M. KENNEDY

For herself, however, Jackie feared serious involvement with a man who was not only a high-profile public figure but a bachelor who relished his independence. She revealed this only in the third person to family friend and later biographer Molly Thayer. The oblique reference is the only known instance in which Jackie wrote of her misgivings about her relationship with Jack Kennedy:

> [She] knew instantly that he would have a profound, perhaps disturbing influence on her life. In a flash of inner perception, she realized that here was a man who did not want to marry. She was frightened. Jacqueline, in the revealing moment, envisaged heartbreak, but just as swiftly determined that heartbreak would be worth the pain.

The most formidable of all Jack's judges, however, remained Mrs. Auchincloss. Jackie recalled, "Jack was something special and I know he saw something special in me, too. I remember my mother used to bring around all these beaus for me but he was different." When, however, the Republican Mrs. Auchincloss coincidentally found herself seated next to the brash Irish Catholic Democrat at a dinner party, she too, independently, was drawn to Kennedy. And let her daughter know it:

> When we left, we were driving down the street and I saw this tall, straight, purposeful young man striding down the street, I said to Hugh D., "There's Jack Kennedy. . . . Shall we see if we can give him a lift?" He didn't seem to have any car or anyplace to go and he was just walking on into the night. So we stopped the car and said, "Can we take you anywhere?" And he said, "Thank you very much. That would be very nice," and hopped in the car. There was something about him not bothering to ask anybody for a lift or not bothering to call a taxi. . . . But just finding him marching on—that was very endearing. I can't describe it to you, but he had a sort of a Lindbergh quality to me at that point. I certainly had, of course, no idea I would ever see him again.
>
> —JANET LEE AUCHINCLOSS

It was a cat-and-mouse game for a while—Kennedy was interested and Jackie was busy, or vice versa, "spasmodic" as she put it. Jackie disliked large social functions, although she began to acquiesce by attending some political functions as Senator Kennedy's date. Primarily, their dating was confined to evening games of Chinese checkers and Monopoly with friends. The only real time they spent alone together was when Kennedy drove her back to Merrywood from the city. The more they were together, however, the more they seemed a likely couple.

> Both loved books and presented them to one another as gifts. Both of them were writers. . . . Both had lived abroad. Both ignored their wealth and made their own way in the world, among people who were not equally affluent. Both kept their personal lives to themselves.
>
> —MINI RHEA

His gifts to her were books on government and history, and biographies of great American military and political figures, including *The Raven,* about Sam

Houston, and *Pilgrim's Way* by John Buchan. Her gifts were books of poetry and art history. They were also similar emotionally:

> She told a friend that she and Jack were both like icebergs with the greater part of their lives invisible. She felt they both sensed this in each other and that this was a bond between them. Another bond was their wit—his perhaps more gentle, hers more biting.
>
> —RALPH G. MARTIN,
> REPORTER AND KENNEDY BIOGRAPHER

Kennedy was also making Jackie a partner in his political work. During his campaign for the U.S. Senate in the summer of 1952, she came up to Boston to attend an Israel bond rally as his escort and made a brief welcoming remark, then went to hear his speeches in Quincy and Fall River, Massachusetts. "I guess I'm a Democrat now," she quipped. After she spent Inauguration Day 1953 covering the events for a full-length article, she went as the new senator's date to the Inaugural Ball. A month later she began translating ten French books on Southeast Asian politics for his first major speech in the Senate.

Jack Kennedy's innumerable girlfriends were no secret in their circle, yet he treated her quite differently from any other woman he had dated. As Laura Berquist Knebel, a *Look* journalist who would become close to the couple, later remarked, "Never once did this suitor propose they go off for a night or a weekend," as he had with others.

> Oh, there were several [girls he was dating], I guess. No one specifically. Now, Ann McDermott he dated. That was during the [1952] campaign. She came down to Washington with the idea of getting a job in government. Nothing really seemed to appeal to her, and she went home in May. He did see her, but he was dating Jackie at this same time. And they [McDermott and Kennedy] had a wonderful relationship . . . [but] I think he knew a year before that he wanted to marry Jackie Bouvier.
>
> I had never met Jackie until I think the early spring of 1953. When Eunice was married in May, Jackie was in England and was coming back the next week, and we were all up in New York for Eunice's wedding. And that was the first indication. Something was said there—I can't even remember what it was—the night after the wedding that there may possibly be something in the wind, that the senator may be becoming engaged to Jackie. But nothing defi-

nite was really said. Then Jackie came back a week or so later. And then there were rumors; it came to our office that he was going to announce his engagement. We didn't quite believe it because actually his courtship of Jackie was just completely apolitical. It was mostly through Charles Bartlett, and he was dating other girls. . . . We knew he saw Jackie Bouvier, and we knew that there was an interest there. . . . I can remember Kenny O'Donnell saying that fall that within a year that he'd be married. And nobody believed it.

—JEAN MANNIX, STAFF MEMBER TO
SENATOR JOHN F. KENNEDY

Jackie wasn't convinced that Kennedy was serious about her. "He couldn't be less interested in me," she told a colleague. Still, her column questions began reflecting what was on her mind:

What is your worst fault as a husband?
Should husbands and wives criticize each other?
Would you postpone your wedding plans if you had to live with your in-laws?
Can you give me any reason why a contented bachelor should get married?
Should engaged couples reveal their pasts?
What changes do you plan to make in raising your children from the way you had been brought up?
Should rich wives pay alimony to poor husbands?
Do you approve of joint bank accounts?
The Irish author Sean O'Faolain claims that the Irish are deficient in the art of love. Do you agree?
What is your candid opinion of marriage?

While she was clearly intrigued, then fond of, and then smitten with, and finally fell in love with Jack Kennedy, at that particular moment Jackie had certainly not made up her mind to marry him—or anyone else for that matter. In an illustrated poem Jackie made for a friend who had just become engaged, she drew herself, "skinny and underpaid, working as a French maid" in Paris while her married friend was burning toast and feeding babies at six in the morning. One verse ran:

"Watch yo' step honey on that path
of roses,"

"There's more thorns 'neath them thar
leaves than you Knowses."

―――◆―――

The inevitable question remained formally unasked by Kennedy. "I don't know if I'll live long enough to marry him," she then joked, and later recalled, "both of us knew it was serious, I think, but we didn't talk about it then."

> He wanted to get married—and [he] didn't want to get married—and then she told me about the night that he finally did [ask her to marry]. And she went off to the coronation.
>
> —JOAN BRADEN, FRIEND

CORONATION

*I*T WAS A CHANCE, SHE LATER SAID, TO DO SOME "REGULAR WRITING" OF FULL-length feature stories, but initially, Jacqueline Bouvier went to the London coronation of Queen Elizabeth in May 1953 as a companion to her friend Aileen Bowdoin Train—and at the instigation of Mrs. Auchincloss, who felt Jackie shouldn't be "waiting for the telephone to ring."

> At the time, her drawings of the coronation appeared on the front page of the *Times-Herald* three or four times, and they were really very good, very clever. I didn't see him [Kennedy] while she was there, but he must have seen them.
>
> —JANET AUCHINCLOSS

As they sailed across the Atlantic, Jackie drew cartoons to accompany her newspaper feature stories, including one about the dogs on board, imagining them with human characteristics when in fact she was satirizing their snobbish owners. In London, Jackie continued with her "Inquiring Cameragirl" column. Fueled by her love of history, she even asked a group at Buckingham Palace, "Do you think Elizabeth will be England's last queen?"

> She was fun to be with because she imagined what it would have been like for her to have been many of the historical characters like the wives of Henry VIII, and the first Queen Elizabeth. She imagined how the lives of the queens underwent dramatic change.
>
> —AILEEN BOWDOIN TRAIN

Besides the column, Jackie also cranked out full-length feature pieces, one of which vividly described London's euphoria:

> Every home one could see . . . bore a picture of Queen Elizabeth—pasted on the outside of the house or in a window. . . . Throughout the city, traffic is unbelievably congested. . . . The Londoners seem amazed at the hordes of Americans here for the colorful event. All the big hotels are jammed with new visitors arriving every day. And the Dorchester, the wartime home of many American officers, is the most beautifully decorated. The facade designed by Oliver Messel represents theater boxes: pale blue balconets with purple and gold draperies. At night gas-fed torches on long white poles blaze above the main entrance, opposite Hyde Park and a block away from the Marble Arch. As I walked thru the Dorchester lobby, one woman turned to another and said: "No, darling, let's lunch at Claridge's. That's where all the deposed monarchs are staying.". . . We went dancing at the 400, a tiny private night club in Mayfair. Lined with accordion-pleated red velvet, it looked like the inside of a jewel box. . . . "I wonder how Elizabeth will change after the coronation," mused a close friend of Prince Philip. . . . We heard the story behind the most popular photograph of the queen . . . of her driving to the opening of parliament on November 4, 1952. . . . The procession was a bit late in starting and she seemed more upset than usual as the photographers crowded around. Then Prince Philip said to her, "Darling, give them one of your best."

"Articles Excellent, But You Are Missed" came a telegram from Jack Kennedy.

Despite the constant rain, Jackie and Aileen reveled in the first great celebration in London of the postwar era, watching the coronation procession from the window at Burberry's. Aileen noticed, however, that Jackie focused on bookstores, with a list of titles on the British legislative process that she was intent on finding.

> She kept buying all these political books and telling me they were for her stepfather. I knew perfectly well they were for Jack. He loved Aldous Huxley, and so she had a whole suitcase full of him.
>
> He had asked her about marriage before we left and she was having a very hard time making up her mind about whether she wanted to marry. After the

coronation, we went over to Paris. We just went out, to bookstores, to antique stores, to the Louvre. I don't think it was indecision about him. She was worried about being taken over by politics and another family, because she always wanted to be herself, and I think that losing her own personality was what she was most worried about.

—AILEEN BOWDOIN TRAIN

He called me up from, I think, Cape Cod, the day she was flying back. . . . I said, "She's landing in New York and then flying down to Washington." He said, "That plane, I think, stops in Boston and I'm going to meet her there." It was the first time that I felt that this was really a serious romance, at least on his part. I had suspected that Jackie cared a lot although she had never really said so because she is the sort of girl who covers her feelings.

—JANET AUCHINCLOSS

Before she left for England, I heard she was running around with the new Senator Jack Kennedy. She had done an interview with him for the column. I called her into my office. "He's a generation older than you. You watch your step." She was very solemn. "Yes, sir," she said quietly. Next thing I knew I got an invitation to the wedding.

—FRANK C. WALDROP

ENGAGEMENT

I took the choicest bachelor in the Senate.

—JACQUELINE BOUVIER

It was upon her return from England, by air, Jackie later recalled, that he formally pressed her, along with a diamond and emerald ring, to marry him. In Newport until the wedding, the senator's fiancée began making plans. With Jack, she registered for their marriage license—and was shocked to discover it was newsworthy enough to be photographed by the press. Over a thousand wedding invitations were sent out to a wide variety of friends, family, colleagues, and political allies, everyone from Mini Rhea to the Nixons.

I'm home one morning, and I get a phone call from Newport, and it's Jackie, and she says "I understand you have a baker in Fall River that's going to make our wedding cake. . . . Do you have the baker available? Could you come down? I want to pick out something I like.". . . So I got a hold of Mr. Plourde and we went down there, and she was in shorts, you know, she was just the typical, excited girl about to be married. So the conversation was about Jack. Of course, she was deeply in love. You could tell by looking at her. She asks us about our family, and the conversation went something like this: "Are you married, Ed?" And I says, "Yes, I'm married." And she said, "Have you any children?" I says, "Yes, I've got three boys." "Oh," she says, "that's wonderful. Jack wants ten children," she says. . . . So anyway, in the course of the conversation, I said, "Incidentally, you're marrying quite a guy." And as I think about what happened and her remarks—and I've got it right in the back of my head exactly how she said it, and every time I say it, it give me goose pimples—she says, "Yes, I'm the luckiest girl in the world."

—EDWARD BERUBE, MASSACHUSETTS POLITICAL FIGURE

Jackie's full-time job at the paper had been a strikingly different life from the conventional life of charity work and social life, of a postdebutante, but when it came time to decide what direction her life would take after marriage, she consciously chose the more traditional venue.

There are friends of Mrs. Kennedy's who believe that had she not met Jack Kennedy in Washington [again] in the summer of 1952, she would surely have been a writer.

—MARIE BRENNER, WRITER

There is every indication that Jackie had thought about continuing to write full-time and discussed the idea with Senator Kennedy. "Well, Jackie," he cracked, "one writer in the family is enough," referring to his authorship of *Why England Slept*. He wanted his wife to meet the public expectations for a Senate wife, as she was already doing as his fiancée. A month after the engagement, she made another political appearance with him, in Worcester, when he presented a check to a church hit by a tornado. Jackie acquiesced but bluntly remarked on the compromise:

Since Jack is such a violently independent person, and I, too, am so independent, this marriage will take a lot of working out.

Another factor in her decision was that she hadn't been given more full-length feature assignments at the newspaper and felt stuck as the "Inquiring Cameragirl." She explained, "I've been getting a little tired of the same format all the time. There wasn't enough chance for real writing. [So,] I'm unemployed." She did not, however, entirely give up the hope of writing. "I always wanted to be some kind of writer. . . . Like a lot of people, I dreamed of writing the Great American Novel." She later mused about the kind of life she had sacrificed by giving up her job:

> If I hadn't married, I might have had a life very much like Gloria Emerson's. She is a friend who started out in Paris writing about fashion—and then ended up as a correspondent in Vietnam. The two ends of her career couldn't seem further apart and that is the virtue of journalism. You never know where it's going to take you, but it can be a noble life.

Jackie also pointed out what was perhaps the greatest reason she acquiesced: "At that point in my life, what I wanted more than anything else in the world was to be married to him." And if Kennedy himself wasn't changing careers to marry, he too had certainly changed his focus. As busy as he was as a freshman senator, he could think of little except his impending partner.

> [He said] "I have never met anyone like her—she's different from any girl I know. Do you want to see what she looks like?" Jack pulled out this strip of four pictures, the kind you get in a penny arcade. The pictures show two people clearly in love.
>
> —DAVE POWERS, KENNEDY AIDE AND FRIEND

ONTO THE FRONT PAGE

*T*HE KENNEDY-BOUVIER WEDDING WAS SET FOR SEPTEMBER 12, 1953. JACKIE asked all of her siblings to be in the wedding party along with best friend Nancy Tuckerman and Aileen and Helen Bowdoin. Among her new in-laws, she was closest to Jean, Robert, and Ted Kennedy, who were all in the wedding, along with Charles and Martha Bartlett.

> The whole Kennedy clan is unperturbed by publicity. We feel differently about it. Their clan is totally united. Ours is not.
>
> —MICHELLE BOUVIER PUTNAM, AUNT

The Auchinclosses, she said, wanted "a simple and very small wedding." The Kennedys invited most of the United States Senate. The bride and her family acquiesced on the size of the wedding, but the press coverage of it was what truly shocked them. Jackie had been amused but surprised when she learned that during her sail with Jack at his family's Hyannis Port, Massachusetts, compound they would be joined by a *Life* magazine reporter and photographer who would cover her for a story entitled "Life Goes Courting with a U.S. Senator."

> Jackie didn't want to have reporters at the wedding. Her mother was so sensitive to having publicity of any kind. She thought it was demeaning and vulgar. Mr. Kennedy said in our case there'll have to be reporters at the wedding because he was a public figure.
>
> —ROSE KENNEDY

The night before the wedding, at the Newport Clambake Club bridal dinner, Jacqueline Bouvier proved that she was up to the Kennedy competition. That night, Jack joked in his remarks to guests that his motivation in marrying Jackie was to remove her from the Fourth Estate, because she was becoming too much of a risk to his political fortunes. Jackie responded by remarking that her fiancé, the great Pulitzer Prize-winning writer, had actually sent her only one missive throughout their courtship. She held up a postcard from Bermuda, with a red hibiscus flower. She read it: "Wish you were here. Jack."

The next morning, after the wedding party headed out of Hammersmith Farm and into town for the ceremony, it was difficult to pull the limousines up in front of St. Mary's Catholic Church. To the bride's amazement, thousands of people were waiting for her.

> I was an usher in the wedding party. The crowds were unbelievable. She didn't want to have her picture taken by all these hordes of photographers. I came up the steps of the church with her and my father. One photographer had this long, telephoto-type lens and pushed it right into her face, almost right onto her. This is as she was coming into the church, to go down the aisle and be married! I had to push the lens back into his camera.
>
> —YUSHA AUCHINCLOSS

It only got worse when Jackie appeared before the crowd for the first time as Mrs. Kennedy. She was gently tugged on the arm by her new husband to stand for a while on the top of the church steps and pose for the Associated Press, United Press, *New York Times*, *Boston Globe*, *Washington Post,* and even *Life* magazine. She grimaced.

The crowd of well-wishing sycophants and curious locals were tired of having their view blocked by the photographers. They literally knocked over the Newport police barricades and rope cordon set up across the street from the church and rushed the Kennedy couple, ripping down NO PARKING signs on the sidewalk of the church that were also impeding their view. Police estimated that there were over three thousand onlookers. The *New York Times* was, of course, there to report that the public "nearly crushed the bride."

Even as a member of the wedding party—you wondered whether you were going to be able to even get into and out of the church. I mean, just masses of crowds outside craning and pushing and crowding in and shoving just to see the bride.

—AILEEN BOWDOIN TRAIN

It was the transition of her suddenly becoming this public figure, but she rapidly went back to being a private person. Or tried to. She was quite caught off guard by the number of people watching. As were my father and stepmother. Jackie was stunned, sort of dazed by it. But it was a good taste of what was to come, what she would have to get used to.

—YUSHA AUCHINCLOSS

I read in one account that "so great was the traffic that cars were backed up nearly half a mile and it took almost two hours for the guests to pass through the reception line to greet the couple." I daresay Jackie must have got a little tired smiling and shaking hands, but I can't think of a more appropriate introduction to her new life as the wife of a political figure.

—ROSE KENNEDY

At the reception, held at Hammersmith Farm, over 1,200 guests sat at tables on the lawn, ate creamed chicken, danced on the terrace to the music of Meyer Davis, and viewed gifts displayed on tables in the house. Each bridesmaid and usher made a toast. At one point the dance floor cleared and the couple waltzed to "I Married an Angel" and "No Other Love."

Jackie gave her bridesmaids monogrammed silver picture frames, and Jack presented Brooks Brothers umbrellas to his ushers.

It was extremely exciting for us, in the wedding party. This glamorous, young senator and this beautiful girl. For her to be the bride that day, however, she had to almost act it out. And, I do think she was really worried about her life and future in politics. She was a woman of great determination, and spirit. In politics, she would need it.

—AILEEN BOWDOIN TRAIN

Jackie Bouvier arriving at St. Mary's Church for her wedding, escorted by stepfather, Hugh D. Auchincloss, with her mother, Janet Lee Auchincloss, behind them, Newport, 1953.

FOUR

Political Partner
1953–1961

I separate politics from my private life, maybe that's why
I treasure my life at home so much. In this business
there's always going to be flare-ups about something.
And you must somehow get so it doesn't upset you. I
think I was always good at it. I can drop this curtain in
my mind.

—Jackie Kennedy

Jackie Kennedy speaking to a group during Senator Kennedy's 1958 re-election campaign in the Berkshires, Ted Kennedy and John F. Kennedy watching.

"MAGIC"

I knew right away that Jackie was different from all the other girls Jack had been dating. She was more intelligent, more literary, more substantial. . . . They were kindred souls. Jack and Jackie, two halves of the same whole.

—LeMOYNE BILLINGS, KENNEDY FAMILY FRIEND

After a honeymoon of several days in Mexico, where Kennedy caught a swordfish that Jackie had hung in his office, the newlyweds spent a week in

Beverly Hills, then headed up the California coast to San Francisco. It was then that Jackie learned of Kennedy's ambition to become president. Her response was to write a poem:

———◆———

Meanwhile in Massachusetts Jack Kennedy dreamed
Walking the shore by the Cape Cod Sea
Of all the things he was going to be.

He breathed in the tang of the New England fall
And back in his mind he pictured it all . . .

He thought with his feet most firm on the ground
But his heart and his dreams were not earthbound
He would call New England his place and his creed
But part he was of an alien breed
Of a breed that had laughed on Irish hills . . .
That surged in the depth of his too proud heart . . .
He turned on the beach and looked toward his house.
On a green lawn his white house stands
And the wind blows the sea grass low on the sands . . .
The lights glowed inside, soon supper would ring
And he would go home where his father was King.
But now he was here with the wind and the sea
And all the things he was going to be . . .
He would find love
He would never find peace
For he must go seeking
The Golden Fleece . . .

———◆———

Kennedy, who'd not yet been exposed to her poetry, was taken aback by the serious piece. When he read some of her satirical illustrated books, he unsuccessfully tried to get her permission to publish them. He did, however, share her poem with his family.

Jackie is a rather quiet and shy person and soft-spoken—at least in comparison with most of our brood—and there may have been doubts about her among one or another of Jack's brothers or sisters or cousins at first, but that marvelous poem, which they read, immediately resolved them. Here indeed was an admirable new member, someone who could contribute a new dimension, who had insights and sensitivities challenging to them, and a fascinating person to know.

—ROSE KENNEDY

She's poetic, whimsical, provocative, independent, and yet very feminine. Jackie has always kept her own identity and been different. That's important in a woman. What husband would want to come home at night and talk to another version of himself? Jack knows she'll never greet him with "What's new in Laos?"

—ROBERT KENNEDY, BROTHER-IN-LAW

Like most young brides, she looked forward to a more or less normal life. She probably wanted to have a home and to have her husband in it. I think it was difficult for her to make the adjustment to the kind of life she has had to lead, but she did make it, and without feeling sorry for herself.

—JEAN KENNEDY SMITH, SISTER-IN-LAW

Jackie was immediately befriended by Jack's father and brother Bobby, but her mother-in-law was a challenge to know. In her, Jackie saw much of her own principled and disciplined mother, and she early on appreciated Rose's deference. "My mother-in-law, she just bent over backward not to interfere," Jackie recalled. "If she gave a suggestion, it was in the sweetest way. She sort of set . . . Jack and me up as an entity."

She admired Mother, saying she was a thoroughbred. Whenever she came over for dinner at my parents, for example, she always complimented Mother on how attractive she looked. For their first Christmas in the White House, my brother and his family came down to spend their vacation in Palm Beach with our parents. They stayed in my parents' home, rather than rent a place. I thought that was quite unusual. If Jackie hadn't wanted to do that, they wouldn't have.

—EUNICE KENNEDY SHRIVER, SISTER-IN-LAW

If she began to meld into his family, he began melding into hers:

Mummy had something with Jack Kennedy. She really, really loved him. He could do no wrong. Lee was crazy about him. From a very, very young age he became my great hero. He and Yusha got on closely. But Mummy, of all people, she thought he just walked on water.

—JAMIE AUCHINCLOSS

They stayed up at Cape Cod quite late that fall and . . . that first winter they lived [in a rented home at 3321] Dent Place. So I did, of course, see them quite often then. And the best book that Jackie has ever written was one she wrote that winter and that she gave to little Janet. It was called *A Book for Janet: In Case You Are Ever Thinking of Getting Married This Is a Story to Tell You What It's Like*. . . . She drew absolutely wonderful pictures of her waving good-bye to Jack as he left the house in the morning and, of course, they were all funny caricatures. There was one of the dome of the Capitol all lit up at night, very dark, and there was a rhyme underneath it about when you saw the light burning there late at night and he wasn't home yet, you knew that the country was safe because he was working.

—JANET LEE AUCHINCLOSS

Though journalists later stressed the differences between the two of them, the couple actually had many bridges. Kennedy had also followed a desire to live in Europe, working in the U.S. embassy in London and traveling extensively on the Continent; his first ambition was also to write; he also had a pronounced talent for writing; and after writing *Why England Slept*, he too pursued journalism briefly, covering the 1945 UN Conference in San Francisco.

I remember one of the great treats when I first came to Washington was when Jackie would call up and ask me to join her and my brother in going out around the region to see some of the Civil War sites—Antietam, Fredericksburg, Gettysburg—a wonderful Sunday pastime. We would tour the battlegrounds, and my brother and Jackie knew everything about the Civil War.

—SENATOR EDWARD M. KENNEDY

Their great intellectual bonds were literature and painting. She painted, and encouraged him to paint—he had some talent. They exchanged books and titles—history, classic fiction, poetry. Kennedy was very proud of Jackie, and she taught him. He learned from her.

—ARTHUR M. SCHLESINGER, FRIEND AND ADVISOR

Jackie goaded him to relax by painting, and took color photographs of local houses for him to use as subjects. She memorized the ballad of "John Brown's Body" because, she recalled, "He loved to hear parts of it recited." She took courses on American history at Georgetown in the spring of 1954 to better converse with him on the subject.

Jack loved her and was proud of her and appreciated her. And it would be hard to imagine a better wife for him. She brought so many things that helped round out and fulfill his character. She developed his interests in art, music, and poetry—especially poetry, in which he had had only a mild interest before. He learned to delight in it because she had such pleasure from it.

—ROSE KENNEDY

She had a fantastic desire for historical knowledge, and she was a sponge once she learned it. She caught every nuance. And she wanted to know American history not just for herself, but for her husband. They were almost competitive in the knowledge they consumed; very much like Henry and Clare Luce, in trying to one-up the other on historical facts and so forth, and I think on many points, well, he almost acquiesced that she knew more about history than he did.

—LETITIA BALDRIGE, FRIEND

That competitiveness emerged playfully in their first year together, but Jackie felt a subtle jealousy when he flirted with other women. She termed his attractiveness "incandescence," and for a time in the mid-1950s teased him about it with the nickname "Magic."

He was very attentive, flirtatious; but if a woman bored him, he would drop her quicker than any known man. He often would talk across a very beautiful girl because she didn't have sense enough to come in out of the rain. I've seen him do it even after he received high position. He would skip people at his own dinner table. It was a perfectly average kind of marriage in many respects. He would be complaining about the price of her clothes. . . . There was that kind of little playback of course.

—WILLIAM WALTON, ARTIST AND FRIEND

In a private note to Zeke Hearin, Jackie provided a glimpse of their life together, and her protective, mothering instinct for a needy husband, joking that among all the delicate and fussy wedding gifts they had received the only ones Kennedy liked and used were the leather coasters Hearin gave. Otherwise, Kennedy said, he might be spotted escaping into the dark away from the precious surroundings she had created. The couple lived in their rented home until the summer of 1954.

> We spent the first four summers of our marriage with Jack's parents at Hyannis Port. We didn't have our own house here. . . . Grandpa wanted to keep everyone together here. He had this [four-bedroom] house for us before we lived in it. . . . I fought against the idea, I thought it was too close, I wanted to be away from the compound.

If anything, as she spent more time with the Kennedys, the more she affirmed her individuality. Paradoxically, Jackie's distinctive personality enhanced the colorful crew.

> She survived because [of] the interests she had . . . in ballet and art and those kinds of things that a lot of the Kennedy sisters aren't particularly interested in. . . . She had her own life; she made her own interests; and she created this atmosphere about herself. . . . I think it helped. She's very strong so she kept her own personality and fitted in at the same time. . . . In the end you bow to Jackie. And they all respected her views about this and that.
> —DOROTHY TUBRIDY, KENNEDY FAMILY FRIEND

SENATE WIFE

> I remember distinctly this beautiful woman coming to my very simple house when she was one of the new Senate wives, for a luncheon. How young she was, and how different from all the rest of us.
> —LADY BIRD JOHNSON, FRIEND AND SENATE WIFE

> Mrs. Saltonstall took Mrs. Kennedy to a meeting of the ladies of the Senate Red Cross. Mrs. Kennedy, putting on her white Red Cross veil, whispered to Mrs. Saltonstall: "I must go up and show Jack this veil." She did, and then returned to making bandages.
> —SENATOR LEVERETT SALTONSTALL, MASSACHUSETTS

In 1981, Jackie discussed her impressions of the United States Senate during an oral history about Senator John Sherman Cooper of Kentucky, a Republican and friend of her and her husband—or "JFK," as he was known in the Senate:

> You never had the feeling that members of the opposite party were unfriendly in the Senate, either with the senators or with their wives. There was always a nice feeling. . . . Don't you think that a liberal Republican and a Democrat felt the same about many things. . . . Not so narrowly partisan, they could appreciate the qualities of the other. You get a lot done in the Senate with bipartisan[ship].

Unsatisfied with remaining ignorant of politics, Jackie learned which senators supported which legislation. Her enlarged political acumen was illustrated in her disagreement with Arthur Schlesinger's idea that Senator Fulbright showed "courage about McCarthy." She remarked tartly, "What was McCarthy to Fulbright. . . . Fulbright never voted for the Civil Rights Bill and campaigned *for* segregation. He is my classic example of the reverse of political courage."

"I wasn't very interested in politics before I married Jack," she admitted, "but I'm learning by osmosis. . . . People say I don't know anything about politics, but you learn an enormous amount just being around politicians." Jackie attended the opening session of each Congress and many of the hearings of committees on which JFK served. She began learning about the African independence movements in individual countries as a frequent front-row observer of the African subcommittee hearings of the Senate Foreign Relations Committee, chaired by Jack. In the spring of 1957 she could often be found in the Senate Select Committee hearings looking into organized crime connections to the labor unions. Nor was she without opinions or a desire to assist her husband on some efforts that appealed to her. "I'm trying to help with this bill to relax the McCarran Immigration Act," she told a reporter later in the decade, "I feel strongly about it. A bill that restrictive might not have let in the Bouviers or the Kennedys from Ireland, or the McCarrans!" She recalled that "one of the most thrilling moments of my life was the time I watched Jack make his speech about the St. Lawrence Seaway."

> She used to come often to the Senate and listen to the speeches and floor action and votes. Mrs. Kennedy would sit, more often than not, in the diplo-

matic gallery, rather than in the wives' gallery or the family's gallery. She would sit right in the center, just dressed very casual, and virtually nobody knew who she was, except inside people, Senate people. The first time I ever remember seeing her, she had on these Capri pants, a sleeveless white blouse and a scarf over her head, and sunglasses—this was outside. But yet here she was going to Senate deliberations! It seemed like a contrast.

I also recall occasions when she was there listening to the proceedings and Senator Kennedy had nothing to do with the debate. She would just be there taking it in from the gallery. She didn't much go to the Senate ladies luncheons and roll bandages. I never saw her in my four years as a page at any meeting of constituents or guests, or having her picture taken with them, because that was a rather frequent thing with the Senate wives in the anteroom. It was generally her interest in the proceedings or getting the senator off the floor to have some lunch.

She used to pack these picnic lunches for the senator. I think it's more to get him out and off the floor. I always assumed it had something to do with his back injury. She seemed very protective, very wifely about that sort of thing, and they would just sometimes go out and sit on the Capitol steps, or they'd go out and sit on the Capitol lawn. I remember one time, the senator was on the floor and asked me to take a note up to her in the diplomatic gallery. And I said, "Oh, yes, Senator, I'll take it right up to her." She was very kind and smiled. She read the note. And then it got to be, kind of, a usual thing. On occasion, I would see her out in the Senate reception room just outside the Senate floor, and she would ask me to go get the senator because it was time for his lunch.

I didn't read the notes, but they had to be clever and romantic because I waited to see if she had a message for him, and as soon as she got them she read them, and they always made her immediately break into a smile.

—DUKE ZELLER, FORMER SENATE PAGE

Jackie chose her Senate activities carefully. She served on the Committee on American Relief for Korea, and offered suggestions to the Senate Committee on the Senate Reception Room in its attempt to choose the five outstanding past senators whose portraits would be hung there. The Senate wives had begun to assist in student exchange programs in the Washington area, and with her skill with Spanish, Jackie tried to initiate exchanges from Cuba. Of those Cuban students whom she did manage to encourage to come to the United States, she helped arrange for their housing in "typical American" homes, invited them to see the Senate in action, and chaperoned them in Washington. She knew the up and down sides of it all—"I was an exchange student myself."

With two homes to run—Washington and Hyannis—and Kennedy's unpredictable speaking and traveling schedule, she was never idle. "Frankly, this takes quite a bit of planning. . . . [It's not] the easiest life to adjust to. But you think about it and figure out the best way to do things . . . usually you find yourself well adjusted." Socializing was not her priority:

> You always hear about Washington—all this going out and party circuit. We never did that; we didn't like it. Then Jack would be traveling a lot, so we just liked to stay home. . . . I never like to say "enjoy the social life" because I think that sounds so trivial and frivolous. . . . Who's in? Who's out? Dinner parties . . . that silly treadmill I have no esteem for. . . . All the big receptions, the cocktail parties—forget that. I think I may have been to one in my life—or the big embassy dinners, even. I'm not sure that anything of substance is really accomplished there. . . .
>
> The French know this—anybody knows this—if you put busy men in an attractive atmosphere where the surroundings are comfortable, the food is good, you relax, you unwind, there's some stimulating conversation. You know, sometimes quite a lot can happen. Contacts can be made, you might discuss something, or . . . you might have different foreigners there and then say, "Gosh, that's an idea. Maybe we ought to see each other next week on that," or whatever. So it can be very valuable that way. . . . Social life, where it's used, is part of the art of living in Washington.

Jackie took pride in her "full-time job" of political wife—even her sartorial influence:

> After their marriage his suits fit perfectly, were conservatively cut and perfectly pressed. . . . From a fumbling person who couldn't tie his own tie, and it was always too long, to an immaculate dresser.
>
> —Evelyn Lincoln, secretary to
> Senator John F. Kennedy

Many mornings, Jackie drove Jack to his office and stayed to help out. She read through the Congressional Record for issues on educational programs. She urged him to lower his voice and articulate his words slowly, for dramatic effect, and to use his hands in emphatic gestures.

Jackie is a perfectionist; anything she did, she wanted to do very well—and she became very, very good at it. That went for politics, too. She worked logically, starting with what she did well. She was excellent with languages. She realized that she could help him with the ethnic mail that came into the Boston office from all over Massachusetts—Italians, French, Portuguese, Spanish, Polish.

—DAVE POWERS

She helped him greatly with translations of French documents when he was preparing a speech on Indochina. I think some of the materials were older books, magazines, scholarly periodicals, very possibly articles that the Library of Congress may very well have rounded up in realizing that some of the articles on Indochina were from the French point of view or indeed from the Indochinese point of view. When he came across something in French, the senator would think—"My wife could translate the research material."

I don't think she herself regarded herself as a political savant or counselor. She had judgments of political figures as people, as individuals, but usually unrelated to their political positions, except that she loved her husband, and people who liked him, and who he liked, she liked. People who were mean to him, she didn't like.

Offhand, I don't recall hearing about her being his political sounding board. In a meeting, or even to me in private, he never said, "I was discussing this with Jackie and it occurred to her that we should do this, or, in her opinion so and so is unreliable." However, their personal relationship was totally private and kept very private. She could have played such a role without anyone knowing about it. And, secondly, it was certainly my impression that he shared a great many things with her and told her a great many things in his life and what was on his mind, so in a sense, her reactions may have had some help or influence.

—TED SORENSON

When the senator was unable to attend many functions where foreign visitors were being honored, Jackie began to attend as his representative, reporting back her observations to him—whether it was the new Soviet minister or Spain's Prince Juan Carlos—but she was increasingly being observed by the press.

Jackie Kennedy working with Senator Kennedy in his office at the Capitol, 1953.

Jackie was never comfortable being asked personal questions to be shared with the voters. After a *Boston Globe* interview in April 1954, she wrote its author, Virginia Bohlin, "I can't tell you what a happy feeling of relief it gives you to pick up the paper with a story in it about yourself and not put it down scarlet with embarrassment." For their part, most reporters found themselves impressed with her:

> I remember a day I spent with Mrs. Kennedy. . . . Everyone we came into contact with that day, from office workers in her husband's office to the cabdriver who drove us to a foster home, seemed to respond to the quietly dressed senator's wife. There was nothing high hat about her—we perched on drugstore stools at lunchtime and had hamburgers.
>
> —FRANCES LEIGHTON, REPORTER

Her father-in-law had built his fortune through diversifying his investments in different businesses, including film production. Joe Kennedy knew how powerfully a picture or image can convey an idea, and he used that power in any publicity related to Jack and Jackie. From newsreels to fashion magazines to network television interviews, publicity became part of Jackie's routine. When it was her call, however, the answer was usually no, as she wrote a magazine editor:

I wish I could either tell you that I would love to do it—or had just been run over by a bus—and couldn't pose for months. . . . If you won't be too angry I think I would just as soon not do one. . . . Every now and then I have to do some kind of political story with Jack—that is all inevitable and part of his job—but I am always embarrassed by them.

Jackie also had to begin to cope with the public, and being a wife in a family whose wealth was widely reported also made her a specific target for appeals from strangers, like one Ronald Munro of Birmingham, England, who wrote her for money after reading a false report that she had hosted a dinner costing $20,000. She responded:

I could not possibly give you that amount of money, were you my closest friend or relative. True, my husband is well off, but taxes in this country are enormous and when he has paid for the household expenses and his business expenses, which are very great indeed, he does give to charity and that goes to the Kennedy Foundation for underprivileged children, and at the end there is not just a great pile of money lying around as you imagine.

As she found herself becoming more of a public figure, Jackie grew uneasy. As she put it simply in 1981, "Some people are made for public life, and some aren't."

PROFILES

THE FALL OF 1954 BROUGHT JACKIE TWO GREAT SHOCKS—FIRST SHE MISCARried what would have been their first child, then, in a final attempt to correct his crushing back pain, Kennedy underwent spinal fusion on October 21 in New York, and infection set in. A priest gave him the last rites of the Catholic church, and it appeared that Jackie would be widowed after just thirteen months of marriage. She recalled, "It was the first time I really prayed."

At the hospital, she spoon-fed him his meals and wrote letters to Kennedy's colleagues in response to their notes and calls—President Eisenhower, Vice President Nixon, Adlai Stevenson, Senate Majority Leader Lyndon Johnson. To Johnson, she wrote in November:

I just wanted to tell you how terribly much your kind letter meant to Jack. It will be so long before he can write a letter or talk on the phone or anything. . . . I never realized how much letters from friends who are thinking about you mean to people who are sick—they give you so much strength and courage for the long weeks when you have to lie in that horrible dark hospital room. . . . He is feeling better now—but he had a bad time in the beginning, which has left him so weak. I guess they won't let him sit up for about five weeks—but at least every day is a step forward.

"My wife is a pretty shy, quiet girl," Kennedy remarked at the time, "but when things get rough, she can handle herself pretty well." His condition, however, did not improve, and he was now completely immobile. Depressed at the prospect of further incapacitation, Kennedy underwent a second operation in February. It proved successful, and with Jackie he went to live in Florida for his recuperation.

> The incision was very large, it was still draining, and the dressings had to be changed several times a day. Jackie did this skillfully and gently and calmly, and made no comment about it to anyone.
>
> —ROSE KENNEDY

> She dressed him in slippers and socks, read books and newspapers for him, brought games, fed him. She constantly lifted his spirits and tried to make him laugh as much as possible.
>
> —DAVE POWERS

On occasions, Jackie took dictation on Senate business and sent it up to his secretary, and when JFK began spouting ideas for a book, she seized on it as a way of keeping him distracted from his pain and scribbled the notions down. In 1953, they had discussed Senator Edmund Ross, who had voted his conscience against the removal of President Andrew Johnson during his impeachment, and Jackie grasped the concepts of the book JFK had in mind. She did some initial research from biographies of John Quincy Adams and Sam Houston she had used in her American history course, and remembering how impressed she had been with her Georgetown professor's teaching of history through biography, she brought Jules Davids into the research process.

She went a step further and made the initial inquiries about publishing the book, researching literary agents and publishers, as well as the process of submission. It was Jackie who finally made the successful connection with Harper and Brothers publishers, who contracted to do the book, titled *Profiles in Courage,* which went on to win a Pulitzer Prize. Kennedy later wrote that he could never "adequately acknowledge" the "assistance and criticisms" Jackie provided, and that the book "would not have been possible" without her.

> *Profiles in Courage* couldn't have happened without Jacqueline. She encouraged her husband, read to him, carried out independent research, and on lined yellow copy paper, wrote down parts of the book.
>
> —MOLLY THAYER

For Jackie herself, however, painting increasingly became an escape into solitude as her husband mended and they returned to public life during the summer at Hyannis.

> Her own paintings are marvelously inventive, done in a semi-primitive style. But what fascinates me most about her painting is her complete absence of pretense about it. There is no studio, or room set aside for painting, she does not wear any special smocks or aprons. She simply keeps a very cheap little easel in a closet, has an inexpensive painting set that anyone can get . . . and she paints.
>
> –JACQUES LOWE, PHOTOGRAPHER AND FRIEND

> Jackie developed the atmosphere where it was very collegial for him—invite a friend over, compare notes as they were painting. In the evening, they'd invite friends for dinner to discuss the paintings. It was all a great source of relaxation and diversion as he regained his strength.
>
> –SENATOR EDWARD KENNEDY

By August, Kennedy was well enough to travel to Europe as part of his duties on the Senate Foreign Relations Committee. On the trip Jackie served as his sole support and correspondent with the Senate office. For the first time, she went behind the Iron Curtain in an extensive tour of Poland, and at a dinner in Rome, she served as the translator between Kennedy and former French President George Bidault. While on the Côte d'Azur, resting during the end of the junket, they were invited aboard the yacht of Greek shipping magnate Aristotle Onassis with the sole purpose of having Kennedy meet his hero Winston Churchill.

We went down to Mr. Onassis's yacht one evening and Sir Winston wasn't recognizing people much. And as we left, Mrs. Kennedy said, "I think he thought you were the waiter, Jack."

—WILLIAM DOUGLAS-HOME, FRIEND

That autumn, the Kennedys bought their first home, in suburban Virginia, Hickory Hill:

Jackie and Jack had been thinking of building at Merrywood. George Howe had drawn plans—Jackie had really drawn all the plans and George had consulted with her as architect. She wanted to have a one-story house with a sort of a courtyard, perched up on a cliff over the river. It all got rather complicated, bringing in water and heat—and rather expensive. When I heard about Hickory Hill, . . . I told her about it. . . . They bought it and moved in there intending to live there always, and they did quite a lot of remodeling. I remember all the effort Jackie went to for Jack's bathroom and dressing room. The shelves had to be just in the right place to reach and the drawers had to be so he wouldn't have to lean over to open them—so that it wouldn't hurt his back. I remember the endless trouble she took over that.

—JANET AUCHINCLOSS

As the recovered Jack threw himself back into Senate work and preparations for the 1956 presidential election, his wife became enthusiastically involved. In fact, so "mad for Adlai" was she that Jackie Kennedy drafted Senator Kennedy's statement of support for Adlai Stevenson in her own hand:

In recent months I have been questioned frequently as to the candidate of my choice for the Democratic presidential nomination. My position can be stated simply. Adlai Stevenson was my choice for the presidency in 1952. . . . His intelligence, farsightedness, and reasonableness have neither diminished nor been matched by any other potential nominee. Consequently Adlai Stevenson remains, in my opinion, the most outstanding choice for the presidency in 1956.

Some have accused him of being too liberal—others have charged him with being too conservative. But Adlai Stevenson is beholden to no man and to no section—only to the welfare of our nation at home and abroad."

Kennedy only deleted the second paragraph and made minor word changes before the statement was issued. There was no question that Jackie supported Stevenson strongly and that he trusted her judgment. Lyndon Johnson's campaign manager Jim Rowe even recalled Stevenson asking Jackie to critique a speech he was planning to deliver. But she was also Jack Kennedy's wife—and knew his ambitions:

> Bill Blair was the best friend and closest adviser of Adlai Stevenson. . . . Blair was making an impassioned pitch for Kennedy to make a serious try for the vice presidency. . . . Kennedy listened hard and said little, but Jacqueline turned to Ken Crawford [*Newsweek* bureau chief] and said, in her soft voice, "Why is Bill trying to persuade Jack to run for vice president when Jack really wants to be president?"
>
> —Ralph Martin, reporter

> I don't think her friendship with Stevenson translated into any stronger political alliance between Stevenson and Senator Kennedy. John F. Kennedy was a Stevenson supporter in '52 before he was serious about Jackie, and really had a whole variety of both political and philosophical reasons for supporting him in '56, so I don't think that she determined or even influenced his decision to support him. I think Adlai, being urbane, and witty, and eloquent, and intelligent, was the kind of politician she encountered all too rarely, and therefore could have been somebody in politics she could speak with and learn from, and get ideas and feel strong about and pleased that her husband was supporting.
>
> —Ted Sorenson

That August, Jackie, who was now pregnant again, joined her husband at the Chicago convention. Of that "frenzied arena" and the booming Kennedy-for-vice-president movement, she remembered:

> I was staying in Chicago with Jack's sister Eunice Shriver. He was staying downtown at a hotel, which was sort of a command post, and the only time I remember being involved was the night before the race when we were down at headquarters. I don't remember Jack there exactly, but I remember a lot of commotion and Bobby saying that we must try to get all the votes we

could for the next day. I remember him asking me if I knew anyone in Nevada or some other states. I can remember being there a lot of that night.

On the night of the vote for the vice presidential candidate, Jackie, watching in a viewing box, became the focus of attention:

> Something I'll never forget was Nancy Kefauver and the beautiful Jackie Kennedy in their boxes during the voting. There was no one around Nancy, and Jackie was surrounded by people. Then Estes [Kefauver] won and suddenly there was no one with Jackie. She was left by herself at the end . . . a forlorn figure.
>
> —Mrs. Dixon Donnelly, Kefauver staff aide

For Jackie, coming just short of victory was devastating, despite the fact that she had not wanted Jack to run as vice president that year:

> I think when something like that starts and gets momentum, then you want it, yes. I know when it was over and we flew back to New York afterward there was kind of a letdown.

In New York, Jackie encouraged her husband to continue as planned on to Europe with a friend, Senator George Smathers, to meet with his father in the south of France.

"Jack's worked so hard and he's nervous about this thing [her pregnancy] and I think you all ought to go off and have a good time," Jackie told Smathers. "You guys should take that trip. You all worked so hard, especially Jack. He deserves a rest." Smathers affirmed, "Jackie insisted we go."

ARABELLA

In Newport, on August 23, 1956, Jackie experienced severe pain. Hemorrhaging, she was rushed to Newport Hospital, where she underwent emergency cesarean surgery. The child died just before delivery and was classified as a "stillborn." To Jackie, however, the baby girl, whom she had carried nearly to full term, was very much her child. And although no legal name was listed, she did name the child for herself. The daughter was Jackie's own

"Arabella." Her death was attributed to Jackie's "nervous tension and exhaustion following the Democratic Convention." Upon being alerted by Mrs. Auchincloss, Robert Kennedy rushed from Hyannis to break the news to Jackie and arrange a nearby burial.

At the time of Arabella's death, Kennedy was sailing with his brother Ted and learned of the loss when he received a message as they stopped on the island of Elba, on their way to Naples. From Elba, he immediately called Jackie. He flew directly into Boston's Logan Airport from Europe and walked across the airfield to a waiting private plane headed for Newport. Asked by a reporter about Stevenson, he snapped, "I'd rather talk politics with you some other time," and left.

> I was at the airport and picked him up as soon as he landed. He was more upset than I'd ever seen him. "Can you get me to Newport Hospital in ten minutes?" If we run all the stop signs, I told him, I can do it. He was nervous and if the light would be yellow, he'd say, "Go through it. I'll pay for all the tickets."
>
> —YUSHA AUCHINCLOSS

Under the best of circumstances, Jackie said that both she and Jack lived with "the public life above the water—the private life submerged," but Jackie was rarely forthcoming with her own feelings, even with her husband and mother.

> There's a certain stiffness about Jackie, even shyness. She was that way even with Jack for a long time. It's not that she's frightened of people, but she's not outgoing.
>
> —JANET LEE AUCHINCLOSS

> It was difficult. I was thirty-six, she was twenty-four. We didn't fully understand each other.
>
> —JOHN F. KENNEDY

After losing Arabella, however, the chasm widened as they grew isolated in their own grief. "Jackie losing the baby has affected Kennedy more than his illness did during that bad year," Joe Kennedy wrote a friend. The emotional isolation became a physical one as well, Kennedy increasingly on the road or on Capitol Hill, somewhere away from Jackie, often with others.

She was alone very much out in the country, because Jack would not get home until very late at night for dinner. When she lived in Georgetown she could rush down and have dinner with him or he could come home late. . . . She couldn't drive the car into town in the middle of the night to join Jack for dinner, and he couldn't get away.

—JANET LEE AUCHINCLOSS

"I was alone almost every weekend while Jack traveled the country making speeches," she later told reporters of that period. "It was all wrong." On another occasion, she said, "Politics was sort of my enemy, and we had no home life whatsoever." His absences caused other strains, imagined and real, and observations and conclusions from others:

I'd say that he was devoted to Jackie. I'd say that it was absolutely unquestionable. But of course—it didn't mean he didn't have an eye for others. He was made that way, but undoubtedly he and Jackie got along like a house on fire; they were always having fun together.

—FRANK O'FERRALL, KENNEDY FAMILY FRIEND

I was aware of the fact that sometimes they seemed more affectionate and sometimes less affectionate. But, you know, for an outsider—and anybody's an outsider in this sort of situation—it's really difficult to know and how to attribute it. It would be pure guessing and largely influenced by gossip, and so it doesn't really add anything to history.

—HENRY BRANDON, FRIEND AND JOURNALIST

Legend claims that Joe Kennedy had a heart-to-heart talk with his son, and then one with his daughter-in-law, persuading them not to divorce. There is no record of any such talk from Jackie or Joe Kennedy, or any other witness, or any person told about it by the family. What is part of the record, however, is Rose Kennedy's talk with Jackie about the inevitable gossip of marital troubles in public life, and how to handle them.

Writing about someone is different from finding oneself written about. So each time, in turn, Ethel, then Jackie, then Joan, I made sure to warn them in advance of what they were in for: that they might be hearing and reading all sorts of scandalous gossip and accusations about members of our family, about their husbands, and for that matter about themselves, and eventually even about their children; that they should understand this and be prepared from the beginning, otherwise they might be very unhappy. They took the burden with the blessing. . . .

I know it must have been difficult for her. But I never knew that they had a serious break or that they were contemplating divorce.

—ROSE KENNEDY

What *did* change in the marriage was Jackie's forcing herself to love Jack Kennedy more realistically and pragmatically, committed to him for his attributes, and with much less of her natural tendency toward romanticizing.

What would you expect of two high-strung, keen-witted intensely conscious and gifted people deeply in love and both of them with notions of their own about almost everything? It was not in the stars for that pair to sink gently into each other's arms in a soft corner, murmuring a note of music in perfect key.

—KATHERINE ANNE PORTER, WRITER

In coming together with her husband again, Jackie had begun to understand him more fully. If she had early on romanticized his strengths and motivations, she now realized his weaknesses. Years later, while Jackie was counseling another woman in a similar public position who was having marital problems because of her husband's assignations, some practical advice was offered at the end of their discussion:

Look, it's a trade-off. There are positives and negatives to every situation in life. You endure the bad things, but you enjoy the good. And what incredible opportunities—the historic figures you meet and come to know, the witness to history you become, the places you would never have been able to see that now you can. One could never have such a life if one wasn't married to someone like that. If the trade-off is too painful, then you just have to remove yourself, or you have to get out of it. But if you truly love someone, well. . . .

—JACQUELINE KENNEDY ONASSIS

In a sense, the overall challenge of the marriage remained for Kennedy to completely understand his wife's complexity:

I think he greatly admired some of Jackie's qualities. But often I think he reacted very differently to things than she did because he had a less introverted nature. At least, this is the way he seemed to me. But sometimes he would look at her with a really puzzled look, but he would never say anything hurting to anybody. She was constantly writing him little jingles and poems and bringing him little presents with appropriate rhymes accompanying them. . . .

Jackie has a sometimes fairly distorted sense of humor, but nobody can be funnier.

—JANET LEE AUCHINCLOSS

Jackie did break some of the grimness with her 1957 wedding anniversary gift to Jack. In another one of her illustrated books, titled *"How the Kennedys Spoil Wedding Anniversaries,"* the first sketch showed Jack in the hospital, Jackie at his side. The second sketch had Jackie in the hospital bed with Jack at *her* side.

Selling Hickory Hill to Robert Kennedy, Jack and Jackie started over again in a rented Georgetown home. Many afternoons she took her younger sister and brother, Janet and Jamie, on adventures, whether to watch ice skating or tour the White House. Jackie desperately wanted her own child.

In the story I did in '57 called "The Rise of the Brothers Kennedy," during the trip to South Carolina when Kennedy was making this commencement address, I was talking to Ted and I said, "Well, let's face it. There are rumors going around in Washington about the senator and his wife, that they're not getting along, that they've been separated. What about that?" Ted said rather heatedly, "Well that's not true. As a matter of fact, I can tell you this in confidence, Jackie is pregnant and that's why she's not traveling with him."

—LAURA BERQUIST KNEBEL, LOOK REPORTER

THE OTHER JACK

ALTHOUGH JACKIE WAS NOW CAUGHT UP WITH PLANNING A FAMILY AND FULFILLing political obligations in Washington, she never forgot her solitary father in his little apartment in New York. On more than one occasion, she persuaded Jack Bouvier to visit her in Washington, and she usually tried to build in some private hours to see him when politics brought her to New York.

At her wedding, it had been planned that Jackie's father would give her away, but all his insecurities surfaced at the thought of having to see his former wife, her husband, the media. That he suffered intermittently from alcoholism was never kept a dark secret. In Newport for the wedding, however, he sank so low that he was unable to play his part.

I think we could have worked things out. It was a very delicate situation. My stepmother could be excitable. She felt awkward about his presence at the dinner the night before the wedding. She didn't want him at the wedding, and asked me to tell him this at his room at the Viking Hotel. I did. I came out of the hotel, got into my car, and just sobbed. I told Jackie what I had done. She was angry. She thought her mother should have gone over herself. She told me, "You shouldn't be the scapegoat on this."

—Yusha Auchincloss

At the last minute, Hugh Auchincloss filled in for Jackie's father, who was slipped into the church to watch. It was a further demoralization for Jack Bouvier, and he sank into a depression.

Jackie wrote to him sweetly, in a tone of obvious affection and deeply ingrained respect. She told him she loved him and that she understood how low he must have felt, and the incredible pressure that the wedding situation had placed on his shoulders. Most important, as far as she was concerned, although Hughdie Auchincloss had walked down the aisle with her, it was really John Vernou Bouvier III who had given her away. Having a daughter as wonderful as Jackie, Jack wondered at once how in hell he had ever lost his dignity. At any rate, he regained it that moment. . . . He swore that one day his daughter would be first lady.

—Kathleen Bouvier

While it was widely known that Kennedy and his father-in-law got on well, talking about "sports and girls," Jackie recalled, she also determined that her father would become integrated to some degree into her Auchincloss family:

Jackie first introduced me to her father in 1946. I had heard uncomplimentary things about him from my stepmother, but never from my father. Jackie had already told him about me when we met at his apartment. He offered me a drink and then we were all going to go out for dinner. Jackie was out of the room and he said, "Thank you for taking such good care of my daughter and making her feel part of your family, and always supporting her in what she wants to do with her life." And that started a long friendship. He asked me to call him Uncle Jack.

In early summer 1957, we had dinner and he looked ill, jaundiced. "I'm not feeling very well," he said, "but please, don't alarm Jackie." I came back up to Newport. I remember telling her by the stairs in the big house. "I just had dinner with your father. When I go back down to New York, why don't you come with me." And she said, "Yusha, what are you telling me?" I said, "You better go down as soon as possible." She did, and she saw him just the day before he died. His friend Pam said afterward, "Jack never had a son, and he almost thought of you as Jackie's brother instead of stepbrother." Jackie wanted to delicately bring together her two families. And she very carefully, eventually did.

—YUSHA AUCHINCLOSS

Jack Bouvier died at age sixty-six of liver cancer on August 5, 1957, at New York's Lenox Hill Hospital. Despite the fact that she was six months pregnant and was told firmly by the doctors to decrease her activity, Jackie assumed all responsibility for his funeral. JFK followed her directions—delivering Bouvier's obituary, which she drafted, as well as obtaining a specific old photograph of him that she loved. In his coffin she placed a gold bracelet he had bought her upon her graduation from Miss Porter's. Bouvier remembered her with an oil painting of two Arabian horses and a French Empire desk, which she would always use as her own writing desk. At the funeral mass in St. Patrick's Cathedral, Jackie arranged for white baskets with white summer flowers, "like Lasata in August."

A CHILD

Another Senate page in the summer of 1957 and I were friends. We went to his parents' house, right next door to the Kennedy's, but were locked out and his parents weren't home. Mrs. Kennedy was in the house and came to her door. "What are you boys doing out so late?" So, the upshot was, she invited us to come in and wait. I don't know if she thought we were going to get into mischief, but it seemed to me to be, a kind of a maternal, protective quality. She was also pregnant. Very pregnant. She wanted us to stay with her, concerned about these two kids sitting on the porch alone. Did we want something to eat? She thought it best that we didn't go anywhere. She asked us, "What was going on in the Senate?" Very motherly.

—DUKE ZELLER

In late 1957 a confident Jackie was reading children's books and books on child psychology and teaching techniques for preschool and grammar school children. A favorite reliable source was Dr. Spock. That year, Kennedy aide and confidant Kenny O'Donnell recalled, "brought the beginning of a new happiness to Jackie and Jack's marriage, which had been under a strain." Part of that happiness, for Jackie, was creating a new home:

I remember that when she got the N Street house, it was going to be just right. It was a house with a lot of feeling about it and a lot of charm, but she did that living room—the double living room downstairs—over at least three times within the first four months they were there. . . . Rugs, curtains, upholstery, everything, was suddenly turned lovely different shades of beige. . . . I can remember Jack just saying to me, "Mrs. Auchincloss, do you think we're prisoners of beige?"

—JANET LEE AUCHINCLOSS

Jackie was in excellent health that November when perhaps the most joyous moment of her life occurred at New York Hospital:

Hugh D. and Jack and I waited in the waiting room at the New York Hospital to get the news. Caroline was born at about eight-thirty in the morning of November 27. . . . I'll always remember Jack's face when the doctor came into the waiting room and told him that the baby had arrived and that it was a girl and that Jackie was fine and the baby was fine. . . . I don't remember that he said anything. But I just remember his sweet expression and sort of a smile.

—JANET LEE AUCHINCLOSS

For Jackie, being a mother seemed to validate her sense of self. It gave her an inner peace and security which nothing else ever had. It opened her heart.

—DORIS KEARNS GOODWIN, FRIEND AND
KENNEDY FAMILY HISTORIAN

Jackie Kennedy holding her first child, Caroline Kennedy, 1958.

> When we first married, my wife didn't think her role in my career would be particularly important. I was already in the Senate and she felt she could make only a limited contribution. Now, quite obviously, that I'm in a very intensive struggle—the outcome is uncertain—and she plays a considerable part in it. What she does, or does not do, really affects that struggle. Since I'm completely committed, and since she is committed to me, that commits her. . . .
>
> She is simply invaluable. In French-speaking areas of the state, she is able to converse easily with them, and everyone seems to like her. She never complains about the rugged schedule, but seems to enjoy it.
>
> —JOHN F. KENNEDY

In a supportive role during Kennedy's 1958 re-election campaign, Jackie nervously participated in a thirty-minute television special, "At Home with the Kennedys," that focused on her husband's career and was hosted by Rose Kennedy. But on the road she flourished:

> She proved herself an aggressive and consistent campaigner in 1958 for the Senate campaign. She went into every single district of the state—from Cape Cod to the Berkshires. She observed people and listened to what they were saying and reported it all back to her husband.
>
> —DAVE POWERS

> She was always cheerful and obliging, never complaining, and to me a very refreshing change from the usual campaigning candidate's wife because she did not bother to put on a phony show of enthusiasm about everything that she saw and every local politician whom she met. The crowds sensed that and it impressed them.
>
> —KENNY O'DONNELL

Jackie proved particularly popular in ethnic neighborhoods. She joined Kennedy in the back of a car at the St. Patrick's Day parade in South Boston. In Worcester, she closed her speech in French to the Cercle Français by remarking, "It was not as frightening [to speak] as it would have been in English." Before a crowd of nearly one thousand in a local school, her command of the language and Mediterranean looks misled people into believing that she was Italian:

When she opened her mouth and introduced herself in Italian, fluent Italian may I say, as the wife of Senator Kennedy all pandemonium broke loose. All the people went over and started to kiss her, and the old women spoke to her as if she were a native of the North End. And I think her talk is actually what cemented the relationship between Senator Kennedy and the Italian-Americans of the district.

—WILLIAM deMARCO, BOSTON DISTRICT LEADER

Politics is in my blood. I know that even if Jack changed professions I would miss politics. It's the most exciting life imaginable—always involved with the news of the moment, meeting and working with people who are enormously alive, and every day you are caught up in something you really care about. It makes a lot of other things seem less vital. You get used to the pressure that never lets up, and you learn to live with it as a fish lives in water.

—JACQUELINE KENNEDY

Kennedy won his Senate re-election campaign overwhelmingly, as he had intended, but as 1959 began, it was clear that the campaigning would continue all the way through November 1960—when he hoped to be elected president. Initially, Jackie balked. "It isn't the right time of life for us," she told Laura Berquist. "We should be enjoying our family, traveling, having fun." As advisers to Kennedy began to map out his campaign, however, Jackie's potential for it became evident. In July 1959 she opened up to a man who would become a close friend:

Although I had met Jacqueline Kennedy several times since their marriage, it was really the first occasion for a leisurely chat with her. . . . In the course of the evening I realized that, underneath a veil of lovely inconsequence, she concealed tremendous awareness, an all-seeing eye and a ruthless judgment.

—ARTHUR M. SCHLESINGER JR.

A month later, on the Riviera, Kennedy finally managed to have a thorough conversation with Churchill about how to handle the potential campaign issue of his Catholicism. Jackie accompanied Kennedy at the meeting, which was arranged by Ari Onassis on his yacht. Earlier that year, the Kennedys had joined Onassis for dinner in Washington, and the senator had dined with him alone in New York as well. It was not in Europe and with Europeans, however, that the campaign would be won, and for the first time, Jackie began to travel widely throughout the United States, her only previous extensive trip having been a

1949 backpacking adventure in Yellowstone Park, where she slept in a tent. She now went to political events in Miami and Atlantic City and traveled extensively through Ohio—Bellaire, Cincinnati, Toledo, Cleveland, Columbus—attending the famous Cleveland Steer Roast two years in a row. In Louisiana she delivered a speech in French at a Cajun rice festival, and September 1958 found her in Nebraska and Iowa auditoriums for Democratic Party dinners. When she appeared with Jack, she always said or did something, or looked a certain way, that unwittingly attracted notice:

> I remember Mrs. Kennedy causing a great stir there because it was one of the few times I think Californians had seen somebody with a hemline above the knee. Her glamour and her unconventional beauty attracted attention and enticed the news media.
>
> —JOSEPH CERRELL, DIRECTOR,
> CALIFORNIA DEMOCRATIC PARTY

> It was just terrific, and it was the Oregon Centennial Year, so we had covered wagons out. I remember Jacqueline Kennedy looked one wagon over and said, "Are we going to ride in the wagon?"
>
> —MARY KELLY, OREGON DEMOCRATIC PARTY OFFICIAL

> My strongest early recollection of her was the day the senator was on his way to Philadelphia. He had a briefcase full of papers. She had the memoirs of the court of Louis XIV.
>
> —JOHN KENNETH GALBRAITH, FRIEND
> AND CAMPAIGN ADVISER

Jackie particularly wanted to campaign in the places where it was most difficult: "It's so boring when we keep going to places where everybody loves Jack. . . . Going into Humphrey territory . . . makes things more fun, more challenging." In 1981, she recalled the importance of the preprimary campaigning:

> Really the way that Jack got it was all those years he'd been going around the country—it was six years of our marriage . . . of every single moment of free time going out. . . . It is that road work and it is knowing every county person or delegate that in the end got him the nomination, when he really had the least chance, I suppose, being Catholic.

Jackie was at his side in the Senate Caucus Room on January 2, 1960, when he announced his candidacy, and her influence was immediately apparent to those in the know. JFK's speech that day was filled with allusions to American life—an idea that came directly from his wife:

> When she read aloud passages from de Gaulle's memoirs, especially the introductory evocation of his image of France, he seized on the idea for his own speeches on America.
>
> —ARTHUR M. SCHLESINGER, JR.

Kennedy's Catholicism was an unknown factor; many still thought Stevenson would be the best Democratic candidate—with Kennedy in the number two slot. Jackie disagreed, however. "Let Adlai get beaten alone," she remarked to an editor at dinner. "If you don't believe Jack, I'll cut my wrists and write an oath in blood that he'll refuse to run with Stevenson." Still, her personal friendship with Stevenson now served an important political purpose as well. "Kennedy became delighted that he could remain aligned to Stevenson without liability because of her friendship with him," recalled Arthur Schlesinger.

As they launched into the primaries, Jackie defined her boundaries, remaining apart, for example, from staff meetings—as JFK, Pierre Salinger, who was his press secretary, and others hashed out strategy on one side of the campaign plane, she remained absorbed in Kerouac's *Dharma Bums*. It was the same at home:

> I was always coming down to breakfast in my wrapper with Caroline and there would be a couple of strange governors or labor leaders I'd never seen before, smoking cigars and eating scrambled eggs.

After a somewhat timid effort in New Hampshire, Jackie emerged in March campaigning for primary day in Wisconsin.

> Kennedy and a few reporters came over to the Governor's Mansion for drinks for a couple of hours starting at ten o'clock. . . . At that point they were keeping Jackie bottled up. My wife thought that was terrible, from a feminist point of view. So she went over and talked to Jackie a lot. And then Paul Ringler, chief editorial writer for the *Milwaukee Journal*, came over and talked to Jackie and

later wrote some kind of editorial comment about it to the effect that Jackie was being misjudged, and she wasn't at all that naive about politics and so forth. She really wasn't. I think they were unnecessarily frightened by that.

—EDWIN BAYLEY, WISCONSIN DEMOCRATIC PARTY OFFICIAL

While waiting for her husband at a Kenosha rally, she managed to keep the crowd there by ad-libbing remarks: "I'm not in the habit of arriving at a campaign stop before my husband, and as I don't have any speech prepared, I can tell you whom *I'm* voting for in November." She went into millinery stores, barbershops, hardware stores, gas stations, and garages up and down the main drag.

Getting out of the car into the snow and wind, Jackie would shake hands and talk with people on one side of the sidewalk on the main street of a small town while her husband worked the opposite side. He kept his eyes on her and often muttered to one of us, "Jackie's drawing more people than I am, as usual."

—KENNY O'DONNELL

In Wisconsin, when the Washington office called to let Kennedy know that a civil rights vote was coming up on the Senate floor, Jackie told him, "You go back to Washington and vote, Jack; I'll carry on for you." That day, Jackie made a blitzkrieg across the state, beginning in La Crosse and ending in Stevens Point, making speeches throughout, including her famous commandeering of a supermarket public address system, where she told housewives to "Just keep on with your shopping while I tell you about my husband. . . ." At a farm, she recalled her own efforts at raising a calf. Before a largely blue-collar luncheon in Marshfield, she pointed out that on the Senate Labor and Public Welfare Committee, Kennedy "has done as much for workers in this country as any U.S. senator." He won Wisconsin. Never, however, did Jackie view herself as political.

Jackie isn't trying to make a part in this for herself, as I think some wives do in politics—busy with women's groups and the like, spending much of their day with such activities. Jackie's satisfaction is totally vicarious. It's all come to her through her husband.

—STEVE SMITH, BROTHER-IN-LAW

I see many politicians' wives who are just as vigorous as their husbands. This may be fun for them, but not for me. I spend my days with politicians—not my nights too. I don't want to come home from the Senate and then have to defend my position to my wife all evening!

As it is, my wife leads, in many respects, a somewhat secluded life, which is the way she wants it. She is rather retiring and is really absorbed in our daughter. I think she has been extremely successful in sustaining me, in fulfilling her responsibility to Caroline, and in enjoying life herself.

—JOHN F. KENNEDY

Still, Jackie offered advice on the practical realities of the campaign—like scheduling:

When I saw his schedule of the trip, I told him it was silly zigzagging back and forth, and he agreed. He told me to talk to [aide] Bob Wallace. I did, and things were changed. That's the first time Jack told me to go ahead and do anything like that.

She also served as a secret liaison:

When he wanted to talk to Galbraith and me, and not upset his hardworking aides, Ted Sorenson and Dick Goodwin, he would have her call us and arrange a meeting.

—ARTHUR SCHLESINGER

On many occasions, she supplied JFK with literary, historical, or poetic quotes to use in his speeches—once supplying quotes from memory of Tennyson's "Ulysses."

She carried around Proust, her favorite author at one point. I remember seeing books by Proust in which she had underlined passages to give to my brother, providing ideas and quotations. She read book after book. I thought, How did she find the time?

—EUNICE KENNEDY SHRIVER

She would listen to his speeches from the podium, or the back of the room, and listen to what he was saying and how he was saying it. And then she would tell him what she thought—what was best, how he sounded, whether he got his message across. He trusted her judgment on speeches.

—DAVE POWERS

Jackie also lobbied for support. At a Liberal Party fund-raiser dinner, she sat with theologian Reinhold Niebuhr whispering about where theology and sociology merged. He later remarked, "She's read every book I ever wrote," and came out for Kennedy. She also helped to set up a meeting between Joe Kennedy and Norman Blitz—a large campaign contributor to both parties and friend of Hugh Auchincloss—who eventually arranged for donations totaling nearly $15 million from Nevada and the Southwest.

I found her neither shy nor disdainful of the political facts of life. . . . She knew precisely what direction to take without ever consulting anyone; she had an appealing personality that she used to its best advantage—in and of itself an armature of steel. . . . She managed to turn many political figures, including [Lyndon Johnson], into devoted admirers.

—KATIE LOUCHHEIM, CHAIRWOMAN,
DEMOCRATIC NATIONAL COMMITTEE

West Virginia was a crucial state. Because it was overwhelmingly Protestant, Kennedy's winning its primary would essentially dissolve the Catholic issue. Charles Peters, who organized county efforts in West Virginia, affirmed that Jackie "wanted to campaign" there, observing that women were drawn to her because she was different from them, as opposed to Muriel Humphrey, who more reflected what they were themselves like.

Jackie, then in the early stages of pregnancy, insisted on traveling throughout the state with Ed King as her driver, and visited miners' wives in their ramshackle company houses, handed out bumper stickers at shopping centers, and shook hands on street corners. One day, driving alongside a stretch of railroad tracks, Jackie saw a gang of railroad laborers sitting on the tracks, eating lunch. She asked King to stop the car, got out and sat down with the workmen and chatted with them for a half hour.

—KENNY O'DONNELL

Besides winning West Virginia, Jackie's effort there opened her eyes a bit more. She admitted to one reporter, "I've never had much of a social conscience, but now I do." She wrote:

> In all the places we campaigned—and sometimes I was so tired I practically didn't know what state we were in—those are the people who touched me the most—The poverty hit me more . . . because I just didn't realize that it existed in the U.S.—little children on rotting porches with pregnant mothers—young mothers—but all their teeth gone from bad diet.

In contrast to the popular notion that Jackie hated speaking to voters, she would often stay and talk individually to strangers despite the tight schedule. In fact, Rose Kennedy said JFK became "irritated" at Jackie for delaying their schedule because she wouldn't rush away from people.

With voters and the press alike, Jackie was ferociously defensive about her husband. She became extremely agitated about one *Milwaukee Journal* political reporter who continued to claim that Kennedy's Catholicism was an issue with voters, without citing examples. "I wonder if that guy does an individual poll at each function on the issues of this campaign. How else could he gather his statistics?" On another occasion she told reporter Peter Lisagor of *Meet the Press* to stop "asking Jack such mean questions."

> She had one concern with public affairs and worked at it—relations with the press. As a loyal, admiring wife she did what she could to sweeten them. . . ."I think," she said, "it is so unfair for Jack to be opposed because he is a Catholic. After all, he's such a poor Catholic. Now if it were Bobby: he never misses mass and prays all the time." She laughed as she said it.
>
> —ARTHUR KROCK

Kennedy was also defensive of Jackie. Despite claims that he feared her style would be a campaign liability, he vigorously praised her intelligence in a heated discussion with reporter Laura Berquist, and in a private memo to his staff, he scribbled a single line to them that made his intentions clear: "We need to promote her more." With all he had to focus on out on the trail, Kennedy remained preoccupied with her:

He asked that the last stop of a long day would be in a town that had something interesting for Jackie, or be someplace she had never before been.

—DAVE POWERS

I remember the occasion when he was speaking at the Charlestown Race Track when his wife was late. He stopped in the middle of his address when he saw her coming up to the front of the grandstand. He turned and looked at her, and I would say that I have never known a man who had a look of more perfect adoration and love in his eyes for his wife than Kennedy did on that occasion.

—CLARENCE E. MARTIN, WEST VIRGINIA LEGISLATOR

While the struggle between politics and home life would always remain, it was also a misperception that Jackie *always* was the one to compromise.

He called me one day when he was supposed to come down [to campaign] and said he couldn't come because he was having—laughingly—trouble with his wife because he had promised to take her on a Caribbean cruise. He had to take her right away because they were about to have a baby, and he couldn't risk wait[ing].

—WALTER HART, WEST VIRGINIA POLITICAL FIGURE

Once the primaries were over, the Kennedys publicly announced that Jackie was pregnant. As she joked to friend Eve Fout, at whose Middleburg, Virginia, farm Jackie boarded a new horse, she knew that as soon as she bought her own horse, she would get pregnant and wouldn't be able to ride it. As the bandwagon rolled toward the nominating convention in Los Angeles, family remained a concern of Jackie's. In June, for example, she skipped an important political luncheon in Washington to attend the graduation of her ninth-grade sister, Janet.

In February 1960 I had just had my first child, but for the first two years of our marriage, we hadn't had a home of our own. Jackie was just then pregnant and going to have to limit her appearances out on the road in the primaries. Jack always wanted one of his sisters or sisters-in-law with him, so I was scheduled to start out campaigning. I didn't have a home, I didn't have clothes or any preparation for campaigning, I had this infant. Then, she stepped in.

Jackie found a fully furnished home for me, two blocks from her own house. She hired an Irish nursemaid for my child, and a maid for the house. Just before I got there, she went out and made sure that there was food in the house. She made sure that there were linens on the beds and in the closets. She even made sure that the heat was turned on. I never called and asked her to do this. She just did it.

Then I had to go out campaigning—even down in the West Virginia coal mines. And, because she was now pregnant, Jackie couldn't wear many of her clothes. So she lent me all of her own suits and dresses, these chic Balenciaga and Chanel clothes. I had this entire wardrobe of things that she knew were appropriate attire for being out on the road with Jack. And she never asked me to return them.

—JOAN BENNETT KENNEDY

CAMPAIGN WIFE

WITH HER HISTORY OF DIFFICULT PREGNANCIES, JACKIE'S DOCTOR, JOHN WALSH, forbade her to attend the Democratic National Convention, which nominated her husband for the presidency on July 13, 1960. In Hyannis Port, she watched the convention on television while reading political fiction like *Democracy* and *The Last Hurrah*, writing several hundred letters, painting, and meeting with reporters.

Just after the convention, Bobby Kennedy asked me for my ideas. The first thing I pointed out was that Jack had forgotten to mention Jackie in his speech, and that this was a great mistake. I said that the first thing the Kennedy campaign had to do was "Bring in Jackie."

She did have her views behind-the-scenes. She had a very strong protective instinct toward her husband with a clear and correct idea of what his proper image should be—and it wasn't being associated with the Hollywood "Rat Pack" crowd. She used her influence when she could to keep them from him. Active campaigning would jeopardize her health and make her lose her child, but she wanted to be involved. With my husband in the newspaper business, I thought she could express her views and provide a glimpse of her family life and who she was by doing a column, "Campaign Wife." She loved writing, and took to the idea. She got to work on it . . . and even made a series of television commercials.

—JOAN BRADEN

Women, said Jackie, "are very idealistic and they respond to an idealistic person like my husband." In October, she kicked off "Calling for Kennedy Week," where she made the first call via a conference hookup with eleven women Democratic leaders across the country, to begin the nationwide telephone-calling effort. In attendance were two hundred women precinct workers, and Jackie opened the floor for their ideas on strategy—adding that she had already advised JFK "to speak more slowly." She made an appeal to pregnant women and young mothers after she heard that Dr. Spock supported JFK, and she invited him to her home to film a political ad with her. There, she also hosted four press conferences with "The Women's Committee for New Frontiers" focusing on political issues of importance to women. She hosted "Listening Parties" for the first two televised debates between JFK and Republican opponent Richard Nixon, and invited press coverage to prompt other women to follow suit. Assiduously, however, she avoided controversy.

> I certainly would not express any views that were not my husband's. I get
> all my views from him. Not because I can't make up my mind on my own,
> but because he would not be where he is unless he was one of the most able
> men in his party.

When asked on television if she advised him on his political decisions, she made a distinction between that and her reactions to his decisions. "I tell him what *I think*."

One issue of her husband's platform that interested Jackie and which she openly discussed was better federal funding for public education. After reading an article in the local newspaper about the temporary use of trailers as classrooms because of overflow, she called it a "resourceful and necessary solution."

> Although I certainly agree that education is primarily a local responsibility
> . . . it does seem imperative that the federal government step in and do its
> share. . . . More teachers must be trained, . . . but they must be paid more
> so they will enter the teaching profession.

At her October 27 press conference, Jackie also discussed the attributes of federally protected medical care for the elderly, via Social Security extension, versus the Republican stance of state and locally appropriated care requiring approved application:

The aged shouldn't be put to the awful indignity of swearing they are in need of medical care. And it's a problem for many women in their middle years. So many of them are faced with the need for taking care of their own children. College education for their children could mean leaving their parents stranded.

During a late September trip to New York for two days, Jackie met with reporters in a rented thirty-seventh-floor Waldorf Towers apartment and dismissed the press speculations about the cost of her and Pat Nixon's clothes with her famous remark that she couldn't spend as much as was claimed unless she wore "sable underwear." Jackie was frustrated but determined to continue campaigning, telling a friend at the time, "I feel very large and slow and inadequate now—but there must be a fantastic effort for the next weeks." She amplified to the reporters:

> I feel I should be with him when he's engaged in such a struggle. If it weren't for the baby I'd campaign even more vigorously than Mrs. Nixon. I can't be so presumptuous as to think I could have an effect on the outcome, but it would be so tragic if my husband lost by a few votes merely because I wasn't at his side and because people had met Mrs. Nixon and liked her.

"I Hope Dick And Jack Fully Realize What Their Destiny Hangs On"

Political cartoon of Jackie Kennedy and Pat Nixon, wives of the presidential candidates, spoofing the "debate" on the style and cost of their clothing, 1960.

The next day, she expressed off-the-record thoughts that reflected her growing consciousness about the cold war, the arms race, and nuclear war:

> A terrible, frightening decade is ahead. People are too complacent about this country's power. Someone has to talk to the Russians. If my country were in Jack's hands, to give the decade a start, I'd feel safe.

From New York, Jackie returned to Washington, where she recorded campaign ads in Polish, French, Italian, and Spanish, encouraging Americans of these backgrounds to register and to vote for Kennedy. Millions of Americans whose immigrant ancestors had not been of colonial stock identified with the ethnic backgrounds of the JFKs: "Kennedy" was obviously Irish, "Bouvier" was obviously French, both nationalities were overwhelmingly Catholic. Jackie particularly capitalized on this difference.

> When he was in a more solidly Polish area, [JFK] would attempt to say a few words in Polish. His Polish was not as good as Jacqueline's.
> —CLEMENT ZABLOCKI, CAMPAIGN OFFICIAL

Jackie also understood the sensitive way in which the campaign needed to reach out to the black community. Early in the primaries, John H. Johnson, the president of Johnson Publications and publisher of *Jet*, an African-American magazine, was highly critical of Kennedy for not assuming a liberal enough stance on civil rights for blacks. With Jackie's help, Belford Lawson, a prominent African American, put together a small brunch in her home—which she sat in on—for Johnson to meet and discuss his grievances with Kennedy. Later, Johnson became a supporter. But it was at an impromptu gathering at Lawson's home where Jackie made a wider appeal:

> At the time I was active in the YMCA, and I arranged a speech at the Press Club for Kennedy. He got sick and couldn't come. He sent Bobby, who read the speech and surprisingly donated a thousand dollars to the "Y." That night Jackie Kennedy went to our house for a little reception—with [Ralph A.] Dungan and some other people from the staff. It was just a small party. . . . But because she was such a charmer here was a chance, as we saw it, to get her to know some Negroes that night. She just stormed the place with her personality. That reception helped to dissipate certain attitudes

toward Kennedy that existed in the black community. That event was not social from our standpoint. It was political business. I don't know of any one single thing locally that did more good.

—BELFORD LAWSON

Jackie consciously pursued the African-American vote: the only fund-raising dinner she attended that fall was one for black women; during the primaries, she was the one who always went to small, black churches; the only nonpolitical fund-raising event during the campaign that she chaired was a black women's fashion lunch for the Roxbury, Massachusetts, Freedom House Civic Center. It was with the Hispanic community, however, that Jackie Kennedy seems to have had her greatest impact. When later asked if Kennedy had been as linguistically skilled as herself, she was unhesitant. "No, he wasn't. He always used to make *me* make speeches in Spanish."

Back in New York again in mid-October, Jackie made perhaps her most influential campaign appearance. In Spanish Harlem, at 164th Street and Lexington Avenue, in the middle of the largest Latino neighborhoods of New York, a stand with bunting was erected for a well-publicized rally. The turnout was tremendous, people jamming windowsills and fire escapes and hanging on street signs. Into this mob lumbered an obviously pregnant Jackie Kennedy with her husband. She climbed onto the stand, sitting among the long row of dignitaries. One by one they rose to speak—Eleanor Roosevelt, Mayor Bob Wagner, and JFK. After Kennedy finished his speech, he told the crowd, "I'd like to have you meet Jackie." After welcoming "*mi amigos*," she delivered a short address in Spanish, beginning:

My Spanish is poor but my knowledge of your history, culture, and problems is better. I can assure you if my husband is elected president you will have a real friend in the White House.

A reporter found her "more effective than all of the other speakers put together," and when Republicans assailed her "pandering to foreign influences," Jackie retorted, "These people have contributed so much to our country's culture. . . . It seems a proper courtesy to address them in their own tongue."

Jackie's role in her husband's election was generally dismissed as mere window dressing, but it may have been her Harlem speech and another that same day to an Italian group, and radio ads that were broadcast in New York, that

Jackie Kennedy talking to reporters after giving a speech in Spanish Harlem, 1960 campaign, with Mayor Robert Wagner, Congressman Adam Clayton Powell, JFK, and Eleanor Roosevelt.

helped Kennedy squeak through to a marginal victory. Statistics on Spanish, Central and South American, Puerto Rican, Haitian, and Italian populations that voted for Kennedy were not recorded, but these groups formed a substantial segment of the New York City voting blocs, all of which he won. Having locked up the New York City districts, Kennedy was able to take all of the state. Without New York's electoral votes, he would have lost the election.

TRANSITION

IN THE MORNING—AFTER WHAT SHE CALLED THE "LONGEST NIGHT IN history"—when Jackie learned that JFK was elected, she slipped away for a walk along the beach, contemplating how her own life would now be changed. When her husband learned she was gone, he ran out to join her, and they walked through the dunes, returning with their arms around each other and laughing. They spent a quiet Thanksgiving in Washington with Bill Walton before JFK flew down to visit his parents in Florida—only to fly back immediately when he got word that she had given birth to a son, named for him.

Despite Eleanor Roosevelt's assurances to her that she would be able to handle the roles of both mother and first lady, Jackie feared the increasing intrusions into her private life—which included a photographer snapping her as she was wheeled out of cesarean surgery. She felt as though I have just turned into a piece of public property. It's really frightening to lose your anonymity at thirty-one.

Already, women's department stores were using models and sketch drawings of women who looked like her, and mannequins were created with her face, figure, and hairstyle. Speculation about her clothing style kept fueling itself. Finally, she decided she would primarily use one designer, her friend Oleg Cassini, and

> have some control over my fashion publicity. . . . I am of so much more fashion interest than other first ladies, [but] I refuse to be the Marie Antoinette or Josephine of the 1960s.

After touring the White House, but before going to Florida for a pre-inaugural rest, Jackie ordered books on White House history, architectural studies, photographs, and drawings of its state chambers and was given detailed blueprints of the rooms. She later revealed:

> As soon as Jack ran for president, I decided that if he were elected, I would make restoring the White House my project. Presidents' wives have an obligation to contribute something. . . . When I knew I'd be living there, it wasn't a matter of wanting to restore it or not; it was something that had to be done. . . . People who visit the White House see practically nothing that dates before 1900. Young people should see things that develop their sense of history.

On Inauguration Day, she was up early. Eisenhower had invited the Kennedys and Johnsons to join him, his wife, and the Nixons for coffee at the White House before the ceremony:

> Jackie was quite enamored with President Eisenhower. When they were due at the White House before the traditional swearing-in, Jackie insisted to Jack that they must be certain to be on time for "General" Eisenhower. They arrived too early, and had to circle around for a bit.
>
> —YUSHA AUCHINCLOSS

From the White House, Mrs. Kennedy, Mrs. Nixon, Mrs. Eisenhower, and Mrs. Johnson went with their husbands to the Capitol, where they sat together in the front row, just behind the pódium. Also at the ceremony were former first ladies who had already made largely flattering predictions:

> There is a great deal more to her than meets the eye. . . . I know she'll do very well.
>
> —ELEANOR ROOSEVELT

> She will find it not too difficult. I think she will be a perfect first lady. Her age is a tremendous asset. . . . But she drops a curtain in front of you. No one will ever get to know her.
>
> —BESS TRUMAN

> I think Mrs. Kennedy will be a great asset to her husband—as she is cultivated and charming.
>
> —EDITH WILSON

> Well, she's awfully young. . . . She's planning to redo every room in this house! There certainly are going to be some changes made around here!
>
> —MAMIE EISENHOWER

As the assembled first ladies headed toward their seats, Jackie strayed:

> [JFK] said, "Could you arrange it so that Mrs. Kennedy and I can have a private word?". . . They went in and had, I presume, their last personal talk. The door opened in three or four minutes, and he said, "Let's go and let's keep it running," and we walked out to the inaugural stand.
>
> —MAJOR GENERAL CHESTER V. CLIFTON,
> MILITARY AIDE

During the inaugural ceremony, Jackie focused on her husband's address, which was read after the swearing-in. "It was soaring," she said, "I knew I was hearing something great." Later she recalled:

> I was so proud of Jack. There was so much I wanted to say! But I could scarcely embrace him in front of all those people. So, I remember I just put my hand on his cheek and said, "Jack, you were so wonderful!"

After reviewing part of the parade, the new president's wife slipped away, to bed. In white cape and inaugural gown that she herself designed, Jackie made it to only two of the four inaugural ball:

> When it was time to get ready for dinner—I couldn't get out of bed. I just didn't have one bit of strength left and felt absolutely panicked. . . . [At the inaugural ball] I just crumpled. All my strength was finally gone. So I went home and Jack went on with the others.

There was no exaggeration about her shattered nerves at the time:

> A cesarean is major surgery and, combined with the sheer physical drain of creating a baby, would knock out most women for a long time. . . . She had moved out of her own home and had very little time to plan a new and much more taxing life. . . . Added to all this, the tensions of the presidential campaign still remained while she was faced by the burden of vast, new responsibilities.
> —JANET TRAVELL, PRESIDENT'S DOCTOR

Right before the election, a drawing had appeared in the *New Yorker* that pictured one man confiding to a friend, "Of course I'm voting for Nixon, but I can't help wishing I could see what Jackie would do in the White House." The world would soon find out.

FIVE

First Lady
1961–1963

My husband loves a challenge, and I do too. I would
hope that when I leave here I will have done something
to help.

—Mrs. John F. Kennedy

THE WHITE HOUSE
WASHINGTON

text before any printing

Jackie Kennedy cartoon of herself as first lady, 1962.

Boss

> A man marries a woman, not a first lady. If he becomes president, she must fit her own personality into her own concept of a first lady's role. People do best what comes naturally.
>
> —John F. Kennedy

In preparation for her public role, Jackie consulted closely with her husband.

> They both realized what a very important side of the presidency the first lady is and they spent a great deal of time making notes.... She already had worked out plans for basic problems and basic organizational patterns before they walked through the doors in January. She arrived at all this after thorough discussions with him.... He was always interested in everything, but he was more apt to know what an important job she would play in his life, and there was no nonsense.
>
> —Letitia Baldrige, social secretary

While there were many occasions when JFK wanted her to make an appearance, and often negotiated by promising "one ballet and one opera" to her in exchange, he never made demands on her, particularly in the beginning when, unknown to the public, she was still convalescing:

I had been in my room for days, not getting out of bed. All the details were getting too much. . . . I was just in physical and nervous exhaustion because the month after the baby's birth had been the opposite of recuperation. I missed all the gala things. . . . I always wished I could have participated more in those first shining hours with him, but at least I thought I had given him the son he longed for. . . . The period . . . was not the happy time in my life that it looks like in all the pictures. . . .

You know, you just sort of collapse. He was born prematurely, because of all the excitement. He was sick. I was sick. . . . They were painting the quarters that we lived in. . . . It's sort of like a big, drafty hotel.

A compilation of her interview remarks following the inauguration recall how she initially viewed herself as first lady:

I didn't want to go down into coal mines or be a symbol of elegance. . . . I will never be a committee woman or a club woman. I am not a joiner. . . . Whoever lives in the White House must preserve its traditions, enhance it, and leave something of herself there. . . . I do have an official role as wife of the president, and I think every first lady should do something in this position to help the thing she cares about. I would hope that when I leave here I will have done something to help, for instance, the arts in which I am so interested. . . . People seem so interested in whatever the first family likes. That is where I think one can lead. One doesn't know whether one leads in the right direction or not, but one hopes one does.

Jackie rigidly limited her public commitments to only issues and projects that fell into her genuine areas of interest—the arts and historic preservation—so as not to dissipate her influence. The only traditional philanthropies she sought to promote were educational, artistic, and welfare endeavors for young children. She brought national attention to Junior Village by visiting the overcrowded publicly funded foster home, sponsoring concerts by young musicians for children, including bossa novas by the Paul Winter Jazz Sextet, and hosting a children's writing contest, the prize being a White House puppy.

Her first order of public business was to change the militaristic formality that had characterized presidential entertaining. She had her friend Bunny Mellon create informal floral designs, had wine connoisseur Frederick Wildman draw up wine lists, requested that guest lists for state entertainments include prominent Americans whose ancestors came from the country being honored, returned to the Jeffersonian custom of round tables, and had eighteenth-century background music played, fireplaces lit, and receiving lines replaced with mingling. The new ambience became an immediate part of her legacy.

> There have been some great wives in the White House—like Abigail Adams and Dolley Madison—so great that you can't think of their husbands, presidents, without thinking of them. It looks as though we are having another one now.
>
> —ROBERT FROST, POET AND WHITE HOUSE DINNER GUEST

Conscious of the imagery she was creating, Jackie made certain that it was recorded properly:

> Jackie . . . had a[n] . . . appreciation, both for the technical problems of picture taking and for the use of the pictures. She wanted a record of White House rooms and activities for history. She asked [White House photographer Cecil W.] Stoughton, for instance, "Don't take pictures of Jack and me. Take pictures of what we are looking at and what we are doing." . . . After viewing Stoughton's movies of the Kennedy tour of Europe . . . Jackie told him that he had been placed too far back in some of the motorcades. Henceforth, she decreed, he was to ride behind the presidential car, where he could capture the emotion on the faces of the people as the president passed. . . . There were certain activities which she saw and made mental notes about, later to dispatch memos to Stoughton about when and where to shoot.
>
> —HUGH SIDEY, WHITE HOUSE CORRESPONDENT FOR TIME

Frequently, however, there was tension between the president's West Wing staff and her own, in the East Wing.

> There were people she liked and trusted, a different set of people than the president's circle. . . . She said, "You know, you were always part of his wing,"

indicating she had her concerns in her domain which sometimes worked at cross-purposes with what the president was up to. And you were either in one camp or the other.

—Laura Berquist Knebel

In Jackie's camp was her staff, headed first by Letitia Baldrige, then her closest friend, Nancy Tuckerman. Running overall operations of the mansion was the chief usher, James Bernard West. Jackie created two new federal positions: curator, which was eventually filled by Jim Ketchum; and press secretary to the first lady, filled by Pamela Turnure. Frequently, the first lady also worked with presidential advisers Arthur Schlesinger and Dick Goodwin, and Press Secretary Pierre Salinger.

Jackie worked from her father's desk, in her bedroom, or in the restored Victorian Treaty Room. Daily the staff sent up work folders, and she responded with handwritten memos on legal-size yellow lined paper, numbering her ideas or instructions methodically, often working late into the night so her instructions would be ready the next morning. If she was out of town, she often telephoned her instructions through the Signal Corps, and the dictabelt recordings were distributed to her staff.

She once dictated a letter saying that the tourists should have some preparation before they went into the state rooms and she decided to place wall cases, "tastefully designed vitrines," in the East Wing with historical items. The dictation was misunderstood, and the architect was startled to find out that he was being asked by Mrs. Kennedy to come up with "tastefully designed latrines." When Mrs. Kennedy found out, she died of hysterics and couldn't stop showing the letter around.

—Jim Ketchum, curator of the White House

Her staff recalled Jackie as a boss:

She was extremely creative and imaginative in all areas of her role as the wife of the president. Her marvelous sense of humor and sense of the ridiculous made working for her great fun. Once she gave Mr. West a pillow and on it was embroidered "You don't have to be crazy to work here, but it helps."

—Nancy Tuckerman, social secretary

She had a will of iron, with more determination than anyone I have ever met. Yet she was so soft-spoken, so deft and subtle, that she could impose that will upon people without their ever knowing it. . . . She had a total mastery of detail—endless, endless detail—and she was highly organized, yet rarely held herself to a schedule. For others, she insisted upon order; for herself, she preferred spontaneity. She took advice readily, but only when she asked for it, and she strongly resisted being pushed.

—J. B. WEST, CHIEF USHER

When Bill Elder left the job of curator, we sat down in the Treaty Room and she said, "Do me the favor of trying." I said I was too young. She said, "That's what they said about Jack." She never lost the ways of a child—humor, imagination, creative energy. She communicated in a straightforward way. In other words, the subtleties and the nuances were there, but you always knew exactly what she wanted. She could instantly read a fraud. She was able to call this up in the rest of us, like the head kid of the neighborhood who figures out what you need for a clubhouse.

—JIM KETCHUM

THE SELLING OF THE FIRST LADY

I seem so mercilessly exposed and don't know how to cope with it.

—JACQUELINE KENNEDY

Composer Rudolf Friml wrote an operetta in her honor. Miss America 1961's wish was to "be more like Jackie." In McMurdo Station in Antarctica, privates pinned up her picture in their lockers. If Jacqueline Kennedy seemed to enter the American imagination as a rather instant icon, she also became one of the most commercially exploited and popularized icons in the world.

Her face was carved in a one-thousand-foot portrait in the snow of Mount Jaillot at Megev, France, by artist Rene Cazassus. She was pictured in a Carnival week float in Basel, Switzerland. Leningrad's fashion magazine *Mody* carried an ad with her image. Louis Foy in the *Paris Press* thought Congress should replace all images of George Washington with Jackie.

Publishers inaugurated a cottage industry around her. Movie magazines offered scurrilous covers, with no story inside. One magazine gave advice on "How to Be Your Town's Jackie Kennedy," with penny-wise advice on buying imitation pillbox hats. Two million paperback copies of a romanticized biography—written before she actually achieved anything—sold out instantly. A Danish firm mass-manufactured Jackie mannequins. Her face was used for ceramic planters, glass pendants, tile hotplates, and dairy creamers. There were Jackie dress-up dolls, cutout dolls, and Barbie dolls, as well as a "Kennedy Game," Kennedy bubble gum cards, and Jackie junk jewelry.

A Jackie look-alike opened the 1962 *Jack Benny Show*, and there were references to her on the *Ed Sullivan Show,* the *Garry Moore Show,* the *Steve Allen Show,* and the *Dick Van Dyke Show.* A *Flintstones* character was created after her—Jackie Kennelrock. Plastic surgeons reported that large numbers of women wanted their noses to be made like hers. Anthropologist Margaret Mead even analyzed the phenomenon.

> She was just outraged about all of it and felt they had no right to exploit her. She wanted us to sue. We couldn't.
>
> —PIERRE SALINGER.

Asked about the movie magazines, Jackie responded archly that the "caliber of their stories remains true to their expected form," but about the comedy album *First Family*, in which comedians impersonated the Kennedys, she told Pam Turnure to phone its creator, Vaughan Meader, "and say that Mrs. Kennedy finds it in appalling taste that he should make money out of a five-year-old child. . . . Tell him I don't care what he says about us."

In time, Jackie found the parodies of her funny—since she herself had always loved doing impersonations. She even once encouraged it in the White House. Nancy Hough, who was on the curator's staff, was known for brazenly doing a perfect Jackie Kennedy imitation on the business phone, often scaring employees with fantastic orders. At a surprise birthday party for Nancy Tuckerman, Jackie had J. B. West wear one of her wigs to impersonate their Miss Porter's School housemother, as Jim Ketchum played the French decorator Boudin restoring the movie theater, and Nancy Hough parodied her. She began to joke about the "silliness" of obsessive interest in her. She did a cartoon drawing showing a White House picket line with signs reading, PUT JACKIE BACK IN AMERICAN CLOTHES! One of her funnier cartoons was one of herself sleepwalking the State Floor.

> I remember working in the campaign with Jackie and we used to get lots of letters then saying, "Why did she wear slacks to the grocery store?" After she was

in the White House everybody thought they were absolutely marvelous. . . . I remember mentioning this to Jackie, and she said, "Yes, you know I'm absolutely the same now as I was before. Before they hated it, and now they love it."

—JOAN BRADEN

Mrs. Kennedy had such marvelous taste that all women in Washington, all the women across the country, copied her . . . the little pillbox . . . the sleeveless shift. It was epidemic, that wardrobe.

—BETTY FORD

I don't think they all loved it. I used to get a good many critical letters about her. . . . But I think it is very silly to try to behave as you think people expect you to, because then you become simply a colorless creature. I think Jackie, on the whole, was right to do what she thought was natural to her.

—JANET LEE AUCHINCLOSS

When an enthusiastic midwestern ladies reading group decided to study the works of Oscar Wilde because the first lady admired him, they were scandalized to discover that he was gay. Others criticized her for foxhunting, wearing a bikini, water-skiing, and going to church in sandals. While there was always a conservative, older element that never warmed to her, most of Jackie's "fan mail" was from young women around the world who asked for her beauty secrets—and their mothers thanking her for improving their daughters' self-image.

I meet young women so impressed by her attitude . . . that many of these young girls now look up to her as an ideal. Whereas formerly they were chasing after moving picture actresses and other popular idols, now they look to her as an example.

—RICHARD CARDINAL CUSHING, ARCHBISHOP OF BOSTON

Consequently, Jackie began to grasp that routine activities were important symbols to the public and had political consequence. She grew conscious of setting a dignified example, particularly with her smoking. The press agreed never to use photographs of her with a cigarette, and she prevented the release of any White House photographs that showed her smoking.

Jackie outlined her press policy as being "minimum information given with maximum politeness," but the less she said, the more the press speculated that she was creating a "mystique." Jackie, who had always kept her thoughts largely to herself, saw no mystique in her being unavailable for interviews because, "the press always covers my official engagements and is kept abreast of my projects and I prefer not to answer personal questions, so that leaves little for a press conference." Still, she often found herself exasperated by the public perception of her:

> What do you suppose they want me to be? I've always been the same person. . . . I always felt I was myself, but with so many reporters watching, listening, how can anyone not seem like someone you're not?

NEW HOME

$\mathcal{J}$ACQUELINE KENNEDY ESTABLISHED HER TURF BY ADAPTING THE SECOND floor of the White House into a home.

> I remember when we did her bedroom. . . . Mr. Boudin, the decorator, wanted to make it real Frenchy, so he had stripes all over the woodwork. . . . She told Mr. West, "You know, I don't think I like it, after all. I wonder if I could do it over in an off-white." She was very definite about the things she liked. . . . [The president]—barefooted, big cigar in his mouth, magazine in his hand. He said, "What in the world? She's doing it over already?"
> —JOSEPH KARITAS, WHITE HOUSE PAINTER

> The effect could easily be that of a refurbished New York elevator flat. It's not, because the great, barnlike corridor has been toned down by an ingenious use of color, objets d'arts, and graceful furniture. Slipcovered French chairs are grouped invitingly on off-white rugs. Lovely chandeliers sparkle overhead. American paintings by George Catlin, Maurice Prendergast, Winslow Homer, and John Singer Sargent hang on tinted walls, and below them are handsomely mounted vases and sculptures, a Louis Quinze desk. . . . The most vivid hues, however, come from book jackets. Altogether there are several

thousand volumes, rising in endless tiers: graceful books on art, histories, multivolume encyclopedias, Churchill's memoirs, a few modern novels—and many biographies. . . . The hi-fi-FM-TV in the west sitting room is long, low, masked. The portable bar there is stocked with Beefeater gin and Ballantine's Scotch. . . . White matchbooks bear the gold inscription THE PRESIDENT'S HOUSE, and the spine of a buckram scrapbook [bears] the simple legend CAROLINE. . . . Flowered drapes have been drawn across the broad west window, masking the rose garden. . . . Tiny points of light twinkle on a hall spinet, on a picture of Princess Radziwill, on a framed snapshot of young Jacqueline Bouvier with her father and another of Caroline romping with hers.

—WILLIAM MANCHESTER

Jackie set out to know every household staff member and generously expressed her appreciation for their work:

Chef Rene Verdon invariably got a memorandum from Mrs. Kennedy after one of these dinners, thanking him for his efforts. The chef would put the memo on the bulletin board in the kitchen for all the help to see. Sometimes, Mrs. Kennedy would draw pictures of canapés she suggested for the next dinner.

—PIERRE SALINGER

When she first moved in, there was a terrible snowstorm and we were trying to get Caroline's room and John's room done before they got back. . . . I couldn't get home if I stayed late, and she asked me if I could stay and finish it. And she told Mr. West that she wanted me put up in one of the guest rooms on the third floor. She had supper sent up and breakfast the next morning. And the next morning she had the florist make up a beautiful cibidium orchid corsage, a double orchid, for my wife.

—JOSEPH KARITAS

FRIENDSHIP

WHEN JACKIE WANTED TREES PLANTED ON THE WHITE HOUSE LAWN TO HIDE her trampoline from the public, she drew J. B. West a cartoon of herself as the smiling Cheshire Cat, her head sailing above the treetops. Despite her humorous ways of coping, the lack of privacy of White House life only heightened her tendency toward solitude, making her pull toward and then withdraw from her friends:

> She was very gentle, but very hard to get close to sometimes. She was truly shy. Once, I remember being at a party. She looked so beautiful, but she stood all by herself in the corner. And then she said, "You don't know how it is. Everyone flirts with Lee and you, but nobody flirts with me." She had a naturally artistic temperament. She would want you near, then need lots of time alone, in thought by herself. That's how she replenished her strength, that time alone.
>
> —JOAN BRADEN

Frequently that time was spent reading. "I can't tell you the peace they have brought me, reading them at night"—she told a friend in a note about books by Archibald MacLeish and John Betjeman—"in these days when I have to fuss with things like mail and evening dresses all day."

She also kept her family and friends in mind, sending off witty notes and satirical cartoons. She did cartoons for Robert Kennedy of his mad household, with his wife dictating poolside, her kids roping in a governess, and a new maid arriving while another, who quit, left by a different door. One for Bill Walton depicted her offbeat artist friend leading the inaugural parade in tight blue jeans. She also humorously captioned otherwise bland snapshots, scribbling under one picture—"The boy with the crewcut, very young, three to your left, keeps taking pictures of me smoking." Her husband wasn't spared the pen either. She drew one of him on the road—washing his socks in a hotel bathroom—and another for their anniversary showing her putting on face cream at her dressing table while he moaned from under the sheets, "I demand my marital rights!" By mail, or phone, Jackie made certain she was in touch with friends in need:

> The unusual thing about her is that she seemed to turn up in life when one could use a friend. When my husband Leland Hayward was dying in the hospital, she heard about it and got herself involved. There was no need for her to get involved in a sad and complicated situation, but she did. When you needed someone like her, she always managed to be there, without you ever having contacted her. She found the best nurses and medical advice. She made it easier.
>
> —PAMELA HARRIMAN, FRIEND, U.S. AMBASSADOR TO FRANCE

Upstairs in the privacy of the family rooms, Jackie found she could nurture old friendships and cultivate new ones. There, some noticed the gap between her public and private personae:

> When she was placed in a formal situation as the center of attention, her voice, and the way she acted, was a retreat from herself—more formal, as perhaps a defense mechanism. She was careful what she did, careful about every word she said. But in private, she sounded differently—relaxed, easy. She was anything but one-dimensional. Whenever we were at the White House—my children were young teenagers—Jackie always really went out of her way to go over and sit down with Dave and Lynn and speak with them while the adults were talking across the room. It just showed an empathy, a subtle kind of caring for other people's feelings. That quiet kind of kindness was stock and trade with her. She didn't look at herself as the great person to whom everyone should come to. She would go over and sit down, and just talk.
>
> —JOHN GLENN

In the family quarters, it was indeed Jackie herself who often proved to be the greatest source of entertainment for friends. It was there—and only there—that she would dance the twist or frequently offer up her latest impersonation—like the French ambassador doing *his* impersonation of de Gaulle. At small dinners and dances, Jackie was able to spend time with close friends in her new home, often combining them with administration figures with whom she developed friendships, like Vice President Johnson—her favorite twist dancing partner—and Deputy Defense Secretary Roswell Gilpatric.

Despite the constraints of her new home, Jackie soon figured out schemes that permitted her to break away from the White House, as well as the Hyannis Port compound. Ever since Norman Mailer had described Provincetown, the bohemian arts colony at the tip of Cape Cod, to her as "the wild West of the East," Jackie fretted, "I suppose now I'll never get to see it." She found a way:

> As first lady, when she wanted to visit Provincetown incognito, she put on a wig with long blonde braids and rode there in an open car from Hyannis Port with Bill Walton.
>
> —SUSAN SHEEHAN, REPORTER, NEW YORK TIMES

"My Project"

OF ALL HER WORK AS FIRST LADY, JACKIE WOULD AFFECTIONATELY REFER TO THE White House restoration as "my project," recalling, "I have worker harder on this project than I ever have on anything." In 1987, she remembered the shabby state she found the mansion in:

> There was reproduction furniture and imitation Renaissance damask on the walls in the state rooms. As far as "antiques," there were two white pottery Scottie dogs with philodendron coming out of them on the mantelpiece in the East Room. Antiques? Well, they must have been at least ten years old.

Having completed her preliminary research during the transition, she announced the formation of a Fine Arts Committee, composed of collectors and curators with Henry DuPont, the nation's leading authority on Americana, as chairman, and that such experts "should put to rest the fears of people who think we might restore the building to its earliest period, leaving out all that came after, or fill it with French furniture, or hang modern pictures all over it and paint it whatever color we like. I don't 'do up' old houses. These things aren't just furniture. They're history."

The first lady successfully lobbied Senator Clint Anderson of New Mexico, Interior and Insular Affairs Committee chair, to create a permanent legal method permitting the White House to accept, solicit, and maintain donations. The result—Public Law 87286—preserved such items as the inalienable property of the White House. When she convened her committee four weeks after becoming first lady, her authority was clear:

> She and [her friend] Jayne [Wrightsman] longed for a French decor, at least in some rooms. . . . Even though Monroe had filled the White House with pieces purchased in Paris, the chairman felt that to suggest the taste of the kings of France would in some way be unsuitable for the home of the president. She and Jayne would summon [decorator Boudin] to their assistance, but because the thought of a Frenchman doing over the White House might possibly cause some question among 100 percent Americans . . . his visits were not publicized. It is not true, as Washington gossip related, that he was carried into the White House wrapped in a rug.
>
> —JOHN WALKER, DIRECTOR OF THE
> NATIONAL GALLERY OF ART

When DuPont wanted to replace a cruder mantelpiece with a priceless one, the first lady overruled him because "it was lovingly made in this house (though it may not be the most beautiful thing in the world), I think it has historic value and should not be removed. We always have to make concessions to history." Even the president was no match for Jackie:

> I don't believe Mrs. Kennedy did any of the restoration at all without first discussing it with the president and getting his approval, and I know that on two occasions he objected to what she was planning. . . . But she usually won out.
> —NELSON PIERCE, WHITE HOUSE USHER

Jackie spent hours every day on the phone, tracking down items from museums and private collectors and cajoling potential donors and contributors. She asked the General Services Administration to search the National Archives for presidential busts, and scoped out the White House storage warehouse herself in Maryland.

> Beyond the items that she knew were out there that had once been in the White House, every time she found herself in New York, which was quite often, she had a list of as many as twenty dealers. She would trudge in and out of every single one and come back with voluminous notes. There's an amazing network within that profession, and if anyone knew anybody who had a piece that they thought would be of interest, either because of the aesthetic value or an historical association, she knew about it and made it very clear that it belonged in the White House. She would have her eye on certain things and come back with a fairly well-defined provenance and photographs.
> —JIM KETCHUM

Eight Paul Cézannes had been willed to the White House by expatriate Charles Loeser, but they had been kept at the National Gallery of Art:

> One day my secretary said, "I have Mrs. Kennedy on the line for you." We had the Cézannes up in the easels in the boardroom, the nicest ones in the shadows. She went like hunting dogs to the best ones.
> —CARTER BROWN,
> FORMER DIRECTOR NATIONAL GALLERY OF ART

Jackie also formed an Advisory Committee of curators and museum directors, a paintings committee, and a library committee, the latter to create a library filled with "great books of all periods embodying the ideas on which American democratic institutions are based." Down the hall from the library, items began coming into the curator's office, Jackie often moving objects around herself to see where they looked best. "When it is done," she declared, "de Gaulle would be ashamed at Versailles."

As the pieces came in, she would sometimes run down to the delivery area. Once, dressed in her jeans, she surprised the moving men by jumping in and lifting off a heavy mirror.

—JIM KETCHUM

Exquisite taste. She seemed to know a lot about everything whether it was materials, paintings, or anything pertaining to art.

—LARRY ARATA, WHITE HOUSE UPHOLSTERER

Just three months after the project began, tourist numbers jumped 27 percent, and Jackie kept the average visitor in mind. She displayed the Vermeil Collection of tureens and bowls around the house for the first time, and put in a prominent place a painting by I. Aivosovsky that depicted American food distribution to starving Russians during their 1891 famine. Her greatest pride was the Blue Room, where she captured the Monroe era of French furnishings and the underlying influence of Napoleon's Egyptian campaigns; however, she remained skeptical of her own decision to make it more white than blue.

When finally the Jefferson life portrait by Rembrandt Peale was donated, she was ecstatic, and placed it in the Blue Room:

It is one of the finest male portraits ever painted. . . . His expression seems to be changing as if he were not only alive but actually looking at you. Everything Jefferson was is there: aristocrat, revolutionary, statesman, artist skeptic, and idealist. Compassionate but aloof, the spirit of the eighteenth century is in Jefferson's face. . . . I wish I could be married to Thomas Jefferson because he would know best what should be done. . . . I'd have liked to study architecture . . . like Thomas Jefferson. Now there was a man! He could do so many things! . . . Jefferson is the president with whom I have the most affinity.

To restore the Treaty Room, Jackie lobbied Capitol Hill to "cut all the red tape" and have a Grant chandelier returned to the White House from the Capitol, prompting Senator Mike Mansfield to introduce a bill to establish a curator of the U.S. Capitol Building.

> She was concerned about the character of some of the quasi-state rooms on the family floor—the Treaty Room, Lincoln and Queen's Suites. She said, "I don't want to leave the walls in such a way that future presidents will hang their Aunt Minnies up here."
>
> —JIM KETCHUM

Throughout her work, Jackie was not only advised by legal counsel Clark Clifford, but *she* advised him. In considering potentially negative press from an editor, she attached talking points about herself, in the third person:

> No other first lady tried and no future one will if this is the way her efforts are received. . . . Sometimes she got very depressed when she couldn't get big sums of money from strangers but she stuck to the difficult task of finding donors. . . . I have spent a year and a half of working to the bone to make the W.H. what it should be. . . . Ask him if he wants to be on my committee and see what drudgery is really like!

On February 14, 1962, a one-hour CBS-TV special, "A Tour of the White House with Mrs. John F. Kennedy," was conducted by the first lady with CBS correspondent Charles Collingswood. Jackie helped develop the script sequences:

> She really knew her stuff. She had done her homework. . . . She didn't worry about her makeup or "best" camera angles. When the director gave her instructions, she followed them exactly. . . . If she was tired, she didn't complain or show it.
>
> —CHARLES COLLINGSWOOD

One-third of the American people watched the special, and Jackie won an Emmy. Jack Gould of the *New York Times* praised "her effortless familiarity with dates and names," but it was she as much as the house that attracted attention:

> I remember watching and listening to Mrs. Kennedy more than thinking about the White House.
>
> —BARBARA BUSH

At the end of the program, the president himself appeared, proudly remarking that "Mrs. Kennedy displayed more executive ability for organization than I had imagined she had."

Jackie had the idea of writing a children's book with Ludwig Bemelmans called *The Mouse in the White House* to benefit a children's charity. He was a friend and had done the famous *Madeline* book series for children, but this idea ended when he died suddenly. In November 1961, however, Jackie established the White House Historical Association as a means of raising private funds for the restoration work, and under its auspices, she was to publish her first book, *The White House: An Historic Guide.* Sold to White House tourists, it raised millions of dollars.

> She thought it was fantastic that it could be copyrighted and that those funds would be used to build and maintain the collection, but she got the idea because she wanted the story of the White House told. *National Geographic* provided the book's printing and photographers. They put together a layout, and two of their senior staff appeared in the West Sitting Hall to present it to her. It was not the kind of book that she wanted to do, and so she really became editor in chief. At that point, the *Geographic* realized there was a *Geographic* way of doing things, and there was a Jacqueline Kennedy way.
>
> As photographers were on scene doing shoots in the Queen's Room, this vision in a turtleneck pullover and jeans came in, saying in the nicest way, "Oh, can I look at the camera?"
>
> And, the next thing you knew, the tripod was being moved a couple of feet, and the perspective was changing slightly, and then she said gently, "Maybe you can try that and see how that works."
>
> There was not a line of text, a picture or caption that didn't reflect her judgment.
>
> —JIM KETCHUM

The first copies were presented to the Kennedys on June 28, 1962, and over the years the book has been updated and sold continuously to the public. In 1962, Jackie did her second book, *The Presidents,* with one-page biographies and their portraits. Eventually, other books were done by the association, its success due in large part to Jackie's marketing efforts:

She wrote to David Finley [of the White House Historical Association] and said she couldn't understand why, whenever she went into anyplace that might have any publications, they had other White House books, but not hers. She knew he felt it would cheapen it, but she said she saw Plato there, and she didn't feel he was cheapened. Many other institutions—from the Capitol to the Supreme Court—copied the format and marketing of her book, and now *The White House Guide* is sold everywhere. Right next to Plato.

—JIM KETCHUM

PRESERVATIONIST

ONCE THE WHITE HOUSE RESTORATION WAS UNDER WAY, JACKIE WANTED TO make certain that surrounding historical buildings would remain as well. Using the clout of her position, she became an activist for historic preservation.

Jacqueline Kennedy gave voice and visibility to the historic preservation movement. With her position as first lady, she provided a moral authority to make a difference. She showed what a lifetime commitment could do. For some first ladies, they were acquired interests while in the White House. She did not come by it casually, and that edge of difference made her a genuine symbol for the movement.

—RICHARD MOE, PRESIDENT,
NATIONAL TRUST FOR HISTORIC PRESERVATION

Preservation also interested President Kennedy, and both he and Jackie were shocked to learn of the imminent destruction of historic Lafayette Square across Pennsylvania Avenue from the White House. They were absolutely true partners in the endeavor, a working partnership.

—JOHN CARL WARNECKE, FRIEND AND ARCHITECT

GSA already had an architectural contract with a large firm to replace the historic buildings with two monolithic government buildings. The drawings were already well along. Congress had approved them, so had the Eisenhower administration. They were ready to start going. I got the call from the White House to stop everything.

—BERNARD BOUTIN, GSA ADMINISTRATOR

The whole thing seemed to be going down the drain when Jackie stepped in and told us, "You white-livered characters need some help and I'm going to get involved. The wreckers haven't started yet, and until they do, it can be saved." Without her . . . we never would have saved the square. . . . She kept us at it . . . and said until the bulldozers move, we're ahead and you can't give up. And she meant it, and we didn't. She really was riding us there.

—BILL WALTON

Jackie intervened at a second point after she found out that JFK and Walton had hastily approved an alternative plan that called for providing needed executive office space in new buildings stylized in a historic look but still calling for the destruction of the original town houses. She advised Boutin:

I think they are totally wrong in this case, as the important thing is to preserve the nineteenth-century feeling of Lafayette Square. . . . Write to the architects and tell them to submit a design which is more in keeping with the nineteenth century. . . . Everyone wants to raze the things and build efficient new buildings.

In February 1962, Jackie implored the Fine Arts Commission to devise a plan to provide the needed office space but preserve the old homes, despite the Commission's resistance. By coincidence, an acquaintance of the president, architect John Carl Warnecke, was in Washington, and he was asked by JFK to propose a plan.

I studied various residential and government squares around the world and informed him it could be done on Lafayette Square within budget. He made the ultimate decision, but unbeknownst to me at the time was the power of Jackie behind him.

—JOHN CARL WARNECKE

Warnecke proposed keeping the nineteenth-century character by placing new but unobtrusive red brick office buildings behind the row houses. It was what Jackie was looking for.

> During the evolution of the plans, I met frequently with Mrs. Kennedy. . . . She was so well informed, and knew everything going on, a result-oriented person. So, there were times I'd go over there with arms full of plans, and we'd meet, away from everyone, once in the Blue Room. We spread the plans out on the floor because she wanted to look at detail. We had to go around on our hands and knees looking at it. . . .
>
> She always had comments to make on whether she liked something or whether she didn't, and would make recommendations or suggestions. . . . I remember in particular the gateway [from the square] to the Executive Office Building through the center of the facade and how we looked at a number of schemes before we came up with one that they liked.
>
> —BERNARD BOUTIN

> I don't think that she was an avant-garde philosopher of the modern movement or expert on the theories of architecture, but she knew about cold, modern glass buildings, and the threat to nineteenth-century architecture. Her focus was preserving that character that revealed the history of the beginning of our country. She had the gut instincts to know what to approve and what not to. The odds were against Jacqueline Kennedy, although she believed firmly that she could change not only the minds of the world's leading architects but the actual direction of architecture in the United States. . . . [At the] public presentation of the design . . . with Jackie's presence at the press conference . . . it received Fine Arts Commission approval.
>
> —JOHN CARL WARNECKE

> She was the one who really deserved the credit for the whole thing. It was her idea. Her imagination. Her drive. Her ability to work with people. She could get you to just break your arm for her. I remember when we finally unveiled the plans. We held it in the GSA auditorium. It was a huge, cavernous room, and it had a lot of press there, and Mrs. Kennedy came over for it, and I met her out at the curb. She whispered in my ear, "Remember, not me. The president. The president. Bernie, the president." And she didn't want to take any of the credit at all.
>
> —BERNARD BOUTIN

Jackie set her sights on the rest of the neighborhood. Her plan to renovate Blair House, the president's guest house for foreign visitors, was limited to a cosmetic renovation because of limited funds. Jackie installed the former Red Room wall damask in a library, installed a high brick wall in the rear to create a private garden for guests, and advised that an adjacent house serve as a potential addition. On the other side of Blair House was the old Court of Claims. Jackie wanted it saved, telling Boutin:

> It may look like a Victorian horror, but it is really quite lovely and a precious example of the period of architecture which is fast disappearing. . . . In the next hundred years, the nineteenth century will be of great interest and there will be none of it left. . . . The Fine Arts Commission and the architects want to tear this down and put a park in its place because they think it makes the block more symmetrical . . . see that this building is preserved and not replaced with a few trees.

It was, and in her short time as first lady, Jackie managed to push through many other local improvements—removal of World War II office huts on the Mall, floodlighting the Jefferson Memorial, scouring clean the Old Executive Office Building. She reviewed the design of a proposed aquarium and even ventured into engineering, exhorting Boutin to stop the planned Three Sisters Bridge over the Potomac because it would destroy nature walks and successfully recommending that traffic problems be solved by widening the existing Key Bridge. With the president, she focused on Pennsylvania Avenue, wanting the Post Office tower and hotels from the nineteenth century saved instead of the plan to replace them with granite monoliths. Eventually, Jackie even involved herself in urban planning at the federal level.

> Hers was among the strongest voices urging her husband to initiate the Pennsylvania Avenue redevelopment, creating the magnificent thoroughfare from the Capitol to the White House that L'Enfant had intended it to be. . . . She played an active role in beginning the revitalization of Pennsylvania Avenue. . . . William Walton said Mrs. Kennedy wanted to use one Pennsylvania Avenue building as "an opera house like she had seen in a trip to Panama City." She worked to make certain that theater and arts uses were a part of the first plans for Pennsylvania Avenue—goals that were eventually realized. . . .
> She was instrumental in having Daniel Patrick Moynihan, then an assistant

to Labor Secretary Arthur Goldberg, draft a presidential declaration ordaining that federal buildings . . . must "provide visual harmony to the dignity, enterprise, vigor and stability of the American government" and should "embody the finest contemporary American architectural thought."

—RICHARD MOE

She was very disturbed about the indiscriminate and constant tearing down that was going on throughout the country. . . . We were building a tremendous number of federal projects at that time all over the country: courthouses, federal office buildings, post offices, you name it; she wanted to see the renderings of these buildings, and learn about who was designing them.

—BERNARD BOUTIN

Jacqueline Kennedy's legacy to preservation went even beyond America. Behind the scenes, she played a crucial role in saving ancient Egyptian antiquities. She recalled in 1987:

I convinced the president to ask Congress to give money to save the tombs at Abu Simbel, which would have been inundated by the building of the Aswan Dam. . . . He would—if I could convince [Republican Congressman] John Rooney of the Appropriations Committee—who was always against giving money to foreigners.

A technical cost analysis was prepared for Jackie. She lobbied Rooney for $10 million and, she recalled proudly, "convinced him."

DIPLOMAT

She would write handwritten letters and go on for pages and pages to General de Gaulle and Prime Minister Nehru. This was an example of her working with [JFK] upstairs and seeing how she could help in her way to further the political gains of the United States of America and its foreign policy. I am sure no other first lady has ever done that, and I am sure no other president has dared let his wife do that. . . . Her own brand of personal diplomacy—she worked [that] out with the president. She was intensely interested in foreign affairs. The president, having seen the enormous success of her trips abroad, realized that she could do a big job for him.

—LETITIA BALDRIGE

No aspect of politics more intrigued Jackie than diplomacy. And nothing seemed to intrigue the world more than Jackie. It began on a short trip to Canada, where a cool reception was expected but the Canadian Parliament actually gave her an ovation greater than the one Queen Elizabeth had received. That reaction was slight compared with the thunderous response on her next trip, in May 1961, to France, Austria, and England.

Prior to departing for Paris, Jackie did a Radiodiffusion-Television Française interview and White House tour in French, pointing out items that had been created by French artists, or given by the French government. "I was at the Sorbonne, and then I went there almost every summer. . . . I was in France as a child, as a tourist, as a student, and now I am going with my husband on an official visit. I love France."

She headed out to France with the thought of her husband and de Gaulle as sort of continuation of the historic association between George Washington and General Lafayette.

—Yusha Auchincloss

He thought that harmonious relations between the United States and France were a fundamental element of world equilibrium. . . . Jacqueline helped him very much to understand France. . . . She asked him to read the memoirs of General de Gaulle. I think her influence was extremely efficient as far as Franco-American relations were concerned.

—Herve Alphand, French ambassador

At President de Gaulle's grand dinner at Versailles that night, Jackie dismissed the translator and acted as interpreter between the two presidents.

It was, of course, very important because it was the first time that we had heard anything of the ideas of the new American president. At that time, the main problems were as always Berlin and Laos—Laos, which really means Southeast Asia. And then, not as a problem of the moment, but as a lasting essential problem was the question of the defense of the West, which means the problem of the atomic weapons, possession, and—if the case may be—use of the atomic weapons.

—Maurice Couve de Murville, diplomat

She played the game very intelligently. Without mixing in politics, she gave her husband the prestige of a Maecenas.

—CHARLES DE GAULLE

Kennedy had been warned that de Gaulle would be distant and difficult to reach. . . . Privately he gave Jackie credit for establishing an easy and intimate understanding between himself and de Gaulle, and it was obvious to everybody in Paris that week that her charm and style gave the French people as a whole a warmer feeling for America than they had shown during the previous postwar years. . . . De Gaulle was captivated by Jackie's knowledge and interest in France, and by her fluency in the subtleties of his language. . . . She drew him into long and entertaining conversations with her husband that probably made him more relaxed with Kennedy than he had ever been with another head of a foreign government.

—KENNY O'DONNELL

She epitomized all the qualities that the French admired; she looked beautiful, had great taste, and she was very feminine—which the Frenchmen particularly like in women. She was just made to be the delight of the French nation. She was knowledgeable not only about French literature and art, but also about the great personalities of France. Perhaps because we had lived there, my brother was more interested in English history, and had many English friends. Jackie had that same affinity for France. I can't think of anything she lacked that they admired.

—EUNICE KENNEDY SHRIVER

The purpose of the next leg of the trip—Vienna, Austria—was for president Kennedy to have his first conference with Soviet Premier Nikita Khrushchev. In the middle of the cold war, the escalation of nuclear weapons was the primary focus of relations between the United States and the USSR. It was an issue of deep concern to Jackie because of JFK's involvement.

I think even all through Paris he was thinking about this meeting in Vienna. The chips were down and I think he was probably very disappointed. . . . Mrs. Kennedy was intensely interested in all of the political successes of his career and reflected it also in herself. . . . She very definitely shared his opinions and interrogated him as to what was going on.

—LETITIA BALDRIGE

The night in Vienna when Jackie first met Khrushchev, he began spouting propaganda on Soviet public education. She smiled, "Oh, Mr. Chairman, don't bore me with statistics."

Kennedy's wife . . . was youthful, energetic, and pleasant, and I liked her very much. She knew how to make jokes and was, as our people say, quick with her tongue. In other words, she had no trouble finding the right word to cut you short if you weren't careful with her. My own conversation with her consisted of nothing more than small talk, the sort you'd expect at receptions or during intermissions at the theater. But even in small talk she demonstrated her intelligence.

—NIKITA KHRUSHCHEV

De Gaulle told the president and Mrs. Kennedy that Nikita Khrushchev would not be the one to watch; he would be focusing on them only, and on the press. It was Nina Khrushchev who must be observed, for she reported back everything to him. In Vienna, Jacqueline put all of her attention on Mrs. Khrushchev, making a good impression on her, which might, in turn, help the diplomatic freeze and tension between the two superpowers.

—JAMIE AUCHINCLOSS

The country that most impressed her personally was Greece. After a brief stop in London, Jackie and her sister toured Greece and its islands, theaters, museums, and villages. She declared that the United States "will always be [Greece's] loyal ally," and at the Acropolis when a curator began to explain the story of how the British Lord Elgin had taken ancient marble carvings to the British Museum, she announced that she would "like to see the Elgin Marbles returned to Greece." She further remarked:

This land is a miracle. It's like a dream. . . . I am literally enchanted with your clear blue sky, as well as with your beautiful sea. . . . Everyone should see Greece. . . . My dream is to have a house here to spend vacations with my children.

If the European trip turned Jackie into an international celebrity, it also helped her to realize that she could be an effective force on her own:

At the end of the year, Jackie made another international tour with the president to several overwhelmingly Catholic nations. After the Bay of Pigs debacle, which had occurred just weeks after the administration began, strong anti-American sentiment began to build in Central and South American nations, and during a weekend in December, President Kennedy sought to dispel some of this with personal meetings and appearances in Puerto Rico, Venezuela, and Colombia. It was also a chance for him to promote his Alliance for Progress, a U.S. funding program of housing, welfare, and educational grants and loans in South America. Advisers saw that Jackie could appeal as much to the masses of poor working people, who would be the first to take up the fight for revolution, as she did to the upper-class political and military dictators. Upon their arrival in Venezuela, she went directly to a program for children of poor families, which also taught mothers about nutrition and other aspects of child care, and the next day, on a wood stand in a cow field, she spoke in Spanish on an Alliance project for rural family welfare:

> I have been very happy to have been able to accompany my husband here. I have been greatly impressed by efforts made here to improve the life of the people. No parents could be happy until they have the possibility of jobs and education for their children. This must be for all and not just for a fortunate few.

The seemingly innocuous, coded words reiterated Kennedy's message aimed at the workers—and the wealthy.

In Colombia, the Kennedys were met by signs reading YANKEE GO HOME, JACKIE COME BACK. She immediately liked President Alberto Lleras Camargo, who was highly educated and versed in history and the arts, and who guided her through the restored sixteenth-century San Carlos Palace.

> Mrs. Kennedy told him [the president of Colombia] that her trip to Bogotá—she felt that in many ways she had gotten more out of that [and was] . . . more touched by the ovation than on any of their trips abroad. She felt this really put the seal on the Alliance for Progress and that she learned a great deal herself.
>
> —ANGIER BIDDLE DUKE, CHIEF OF PROTOCOL

At dinner in the palace that night, Jackie spoke, the portrait of Colombia's first democratic president, Simón Bolívar, strategically placed behind her:

> I know that we share the desire of bringing to all the peoples of the hemisphere a better life for themselves, and know that you agree that the good things in life—education, housing, and employment—should be within the reach of all and not just a few blessed by fortune.

Three months later, Jackie made a long-anticipated solo trip to India and Pakistan with her sister. Although southern Indian states Mysore and West Bengal were insulted when her itinerary cut a visit to their region, most Indians treated her as royalty. A woman who walked sixteen miles to see her said that Jackie was "Durga, the goddess of power." A so-called lawyer-poet from Bharatmata presented her with a several-hundred-line Welcome Poem. One overzealous admirer wrote her a letter in his own blood, another burned votive candles before pictures of a Hindu god, the Virgin Mary—and Jackie. Rosewater was sprinkled at her feet, lotus garlands were strewn around her neck, a red tilak dot was imprinted on her forehead. She traveled to see the Taj Mahal in an historic train and cruised down the Ganges under a canopy of thousands of marigolds.

Jackie immersed herself in Indian customs—she threw holi chalk powder, ate wild boar and candies wrapped in pounded silver, watched endless folk dancing and singing, rode an elephant, removed her shoes in mosques, and placed roses at Gandhi's cremation site. She even tried standing on her head after Prime Minister Nehru first introduced her to yoga.

> She was completely captured by the Indian culture. It was new to her, but it
> never left her and she always wanted to make another private trip—which she
> later did. She was most fascinated as well by Hinduism.
>
> —JOHN KENNETH GALBRAITH

Accompanied by Galbraith in Delhi, Jackie toured the All-India Institute of
Medical Sciences, which had received partial U.S. federal funding. As she
exited, she was overwhelmed by the hundreds of children lining the street and
joked to Galbraith, "I hope nothing prevents you from talking about family planning." She was dazzled by Nehru's gift—and it was the first piece of what would
become a collection of miniature paintings she maintained throughout her life.
Each picture told a story reflecting Indian culture, legend, and mysticism.
Galbraith chose the gift at Nehru's request.

> The painting has a certain life of its own, which she particularly loved. It was
> of a burglar breaking into a palace—and he is completely overtaken as a captive by the princesses.
>
> —JOHN KENNETH GALBRAITH

> There were times when we were so completely exhausted by our schedule that
> at the end of the day, laughter overcame us as we exchanged stories of whom
> and what each of us had had to cope with. Then it was back to smiles and nectarine juice at the banquet table until I thought I would collapse. But we survived, and it was great.
>
> —LEE RADZIWILL

After ten days in India, Jackie left on March 21 for Pakistan, proceeding as
far as the Khyber Pass. In the famous Shalimar Gardens, she gave a speech,
praising "the reverence that you in Pakistan have for your art and for your culture, and for the use that you make of it now."

Behind the scenes, there had been considerable tension for Jackie. In India,
she had to constantly, but delicately, avoid a myriad of political frictions, primarily disenchantment between the United States and India after the latter seized
Goa, an action that Kennedy vigorously abhorred.

> She made no comments about the obvious caste system. She took in all levels of
> Indian society from the maharanis and the maharajas down to the people on the

street. She was very much taken by these places as centers of art and architecture, but she didn't make any political play of any sort. What was accomplished was a sense of the friendship between the Kennedy family and Prime Minister Nehru.

—JOHN KENNETH GALBRAITH

Jackie's ambivalence about being a public figure, however, emerged again with her exhaustion on the flight home.

Jack's always so proud of me when I do something like this, but I can't stand being out in front. I know it sounds trite, but what I really want is to be behind him and to be a good wife and mother. I have no desire to be a public personality on my own.

Although she visited Mexico in June 1962 with JFK, and Italy in August with her daughter and sister, Jackie made no more solo international trips as first lady. Although her overseas activities were strictly ceremonial, the goodwill generated support toward the United States from the native peoples, a "bettering of already good Mexican-U.S. relations," as Senator Mike Mansfield put it in

Jackie Kennedy receiving traditional Indian tilak during her tour of India and Pakistan, 1962.

regard to that country. At the White House, she moved the traditional welcoming ceremonies from the barren airport tarmacs to the South Lawn, and invited the heads of state into the family quarters before the state dinner. The impact of such sensitivity was real. After attending a dinner with Jackie as his table companion, Australian Ambassador Howard Beale said that "if anything can be said to have cemented Australian-American relations, it was this irrelevant social event. . . . I don't think you can ignore the value of a contact of that sort. . . . She was great company, bubbly and just nicely irreverent."

In her efforts to adapt to the customs of the countries she visited, Jackie earned respect as an American and, consequently, for America. It was a rare case of "style" translating into substance. A *New York Times* columnist observed of her symbolism:

> She stands for . . . foreign languages and an effort to understand foreign people in a country that tends to think it is the only country and that English is the only language. She stands for a sensitivity to art and beauty despite pragmatic politics, nuclear tests, and the cold war. She is one of the few independent spirits left in an age of conformity.
>
> —CHARLOTTE CURTIS

Jackie Kennedy in the Vatican on her way to being received by Pope John XXIII, 1962.

WHEN ASKED WHAT SHE HOPED TO ACCOMPLISH IN THE SECOND HALF OF Kennedy's term, Jackie's answer came easily: "More time with my children, for they are both at an age where it is important that their parents be with them as much as possible." She asserted:

> I think it's hard enough to bring up children anyway, and everyone knows that limelight is the worst thing for them. They either get conceited, or else they get hurt. . . . They need their mother's affection and guidance and long periods of time alone with her. That is what gives them security in an often confusing new world.

Jackie focused intently on asserting her priority:

> The emphasis in the nursery was on the quality of human relationships. While the children were watched closely and supervised critically, they were not waited on nor coddled beyond infancy. They were lavished with affection and love, but in adult language and reason.
>
> —HUGH SIDEY

> I was always struck by her calmness and how clearly and simply she spoke to the children in this soft voice. She would say to me, "I want John and Caroline to grow up to be good people." That truly was her goal.
>
> —SUSAN NEUBERGER WILSON,
> PARENT OF PLAYMATE OF CAROLINE KENNEDY

> There came a number of times when I could help her simply by taking over the hospitality of a wife of a visiting head of state. Any number of obligations I could relieve her of, I was happy to do. She had two very young children and had her hands full.
>
> —LADY BIRD JOHNSON

> She did her best, . . . taking them off in her blue Pontiac station wagon on quiet expeditions to shops or parks. On Halloween evening in 1962, the doorbell rang at my house. . . . My fourteen-year-old daughter opened the door to the trick-or-treaters . . . small hobgoblins leaping up and down. . . . After a

moment a masked mother in the background called out that it was time to go to their next house. . . . It was, of course, Jackie.

—ARTHUR SCHLESINGER

One of the most vital innovations that Jackie instituted was a kindergarten in the White House solarium for her daughter and her friends. Jackie even arranged to have a live—and pregnant—rabbit in the class, so the children could watch a mother bunny and her babies.

The first year it was a cooperative nursery school with mothers, and Mrs. Kennedy included, taking turns as teacher. . . . Their school life would be integrated into what was going on in the White House. If there was . . . going to be a ceremony on the lawn, then part of the day's activities would be to watch from the balcony.

—PAM TURNURE

Mrs. Kennedy had gone to Greece. And while she was away you could see that Caroline was missing her mother. I said, "Well, what about learning a full-fledged phrase for your mother when she comes back—to greet her in French?" So the next day . . . she got so excited about saying the phrase in French. When she returned, Mrs. Kennedy said, "Jack, did you hear that?" She was so pleased. I have never seen two people so happy about children's achievement.

—JACQUELINE HIRSH, KINDERGARTEN TEACHER

She also made sure that their father's work didn't preclude his involvement:

The day began at a quarter to eight. George Thomas, his devoted . . . valet, would knock at the door of the Kennedy bedroom. The president would then ordinarily go over to his own room for breakfast, leaving Jacqueline to sleep for a few more moments. As he sat down before his breakfast tray, surrounded by the morning papers and urgent cables and reports . . . Caroline and John would rush in, greet their father, and turn on the television to watch animated cartoons. When he took his bath, they followed him into the bathroom and played with the little floating animals, yellow ducks and pink pigs, that littered the tub. Then more presidential reading with the television going full blast. At nine o'clock a calisthenics program came on, and Kennedy liked to watch the children tumble on the bedroom floor in [rhythm] with the man on the screen. In a moment, he would go back to see Jacqueline, now awake and having her own breakfast. Then, taking one of the children by the hand, he would walk over to the presidential office in the West Wing.

—ARTHUR SCHLESINGER

The real home life for the Kennedys was lived at an old house, called Glen Ora, two hours from the White House, in Middleburg, Virginia. Often there four days a week, she snapped pajamas and changed diapers, gave her children baths, read them to sleep. She referred to Middleburg as "home"; Washington she always called "the White House." The sign at the end of the road, with stone gateposts, leading to the yellow stucco house said it all: POSITIVELY NO TRESPASSING.

It was very simple there at Glen Ora. The kids had a wonderful cave to play in. A wonderful man David Lloyd took care of the horses for her, and of a pony for the kids. The Secret Service would park at the end of the driveway, we'd go off and do our thing, go riding, and then come back and they'd drive her off. She lived like everybody else. Wait in line at the store, go right into any of the shops.

The press would poke around usually when there was a big event down here. Sometimes someone would call me and tell me more about what we had just done. Jackie said, "Look, if I worried about what people said about me every day, I couldn't get up in the morning. I learned very quickly."

She wrote me a very defined outline of what her home in Middleburg meant to her. She always had meals at home. Only four times did she go out to eat, two times at a restaurant, two times at friends' homes. Her only real friends were those whose children were Caroline's playmates. Her life here was spent at her home, and she wrote that if that sounded antisocial then that was what she was, and should be, at that period of her life. She appreciated that people let her alone. She said she saw too many people all week to want to socialize on weekends. She didn't consider herself part of the social set, and said that if they had not gotten into the White House, they wouldn't have gotten Glen Ora because they would have had a normal home life. She said that it was the open sky, and the countryside and quiet that she loved here. And, like many an American housewife, she had a budget at home. Remarking on a "hell of a bill" for her horses, Jackie said it came after a long lecture from the president on living within a budget—and she didn't want to be left riding the pony.

—EVE FOUT, FRIEND AND FELLOW FOXHUNTER

Jackie also wanted her children close to the larger family—at Hyannis and Palm Beach with the Kennedys, and Newport with the Auchinclosses. Having felt such a fierce attachment to her own grandfather, she made even greater efforts to foster close family ties following Joe Kennedy's 1961 stroke.

> Mrs. Kennedy was so marvelous with him because she could be even more natural. It pained the president to see him as he became after his stroke. I can remember . . . Mrs. Kennedy had taken the children out to the airport to meet Grandpa, and the children never thought anything about it. . . . Mrs. Kennedy was marvelous about keeping the atmosphere relaxed.
>
> —Pam Turnure

Her sensitivity to other family members emerged at large gatherings:

> At one Thanksgiving, the whole family gathered for one of those Kennedy living room games, but kind of like a variety show. I played some Chopin. Jackie read a poem, probably Edna St. Vincent Millay. Jack then decided that he was going to sing and said, "Joansie, please accompany me on the piano." I managed to follow his voice, but Jackie knew what I was doing. "Joan, you are a terrific musician because you made Jack sound great. I guess it's us against them!" she said in reference to the fact that we did poetry and music and the others did skits. "We're different from the rest. We did our own thing."
>
> —Joan Bennett Kennedy

> When her children were just beginning to grow up, she and my brother developed a great desire to be able to spend some precious time with them, and have fewer distractions from the larger, rambunctious family. They wanted to develop relationships with both of their children. On the other hand, when there was going to be a head of state visiting, Jackie would gather the various suggestions for gifts for them which she solicited from the State Department, Library of Congress, and other art societies, and bring them up to the Cape and talk it out with the family—things that would be interesting for them. In all of us going through the ideas, Jackie led the discussions. It was engaging. She permitted everyone to offer their creative ideas.
>
> —Senator Edward M. Kennedy

When they were staying in Hyannis, the media were always ready and waiting:

Jackie Kennedy decorating Easter eggs with her two children and unidentified others in the kitchen of Joseph P. Kennedy's house, Palm Beach, Florida, 1962.

We decided to go water-skiing. But the press had these long-range cameras and took pictures of us. The next day, there we were in the *New York Times*—a big picture of us out water-skiing and continuing write-ups. Then came all sorts of mail critical of her, and critical of me, though I never quite figured out why some people thought it was unbecoming that she was water-skiing in a bathing suit. She got a huge kick out of it. She was also very apologetic, thinking that she had gotten me in trouble.

—JOHN GLENN

If Jackie hammered out compromises with her press, she remained adamant about preventing publicity about her children, often battling her husband, who disagreed. On one occasion, she handwrote a letter to reporter Ellen Kay Blunt for the "incredibly decent gesture" of not having Caroline photographed for a news story.

(right to left) Jackie Kennedy, Caroline Kennedy, Will Smith, Jean Kennedy Smith, in Halloween costumes sitting on the Lincoln Bed in the White House, 1961.

Mrs. Kennedy had a way that strikes terror into your heart. She was a very strong-minded girl and tough. . . . She caught my eye and said, "Oh, now you're not here to photograph us, are you Stanley?. . . Or Caroline either?"

—STANLEY TRETICK, LOOK MAGAZINE PHOTOGRAPHER

THE NATION'S MUSE

What she liked about history was that it was sometimes an explanation of culture, of the life of a people at a time. To her, history helped people to understand what an artist might have been trying to express at the time of his work. "Culture" to her was more adventurous than history, more expressive in the life of a people.

—CLAUDE DE RENTY DU GRANRUT

She saw the performing arts and the world of the intellect, and the world of the scholar, and the world of the spirit . . . as being extremely important. This was not publicized, but if you ever had the joy of speaking to her, and hearing her passion, you realized that she was really remarkable in the sense that she was a true intellect, and a true "people person."

—DAVID AMRAM

The *New York Times* said she qualified as minister of culture, and Norman Mailer called her "The Nation's Muse," but Jackie wanted to proceed carefully in promoting American arts. After she asked George Balanchine, director of the New York City Ballet, how she could best promote the arts, he recommended she become a sort of "spiritual savior" of America, "to distinguish between material things and things of the spirit—art, beauty." While she said that promoting American arts appealed to her more than any other project, "emotionally and intellectually," she avoided imposing a fixed public standard based on her own tastes. Privately, however, Jackie did exercise considerable power. In the autumn 1961 dispute between the Metropolitan Opera and the musicians' union, for example, when the Labor Department took the unprecedented step of negotiating, "it was Jackie Kennedy not John F. that got us into it," said Assistant Secretary Reynolds. And she did immediately persuade her husband to appoint the first presidential adviser on the arts, explaining in 1987:

> President Kennedy and I shared the conviction that the artist should be honored by society, and all of this had to do with calling attention to what was finest in America, what should be esteemed and honored. The arts had been treated as a stepchild in the United States. When the government had supported the arts, as in many WPA projects, artists were given a hand, and some wonderful things emerged. It had been seen in Europe how proud those countries were of their arts and artists. Of course, they had a longer tradition of patronage, going back to kings, popes, and princes, but modern governments continued this support. Our great museums and great performing companies should of course be supported, but the experimental and the unknown should also be thrown a line. Our contemporary artists— in all the media—have excited the world. It was so sad that we couldn't help them more.
>
> Of course, the president and I talked of these things. It was something he responded to and cared about for his country. Who else had had a poet read at his inauguration, and so many great writers invited to it?
>
> The public had to feel the need for support of the arts; you couldn't just jump in and name someone as an "arts Czar."

Jackie had an in-depth conversation with Senator Claiborne Pell on the position of arts adviser and on creating an advisory council—all of it the groundwork of the National Endowments of the Arts and Humanities.

We discussed who was the best person to take on the job of the president's adviser on the arts for the long run, how Congress would function in the funding of regional arts and humanities projects. She expressed high regard for Malraux and had several quite long talks with him . . . [on] the idea of an American version of the French Ministry of Culture and what kind of shape it would ideally take on and what was realistic in America.

—SENATOR CLAIBORNE PELL, RHODE ISLAND

She was always appalled that America spends billions at the Pentagon, but had no Ministry of Culture. No support of the museums on a regular basis, no educational television—all these things troubled her. She was a great influence on Jack in that regard. She did not want this known, she did not seek credit for any of it, but she discussed it with him.

—VIVIAN CRESPI

I had become interested in art and its economic role, and eventually had a seminar at Harvard on the economics of the arts. Jackie was attracted to the whole idea of how one guarantees appreciation of the arts, financial appreciation of the artist, how artists live.

—JOHN KENNETH GALBRAITH

August Heckscher was appointed as the first arts adviser in November 1962. He recalled:

Mrs. Kennedy had made her famous tour of the White House on television, and . . . the reporter asked, "Mrs. Kennedy, what do you think government's relation to the arts ought to be?" And I thought to myself, Oh, gosh, she's going to say something, she's going to ruin everything or make my job much more difficult. And she answered it so perfectly. . . . "That's much too complicated a question for me to answer.". . .

Mrs. Kennedy herself was much too wise to be busy every moment promoting the arts. She would do one thing with superb taste and it would have a tremendous impact. Of course, I saw Mrs. Kennedy . . . informally on many occasions . . . [but] I didn't want to be thought of as being down there to help Mrs. Kennedy decorate the White House. . . . We were thinking in terms of national policy. . . . Mrs. Kennedy was awfully nice to me. She said, "Mr. Heckscher, I will do anything for the arts you want . . . except read bills. . . . I can't be away too much from the children and I can't be present at too many cultural events. . . . After all, I'm not Mrs. Roosevelt."

—AUGUST HECKSCHER, ARTS ADVISER TO THE PRESIDENT

Nearly all of the first lady's 175 public appearances were at cultural events, ranging from a New York Philharmonic concert to a reading by Irish playwright Michael MacLimmoir. The *New York Times* dubbed Jackie the "guest star [who] . . . never left her seat" when she attended the New York City Center Ballet for her favorite "Liebeslieder Waltzes" based on Brahms's selections, and Pas de Dix from Glazounov's "Raymonda Symphony in C" with music by Bizet. Asked if she enjoyed the ballet—before which the press flashed their cameras—she quipped, "Yes. Once the lights went down." Her attendance at the opening of New York's Lincoln Center for the Performing Arts was even telecast nationally:

Jackie asked if I would go with her because I was a good friend of Governor Nelson Rockefeller, and his family had largely underwritten the center and would all be there. Once there, everyone wanted to have their picture taken with Jackie. I had the assignment of keeping her from being photographed with the governor, a Republican running that year. Somehow, this was managed. Then, we were backstage when Leonard Bernstein was conducting. He later told me that as he was conducting, he kept telling himself, I will not kiss Jackie Kennedy, I will not kiss Jackie Kennedy. And then, with all the television cameras focused on him, he finished and came right up to Jackie. And kissed her on the lips!

—JOAN BRADEN

Jackie served on the advisory board of the new American Symphony Orchestra, because it would develop international collaborations and commission works by new composers of the Americas, and as chair of the Washington School of the Ballet Foundation, because it awarded scholarships without regard to race and created a foreign student exchange. She sponsored the Festival of Performing Arts for students and the Cabinet Artist Series, which was a series of performances and lectures hosted by cabinet members. She also wrote letters supporting new cultural efforts—from the new Arkansas Arts Center, whose formation she found "exciting new evidence of growing community interest and support of the arts," to the New York Shakespeare Festival's new amphitheater for free public performances.

> When I worked for Shakespeare in the Park, we passed the hat. She was one of the early supporters, but never used her name. She was the person who helped to make that possible.
>
> —DAVID AMRAM

The thirty-one-year-old first lady also kept up with the contemporary scene. She had a collection of bossa nova, samba, hot jazz, and Chubby Checker records—and reportedly one 1963 Beatles recording import. Her favorite movies at the time, which were shown at the White House, included *Breathless, Jules and Jim, Last Year at Marienbad,* and Fellini's *La Dolce Vita.* She collected contemporary art by Walt Kuhn and Robert Goodnough, and helped the fledgling Washington Gallery of Modern Art get necessary publicity. She told an aide, "It's wrong to identify oneself solely with art of the past, and never encourage what is happening now."

> I remember once talking to her about the WPA, and she felt that the 1930s was such an unbelievable period as far as what the federal government was able to do in fostering art, and how close to tragedy much of those efforts came as far as their preservation.
>
> —JIM KETCHUM

The National Cultural Center was only a concept when Jacqueline Kennedy entered the push for it, but her commitment to its mission, fund-raising, and building became part of her legacy. She was almost as mortified as she was angry that the nation's capital lacked the professional facilities needed to attract national and international talent and to nurture young artists. She supported the movement of creating an arts complex of separate buildings in a downtown theater district, but once it became clear that the complex had to be built on a certain site that was deeded land from the government, she pushed the president to seek large contributions for the center there. He cracked, "All right, Jackie, I guess now we've got to call in all the fat cats that I've been saving up for the campaign."

To help raise funds, Jackie painted two watercolors—one of an angel, and one of the three kings—for reproduction and sale as Christmas cards, and headlined the American Pageant of the Arts, live at the armory, where nearly six hundred guests at $100 a seat watched, while other citizens paid admission fees at universities, clubs, and theaters to watch her speak on closed-circuit TV.

Her most publicized effort, however, was her use of the White House as "a showcase for American art and artists," and she had Lincoln Kirstein, who was then with the American Shakespearean Theater, design a portable stage for the East Room.

> She wanted everything that was the finest in music, drama, ballet, opera, poetry, and set a tone that would encourage culture around the country. . . . She called me in on music, because it was an area of experience, but she made the final decisions.
>
> —PIERRE SALINGER

Her most famous performer was cellist Pablo Casals. Breaking his ban on performing in the United States because of its support for Franco during the Spanish Civil War, he relented for Jackie. Leading American composers and conductors were invited as guests:

> It was very cold that evening, but Jacqueline Kennedy insisted on accompanying Marita and me to our car. She was without a coat—she was wearing an evening dress—and I was afraid she might catch cold. I asked her please not to come outside. But she said, "The president would want me to—and I myself want to." She stood there, in the cold, waiting as we drove away.
>
> —PABLO CASALS

Another performer's appearance signaled a message on civil rights. Before African-American mezzo-soprano Grace Bumbry sang operatic selections, she sat at the president's table for dinner. Daughter of a railway clerk, she had begun singing in her St. Louis Methodist choir.

> Tish Baldrige actually had an assignment from Mrs. Kennedy to find unsung artists. They found [Bumbry] . . . at a Wagnerian festival in Europe. . . . She became a name in her own country for this one appearance.
>
> —PETER LISAGOR, REPORTER

The most stellar array gathered at the White House was at the Sunday night, April 29, 1962, dinner when Jackie honored all forty-nine living Nobel Prize winners living in the Western Hemisphere, and persuaded Ernest Hemingway's widow to release some of his unpublished works to be read that night. The event most personally important to her was a May 1962 dinner for

French Minister of Culture André Malraux, for whom she even arranged full state honors. Malraux had an heroic political, military, and literary career, but it was his emerging theories on the purpose of art to stimulate the modern masses that intrigued her. "He's a true Renaissance man," she said, later recalling:

> He spoke of the larger purposes of culture to society—how public spaces with sculpture can affect someone rushing off to work, and maybe change their perception of themselves, even slightly. That somehow government should carefully assist in efforts of culture that went outside of the museums and galleries and into the streets. . . . It was rather abstract—art . . . in its largest concept, is a universal language. The new humanism of it came in some form of daily understanding or exposure to art—or music, or film, or even advertisements and buildings and placards on the street [which people saw] on the way to work or home. . . . I worked carefully on the guest list for the state dinner, wanting to include artists admired abroad, not only the traditional, established ones. . . . I hoped his visit would call attention to the importance of the arts.

Her guests included fathers of modern abstract painting Mark Rothko and Franz Kline; poets St. John Perse and Robert Lowell; writers Saul Bellow, Anne Morrow Lindbergh, Archibald MacLeish, and Thorton Wilder; artist Andrew Wyeth; dramatic writer Paddy Chayefsky; producer Elia Kazan; playwright S. N. Behrman; and choreographer George Balanchine. Despite the false accusations that playwright Arthur Miller had been a Communist, Jackie wanted him there as a guest—and he came. Tennessee Williams first said it was "too far to go for dinner," but Jackie phoned him, and he too accepted.

Wanting to personally guide Malraux through the National Gallery, Jackie sent ahead for a catalogue so he could choose which paintings and sculptures he was most interested in. He brought the *Mona Lisa* as a personal loan to Jackie, but as the gathered president, vice president, cabinet, Supreme Court, ambassadors, and French officials awaited the unveiling and what was expected to be Malraux's eloquent speech, the loudspeaker system failed. The next morning, Jackie reassuringly wrote to the devastated director of the gallery:

> It is, as Malraux said, part of the magic of the *Mona Lisa*, almost an evil spell. . . . And if you think a mike going off was bad—wait until you see what happens when they see the Blue Room white!

President Kennedy, Mme. André Malraux, French Minister of Culture, and Mrs. Kennedy at unveiling of public loan from France of the Mona Lisa, National Gallery of Art, Washington, 1962.

Ultimately, Jackie's influence affected the president and his commitment to the arts:

> I think he was quite conscious and deliberate about elevating the taste of White House entertainment in the hopes that they would create ripples that would improve tastes generally. I think that he admired and appreciated and respected and perhaps loved his wife for doing this. . . . His aides always led you to believe, "Well, of course, the madam has arranged this, and he's going through with it. . . . "
>
> —Peter Lisagor

When Heckscher left the arts adviser post in June of 1963, he issued his official report on how the administration could initiate the link between government and the arts, which the president publicly released. At the time, Jackie was away, and presidential aide Kenny O'Donnell delayed action on the recommendations, considering it far from a political priority. The evolution of what Jackie hoped would someday be the U.S. cultural ministry resumed when the appointment of aide Richard Goodwin as arts adviser was scheduled for November 25, 1963. Of course, it never happened.

In 1987 Jackie recalled, "I hoped one day to have a minister for the arts in the cabinet. Much groundwork would have to be done before that would be possible." The National Endowments for the Arts and Humanities, created by President Lyndon Johnson, she added, "achieved all this." Public consciousness, however, would ultimately associate her less with the politics and more with the spirit of the arts.

> In her own fashion she lifted our ideals. She reminded us that art is a source of spiritual power in any people. Grossness, the commonplace, even folksiness were impossible to her. . . . Culture was no longer a dirty word or even dangerous.
>
> —PEARL S. BUCK

> She introduced for the artist a whole new world of surprised self-respect.
>
> —THORTON WILDER

> She . . . enjoyed being with creative people, and felt that artists are very central figures in the health of a country. . . . She represented all at once not a negation of her country but a possible fulfillment of it, a dream of civilization and beauty, a suggestion that America was not to be trapped forever in the bourgeois ideal.
>
> —ARTHUR SCHLESINGER

THE POLITICIAN

> Whenever there was a discussion going on about the Far East or Mideast or Russia, or any world affairs, she was very well informed and could hold her own in any conversation. She never made any public knowledge of this, and it wasn't the way most people viewed her. Behind the scenes, once you got beyond this veneer that she had been pigeonholed in, you realized this.
>
> —JOHN GLENN

Jackie said she resisted political identity because such commitments would take her from her children, but it was wrong to read that as lack of interest:

> She had a distinct dislike for the business of politics, [but] . . . undisguised admiration for those who practice it with excellence. . . . She [gave] the appearance of detachment from the hurly-burly . . . while demonstrating a keen understanding of the problems which beset mankind.
>
> —PIERRE SALINGER

Jackie disliked the constant change in alliance of politics and, for example, still felt slighted over Eleanor Roosevelt's initial refusal to support Kennedy. Jackie told Bill Walton, "Well, you know, you liked Mrs. Roosevelt better than we did." On the other hand, she admired Eleanor Roosevelt's political might, for while Jackie played the traditional wife, she often resented assumptions about the limitations of women's professional abilities.

> President Kennedy was one of those who thought women should have full rights and privileges in our [press] club, and he never let up the pressure on me to see to it they were admitted. But I was as direct and blunt in saying no to Kennedy. . . . "I must sleep with them, but I'll be damned if I'll eat lunch with them." About a year later . . . I was having a long talk with Mrs. Kennedy on the broad veranda of her parents' home, . . . urging her to join me on a projected ABC early morning program. But she would have none of the idea. "Look, Bill," said Jackie, "I have the same feelings about career women that you do." I was genuinely confused, and said I didn't know what she meant. . . . "Yes, you do," Mrs. Kennedy insisted. "You told Jack you might sleep with those Washington newspaperwomen, but you'd be damned if you'd have lunch with them." I knew enough to quit when I was behind.
>
> —BILL LAWRENCE

> If she had gone into the White House with Jack Kennedy twelve years later, she would have been a rebel; particularly with that brain of hers. She rebelled against the status quo. The West Wing was so macho. We just lived with it. So, she got things done by making a telephone call, instead of going down to Congress.
>
> —LETITIA BALDRIGE

It was 1961 but Jackie was not a person who would have been jealous of working women in the White House or disapproved of them or had any of the reactionary responses of some traditional women.

—GLORIA STEINEM

Both Kennedys viewed Jackie's half of the partnership as the supportive role, but because her husband's business was the presidency, her support was bound to carry over into politics.

Perhaps her greatest influence was to confirm his feelings . . . not to let his public role stunt or stifle his inner existence . . . a distinction between the totally absorbed professional, for whom politics was the whole of life, and those who enjoyed the game and art of politics but preserved a measure of detachment from it.

—ARTHUR SCHLESINGER

Jackie herself was hardly detached from the presidency. "He seldom brought home his working problems," she said, adding almost as an afterthought—"except the serious ones."

JFK turned to his wife for advice whenever a crisis arose: the Berlin Wall, the Cuban Missiles, the Bay of Pigs. He would talk with her about it and she would talk with him. She wouldn't advise his staff, she would advise him— that's why nobody knew about it.

—MAJOR GENERAL CHESTER CLIFTON

From time to time, of course, she did, as one crisis or another dominated the headlines [inquire about political problems]. He would say, "Oh gosh, kid, I've had that on me all day—ask [McGeorge] Bundy to let you see the cables." She would read the cables for a while until the flow of problems depressed her.

—ARTHUR SCHLESINGER

From her travels, JFK also began to rely on her "eyes and ears" role:

Her letters to Jack while she was away in foreign ports were full of subtle political observation. Her sharp eye for detail made her an excellent troubleshooter for the administration. Her letters, reports might be a better word, held back nothing by way of praise or criticism.

—SENATOR GEORGE SMATHERS, FRIEND

Though only thirty-two years old, Jackie found herself in a position to influence world history, though the extent of that is unclear.

She made a point of not calling me up or anybody else on the substantive side to say, why don't you do this or make sure you do that. I don't think she saw herself as somebody who was involved substantively in policy questions beyond the specific areas—the arts or preservation. She was not involved except to the extent that dinner table conversation or pillow talk might involve her. And that—we'll never know.

—TED SORENSON

The instances of Jackie's changing policy were rarely documented. When she learned, for example, that an IRS tax exemption awarded to the U.S. Olympic Equestrian Team was revoked, she expressed her disapproval to the IRS board of examiners and had the exemption again awarded. Jackie was "sure this reversal of their decision will stick," but warned a friend to "let me know if it doesn't!"

I remember there was one mutual friend that we had who had a speech impediment, and was up for a job that was going to mean that he was going to be meeting the public, and the people who were considering him were very negative about this aspect. I happened to talk to her about it, and she said, "I think I'll write a note." And I said, "Is this something that you really feel you should do?" And she said, "Isn't it the just thing, the fair thing to do?" The next thing I knew, she gave me some remarks which I then typed, and she signed it, and it was put in the mail. She did not want anybody else to interfere or question it.

—JIM KETCHUM

There had been a terrible earthquake in Italy. She called me and said wasn't there something the Defense Department could do? I thought, no, what could we do to help? And she said that we had all the planes and helicopters, the soldiers, the ability to get in and out of a devastated site and immediately provide some relief. And she was right. And we did it.

—ROBERT MCNAMARA, SECRETARY OF DEFENSE, FRIEND

From her grandfathers to her father to her husband, Jackie had always been fascinated by powerful men, and she developed personal friendships with many policy makers:

> I really first began to see Jackie as a friend on a personal basis in 1961. We were part of a group, the Hickory Hill seminars. These were a group of about fifteen or twenty people who gathered at Treasury Secretary Douglas Dillon's house, or Robert Kennedy's home—Hickory Hill—for a special discussion of current events and issues. Jackie was an intent listener, always asking questions. She also liked to talk about the concept of personality in politics. She was interested, for example, in learning about Nelson Rockefeller, who was a personal friend of mine. She used to ask me a great deal about him, because she was convinced that in 1964, he [JFK] might be running against Rockefeller. Jackie would ask me if I knew when Nelson was next coming to Washington, so I could invite him to the White House, hoping to disarm him. She just had a natural curiosity about how the government worked. That would come up in gatherings, when she was not acting in an official capacity or had to perform. She loved the company of men, the rough exchange of ideas. She did not protect herself with some coterie of admiring women.
>
> —ROSWELL GILPATRIC, ASSISTANT DEFENSE SECRETARY

Although she was personally fond of LBJ, she was certainly capable of viewing him with a jaundiced eye, stemming from his 1960 primary challenge to JFK. When Schlesinger mentioned LBJ's "mild personal thrusts" at JFK, Jackie retorted, "Were they mild? Didn't he say his father had been a Nazi? And having Connally talk about [JFK having] Addison's disease?. . . They were not mild." Because she didn't want to "stir up the controversy" about LBJ's fight for the nomination, Jackie suggested that Schlesinger should record that Kennedy "did not think Stevenson was a political whore like many politicians he knew." She reflected on LBJ:

> He was an effective vice president. . . . He had such an expansive personality. . . . [JFK] thought it would be a very frustrating job, and I think he tried to do everything to make Vice President Johnson feel as comfortable in it as possible. . . . I don't think the vice presidents before had automatically come to state dinners, but . . . they would always come upstairs . . . so that we would receive the state guests as a foursome, the president and the

vice president. Every time we had a private party, . . . we'd always ask the Johnsons to be with us and our friends.

As far as cabinet and executive staff were concerned, Jackie had not weighed in on their appointments, but she had been kept apprised by her husband, later defending him by emphasizing that "toughness was a criterion but that wasn't what JFK really was looking for—character was." For those who paid close attention, Jackie's opinions could be very useful:

> There was a general, a senior figure in the Pentagon, and I remember Jackie saying, "Well, Jack had a very good opinion of him, until last Saturday when he came to the White House in a sport jacket. I guess the uniform was no longer holding him up." This is something that I've often reflected on, and it's very important to catch. Jackie did not take a strong position on political issues. She was broadly in support of the liberal spectrum of ideas, but she was not, and did not present herself, as a guide on that. She was wonderfully shrewd. We all depended on—and the president very much was dependent on—her sense of people. What they believed in. What they were driving for. What their motives were. What their ambitions were. This was where she was extremely incisive, perceptive, shrewd, and we all respected and in some measure feared Jackie's opinion. She cared little for the policy and theory, but very much as to what the people were up to. We heeded her view of people, politicians, and their motivations.
>
> —JOHN KENNETH GALBRAITH

At times, her defensiveness about press attacks was vehement. She contacted journalists when they wrote pieces with factual errors on topics as far-ranging as the attorney general's private communiqué with a Soviet official to the famous forty-mile "health hike" undertaken by administration officials.

> One day after I had lunched with Kennedy, the guard at the gate I was exiting from informed me the president wanted me to return to the mansion. When I reached the third-floor family quarters, however, I was received by Mrs. Kennedy, who explained that the president was having a nap and the summons had come from her. "If you have anything critical to write," she said, "don't pin it on the poor president; pin it on me."
>
> —ARTHUR KROCK

Despite the fact that she never discussed politics with the press, Jackie paid vigilant attention to each victory and error of the president. Her gifts to him on their anniversary were three scrapbooks on her projects, each with headlines about his work as president. She kept tabs on who in Congress voted for the administration, once yelling out of her limousine to a senator she knew who wasn't going to vote for the Education Bill, "If you're not, I won't let you take out Tish Baldrige anymore." Of all JFK's initiatives, the Space Program most intrigued her, largely because of the astronauts themselves. Publisher Punch Sulzberger noted in his diary:

> Jackie is vastly impressed by John Glenn the astronaut. She says he is the most controlled person on earth. Even Jack, who is highly self-controlled and has the ability to relax easily and sleep as and when he wishes, to shrug off the problems of the world, seems fidgety and loose compared to Glenn. Glenn is the most dominating man she ever met. . . . Glenn could do anything: . . . for example, he would be a fine ambassador in Moscow. Jackie says it isn't true that the spacemen are specially quizzed on their marital relationships. The wives apparently all pray a great deal when a launching is about to take place. Says Jackie: "Even if you didn't believe in God, wouldn't you pray?"

Jackie watched the splashdown of Glenn's spacecraft on television with the president in the Oval Office, and the astronaut eventually became a personal friend of hers:

> I first met Jackie before my flight in '62, at the second briefing I did for the president, to which I brought models and diagrams. She was very interested in the space program! It wasn't an affectation. She'd obviously done quite a bit of reading about it and had good questions, which surprised me, and we discussed it a number of times. She asked about the controls, how it propelled, was it engineered as an airplane is? Everybody can imagine themselves being an Indy racer because they've driven a car. But this was something new, and she wanted to know what it was like to launch and orbit in space, to be weightless, imagining herself in the capsule. She also saw the space program as a symbol of inspiration for young people, and part of their education—the big picture. I told her she should have applied to be an astronaut!
>
> —JOHN GLENN

One of Kennedy's most complex challenges—civil rights—drew Jackie in personally. She and JFK discussed at length the resistance to his civil rights bill in Congress and to school integration in Alabama, and she watched the famous 1963 March on Washington intently on television—from a bed where she was recovering from cesarean surgery. When the Metropolitan Club refused to change its discriminatory policy toward blacks, Jackie suggested that members from the administration who resigned from the club form a new, nondiscriminatory one and hold their meetings in the White House family quarters. At a Lincoln's birthday reception for African Americans, she even defied JFK to express her anger at his choosing political expediency over racial tolerance:

It was [Sammy Davis Jr.], the president focused on before he came downstairs to the reception . . . a talented song-and-dance man whose marriage to a Swedish actress named May Britt was considered a scandal or worse by Americans who disapproved of all interracial marriage. . . . A photograph of the black man in the White House with his white woman could be a political disaster. . . . [JFK] told one assistant after another to tell his wife to take May Britt aside so that the Davises would not be together before the photographers were pushed out of the room.

Jacqueline Kennedy refused. She was so angry at the suggestion she did not want to go downstairs at all, and the formal reception began without the president and his wife. He was still upstairs trying to talk her into going down. She finally did, agreeing to sit next to her husband for a formal portrait with Vice President Johnson and his wife, as well as Mrs. Robert Kennedy and eleven Negro leaders. Then she stood up, said she did not feel well, and left.

—RICHARD REEVES, HISTORIAN

Disgusted by the use of violence against civil rights supporters, Jackie publicly revealed her views on integration by inviting the assistant press secretary's son, Andrew Hatcher Jr., an African American, to join Caroline's school group, desegregating the White House in one swoop.

What was happening in civil rights concerned her, and she was certainly ahead of the curve in her thinking on it. It was important to her that her youngsters have minority children represented in their unofficial play groups as well as their school groups. I've just really always been mindful of how she communicated with blacks and other minority staff members exactly the way that she did with the whites—just as people. No matter what a person's race or station may have been, it was not only important to her that they be treated with respect, but important to her that her children similarly respond. They were taught to speak respectfully to all people.

—JIM KETCHUM

Jackie proved invaluable in warmly asserting the welcome to African leaders of recently independent nations. Tish Baldrige recalled her drawing out a "shy, nervous African president" in French, "completely putting him at ease in what were terrifying surroundings for him."

Her animated chatting in French with the new heads of embassies from French Africa may mark a revolution in American relations with underdeveloped countries. She may be worth more than all the military and economic aid America might send them. What people want is to be accepted, not bullied or bought.

—LAURA BERQUIST KNEBEL

JFK discussed with Jackie his growing discomfort with Vietnam intervention, telling her about General Douglas MacArthur's warning that he must limit commitment there.

So few people were aware of Jackie's involvement, the fact for instance that she often observed the meetings of the National Security Council.

—DAVID ORMSBY-GORE, FRIEND AND
BRITISH AMBASSADOR TO THE UNITED STATES

JFK turned to Jackie as his confidante during the greatest disaster of his presidency, his approval of CIA plans to invade Communist Cuba by landing troops in the Bay of Pigs, a debacle that ended with their being captured by Castro's forces.

Jackie walked upstairs with me and said he was upset all day. Had practically been in tears, felt he had been misinformed by the CIA. . . . Jackie seemed so sympathetic and said she had stayed with him until he had lain down, as she had never seen him so depressed except once, at the time of his operation.

—ROSE KENNEDY

She told me that Kennedy had cried when the news of the Bay of Pigs came in. This was obviously a great blow, especially so early in the administration when it showed the highest promise. She was enormously concerned about his well-being.

—ARTHUR SCHLESINGER

She was always asking how the Pentagon worked and about the relationship between the Joint Chiefs of Staff and civilian officials. When I wrote about duplication in the armed forces, she responded that she hoped recommendations for change would be followed. She worried about incompetence at the Defense Department, the CIA—and who should be removed and what military personalities were irresponsible, and how to implore the president to remove them.

—ROSWELL GILPATRIC

Jackie later criticized the Joint Chiefs of Staff for their bad advice to JFK, pointedly remarking that Curtis LeMay was a "mad bomber" with "tunnel vision." Several weeks later she was trying to protect her husband by ensuring that the subject was closed and chastised a friend who had "Jack go through another one of those sessions on the Bay of Pigs at dinner." She later proudly made a speech in Spanish to thousands of Cubans in Miami's Orange Bowl who had gathered to honor the recently freed troops.

She played an even more important role for the president, however, during the Cuban Missile Crisis. Personally, she had in Vienna found Khrushchev devious, but in observing the Soviet delegation, she told her husband that she sensed sincerity in Andrei Gromyko and that perhaps he was the most trustworthy person in the Kremlin. When she insisted that Basil Rathbone recite the St. Crispen's Day battle speech for a dinner honoring the duchess of Luxembourg, Jackie said, "The only person I would not wish you to say it in front of is Khrushchev, as we are not united in purpose. . . ." Publicly, her only remark on the cold war nuclear threat was a blandly cautious support for the Women's Strike for Peace. Privately, however, during the October 1962 standoff with the Soviets, who built up missile sites on Cuba, Jackie was a crucial confidante:

On a Friday—October 19—President Kennedy was leaving on a trip west. At my office window . . . I watched him walk briskly from the West Wing across the lawn to Chopper Number One. The usual retinue . . . trailed behind him.

They boarded the helicopter and I waited to see the steps drawn up. . . . Instead, the president unexpectedly reappeared in the doorway and descended the steps alone. How unusual, I thought. Then I saw why. Jackie, her hair wild in the gale of the rotors, was running from the South Portico across the grass. She almost met him at the helicopter steps and she reached up with her arms. They stood motionless in an embrace for many seconds. . . . Perhaps no one else noted that rare demonstration of affection. A few days later in the publicized hours of the Cuban missile crisis, I remembered it. I thought of its deep significance—the unbreakable bond of love between them that showed clearest in times of trouble.

—JANET TRAVELL

Before the president relayed his ultimatum to Khrushchev to order back his missiles, aides saw only one crack in his stoicism during the famous Thirteen Days in October of the crisis:

He telephoned Jackie at Glen Ora . . . and asked her to come back to the White House with the children that evening so that [they] could be together if there was a sudden emergency. Later that week, the president asked Jackie to move out of Washington so that she could be closer to their assigned underground shelter if a sudden attack came, but she refused to leave him alone.

—KENNY O'DONNELL

I remember there was a little squib . . . in the *New York Times*. It said that "at four o'clock in the afternoon, the president had called up Mrs. Kennedy and they went and walked out in the rose garden." He was sharing with her the possible horror of what might happen.

—CHUCK SPALDING, FRIEND

I was the unofficial minister of disarmament for the British government at the time. . . . The Soviets didn't want nuclear war any more than we did, because they knew what the holocaust would be, just as we did. Jackie . . . took notes when Jack and I talked about this.

—DAVID ORMSBY-GORE, FRIEND AND
BRITISH AMBASSADOR TO THE UNITED STATES

At night after the long hours of secret planning Kennedy would walk alone on the grounds of the White House trying to clear his mind. Jackie would walk out to meet him and the two would go back inside for dinner where he would tell her everything that was happening. When Kennedy gave his key men silver calendars with the thirteen crucial days of October marked off, he made a special point of giving one to Jackie too.

—HUGH SIDEY

After the nightmare of that October, Jackie considered the Nuclear Test Ban Treaty to be her husband's greatest achievement.

There was nothing that caused greater concern in 1961 and 1962 [than] that there was no control over nuclear weapons. . . . So many countries would have atomic weapons and be testing them, and the world would be that much closer to total destruction. . . . The Test Ban Treaty was finally signed. . . . It was more of a sense of enormous relief, and our future generations, and our children and theirs would be safe.

Jackie felt that a cold war retreat went beyond being political, and was one issue that she did press her strong opinion on with the president:

She pushed him to join the Test Ban Treaty with Great Britain and the Soviet Union. A few of his people were against it because they felt he would have to make too many concessions. But Jackie prevailed. . . . She was all for normalizing relations between the United States and the Soviet Union. In 1963, for example, there was opposition among the president's brain trust to the proposed sale of 150 million bushels of wheat to the Soviets. Jackie wanted the sale to go through. . . . She knew which people to push and how far to push them. The sale took place.

—DAVID ORMSBY-GORE

She was intensely interested in the limited Test Ban Treaty and thought it an immense achievement. I had been very involved in pushing for it, so he gave me one of the pens he used to sign it. Subsequently, because she spoke of it with such pride, I gave her the pen.

—ROBERT MCNAMARA

Schlesinger thought Jackie was a "realist without illusions," but in writing to a friend at the time, she concluded with hope:

Perhaps saving old buildings and having the new ones be right isn't the most important thing in the world—if you are waiting for the bomb—but I think we are always going to be waiting for the bomb. And it won't ever come.

Jack's Wife

The one thing that happens to a president is that his ties with the outside world are cut. And the people you really have are each other. . . . I should think that if people weren't happily married, the White House would really finish it.

—Jacqueline Kennedy

For all but ten years of his forty-six years, Jack Kennedy was a bachelor, and he was never to completely lose his habits from those years of freedom. Particularly in the beginning of their marriage, his proclivities provoked insecurity in his wife, and at one point, she had only half-joked to him that "he had met his love too late in life."

She had the kind of awareness that Jack obviously found attractive, but it also made her more vulnerable. She has a toughness, like a fighter who doesn't go down, but gets hurt. I think she probably suffered to beat the band, but nobody ever saw the hurt. But she filled out the picture for Jack. If you look at a picture of the two of them and take her out of the picture and put somebody else in, then you'll see what I mean.

—Chuck Spalding

By the time she became first lady, Jackie was largely unthreatened by anyone:

Jackie would pick out the two prettiest, brightest women—if they were dumb, he would ignore them—and put them on either side of him.

—Bill Walton

Throughout their marriage, the couple affectionately needled each other to subtly make their points. After teasing him about a woman friend of theirs as his "ideal," he retorted, "You're my ideal." Their humor served as the framework even for their disagreements. "Jackie is the one who can make the president laugh," said a friend. "He can never really get mad at her about anything."

To everyone they were the president and his first lady, but they were each other's husband and wife. Once in Newport, I had dinner with them and Lem Billings. Jack wanted Jackie to attend an event. She said, "I just can't with my schedule right now." And they bantered back and forth. There was nothing to hide. They didn't try and act perfect. It was just one of those touchy moments that naturally happen between husbands and wives.

—Joan Braden

Jack always said how smart Jackie was, and she really was. What they had going between them was this sense of humor. And she could cut him down, and did—no question about it. When she felt strongly about something, she let him know it and let everyone else know it.

—Stephen Smith, brother-in-law

She could deflate any pompous presidential posture he did not immediately deflate himself.

—Ted Sorenson

[Military Aide] Clifton remembers the night that Kennedy summoned him to his table in the State Dining Room and muttered a mild complaint about the music the Marine Band was playing. "Let's get something livelier," he said. [Clifton] went to Jackie . . . and he relayed the president's request. "Oh, he does?" she said, surprised. "I chose that music myself, but, if he insists, have them play 'Hail to the Chief' over and over. That should amuse him." Clifton abandoned the mission.

—Hugh Sidey

Kennedy, like many men of his time, was uncomfortable with emotional conversation or revelation. He never talked about his childhood, his relationship with his parents, or his frightening confrontations with death three times in life, once as a child.

I once asked him if he'd ever fallen desperately, hopelessly in love, and he just shrugged and said, "I'm not the heavy lover type."

—JAMES MCGREGOR BURNS, FRIEND, ADVISER, HISTORIAN

My husband was a romantic, although he didn't like people to know that.

—JACQUELINE KENNEDY

In 1964, Jackie revealed to Dorothy Schiff that the president "never kissed in public or anything like that and really hated public demonstrations of affection." Upon her return from Europe in 1961, for example, when Jackie greeted him with a kiss, he—aware of a nearby photographer—groused to the driver, "Let's *go!*"

Despite the constant entreaties of the photographers, the president was never seen to kiss his wife in public. Such displays of affection before cameras he considered to be in bad taste.

—HUGH SIDEY

When he wasn't in public and knew he could not be photographed, however, President Kennedy eventually learned to relax—both with himself and in allowing Jackie to show affection:

When she was married to Jack, we'd go sailing together. I'll always remember her sitting there so peaceful, putting her bare feet in his lap. She was so genuine.

—WILLIAM STYRON, FRIEND AND AUTHOR

One friend . . . had been conferring with the president, and then JFK met his wife in a corridor of the White House. They joined hands and walked away, hand in hand, oblivious of servants and Secret Service agents. Jackie had become to John Kennedy what she had always hoped to become—his haven, his refuge, his separate world.

—LAURA BERQUIST KNEBEL

One guest, who wished to remain anonymous, recalled a small scene between the couple as a private dinner was breaking up, and JFK "put his arm around her waist in the most natural, husbandly manner imaginable. It could only have been a spontaneous gesture and it could only have come from a husband who was getting along with his wife just fine."

Jackie often kept an eye on the Oval Office from her sitting room window, watching JFK's rose garden ceremonies during the day, and waiting for the light to go out in the evening. Occasionally, she slipped into the Oval Office dressed casually in a sweater and jodhpurs to surprise him, and they once sneaked outside together and around half the perimeter of the White House fence, considering it a liberating feat.

She forced a separation between his private life and work. That was the deal. Unlike Johnson, when Kennedy was finished, once he went back upstairs, he went to his wife and that was the end of it. No staff, no more interruptions every half hour.

—Pierre Salinger

Jacqueline watched with fascination how White Houseitis affected their acquaintances, leading some to grievance and others to sycophancy. She sometimes thought that if she ever wrote a book, it would be called *The Poison of the Presidency*.

—Arthur Schlesinger

Her routine when the president returned home from work was not unlike that of thousands of other young wives of that era. She would avoid disturbing subjects, have his favorite daiquiri ready and record album playing. Sometimes she scheduled a family movie or swim in the pool. On the rare nights when the children were already in bed before their father came home, usually about seven-thirty, the couple often had friends and family over for small dinners. Several individuals observed how the couple interacted:

The president kissed his wife, asking about the children, and wanted to know how Jacqueline had spent her day. He noticed, and complimented, her hairdo. . . . This led to a discussion of fashions, and JFK seemed completely informed on the subject. The hi-fi softly played classical music as we sat down. Jacqueline, who is somewhat reserved even in small groups, is a fascinating conversationalist when drawn out, and her husband knows exactly how to do this. . . . That night, I remember the president asking Jacqueline if a particular painting had arrived for the Lincoln Room. Her reply was animated and enchanting.

—Peter Lawford, brother-in-law

Mrs. Kennedy provided a whole new . . . set of interests that were relaxing for him. He was as fascinated talking to somebody like, I don't know, a noted choreographer, a noted painter, a noted photographer about his work, and could get relaxation from that as well as talking to Dave Powers. . . . They didn't go out very much, I remember that. . . . it was a difficult thing to do, and it got to be a strain.

—PAM TURNURE

Jackie would leave cartoons and limericks for Jack in unexpected places to cheer him up when the nation's affairs were going badly. She would arrange for a special treat—like Joe's Stone Crabs from Miami—old friends would pay morale-boosting calls at her prompting. Her most effective weapon was a surprise visit to his office with the children. And she labored more over his birthday celebrations than over any state dinner. Many days she would be waiting by the elevator to help him when he emerged from it, dragging himself on crutches.

—LETITIA BALDRIGE

She was very affectionate in referring to the president and I was struck by it. We were discussing some dinner . . . and she said, "Well, we can do it almost any time but not in the early weeks of April, because that's near Easter and that's going to be Jack's vacation and I want to keep that absolutely clear." She was thinking ahead and very thoughtfully about him.

—AUGUST HECKSCHER

In moments of discouragement she sometimes cried, "Oh, Jack, I'm so sorry for you that I'm such a dud." He would tell her that he loved her as she was.

—ARTHUR SCHLESINGER

Kennedy frequently lavished his focus on her. He enjoyed her reaction when he surprised her in the family quarters by bringing up guests that she revered, like Robert Frost. On a photo of him and Jackie, he inscribed "For Mummy and Uncle Hugh D—with thanks for helping to create the best half of this photograph." He told one friend, "You have no idea what a help Jackie is to me, and what she has meant to me. *Didn't* she look beautiful?" While the cost of her tastes often set him off, in fact, it was he who usually surprised her with gifts of the sort she cherished—a Renoir drawing, for example, was his first White House Christmas present to her.

Cartoon illustrating Jackie Kennedy's popularity as contribution to positive foreign perception of Kennedy administration, 1962.

Her husband's delight in her was visible. His eyes brightened when he talked of her or when she unexpectedly dropped by the office. . . . He loved picking out presents for her; her birthdays would be a profusion of boxes from Klejman and drawings from Wildenstein.

—ARTHUR SCHLESINGER

The night of the state dinner for the shah of Iran he twitted Mrs. Kennedy by saying, "You'd better watch out, Jackie. You'd better watch out and see what kind of jewels come out. . . . I bet her clothes bill is more than yours." He was very proud of her taste. He loved beautiful clothes. He didn't love all the publicity she got for being a clotheshorse.

—LETITIA BALDRIGE

He turned to me suddenly and asked: "Is that a Givenchy you're wearing?. . . I'm getting pretty good at it—now that fashion is becoming more important than politics and the press is paying more attention to Jackie's clothes than to my speeches."

—GRACE DE MONACO

I remember the day that young Franklin Roosevelt was sworn in as assistant secretary of commerce. . . . Jackie was in a pair of slacks and a funny-looking windbreaker and really untidy hair. And at that point, she was . . . in a period of more exaggerated hairdos. . . . She said, "I'll just jump out of these slacks into a dress.". . . She emerged in a dress but her hair still looking really quite long and loose and slightly untidy, I thought, but I did not say anything because I thought it would make her self-conscious. We went over to the president's office very quickly . . . and he said to Jackie, "I really think we ought to go in now. . . . They've been there for quite some time in the Cabinet Room—do you want to fix your hair first?" Jackie looked at him in complete amazement and said, "But I just did." His face fell a little bit, but he just said, "Oh, all right," and in we went. She was perfectly oblivious to the fact that her hair did look a bit wild.

—JANET LEE AUCHINCLOSS

With the boundary between home and office blurred in the White House, the strengthening of their relationship was increasingly evident to the staff:

In the White House husband and wife were very close. His election, to her surprise, strengthened instead of strained their marriage. Those were their happiest years. . . . Contrary to her fears during the campaign, [she] saw more of her husband than ever before, and he found with her a happiness and love he had never known before. He became more relaxed, less demanding and very proud of his wife. . . . I would see Jacqueline walking with her husband to his plane, hand in hand, without regard to the police or politicians all about them. . . . Jacqueline possessed a quality of strong independence and, occasionally, saucy irreverence that made him all the more pleased to impress her in his work. . . . Their marriage was not always smooth in its early years, but it brought them both an increasing amount of happiness, particularly in the White House. They learned from each other. . . . Jacqueline remained essentially unchanged by either adulation or adversity . . . even when not everyone wanted her to be herself . . . sensitive but strong-willed. . . . [She] had no desire to be anyone else.

—TED SORENSON

It was in the middle of the day, however, that husband and wife had their time completely alone together, in the larger bedroom that remained primarily hers (presidential couples were then traditionally given two separate bedrooms). As far as their staffs then knew, they were simply having lunch together. It was only the chief usher, valet George Thomas, and later Arthur Schlesinger, whom Jackie personally told, who knew what happened after lunch. If Jackie was occupied with others at that moment, then Kennedy told his valet, George Thomas, to get her. "The president says that if you don't hurry," Jackie recalled Thomas telling her, "he'll fall asleep."

> After luncheon . . . Jacqueline drew the curtains and opened the windows. . . . This was her hour of the day, as the morning was the children's.
>
> —ARTHUR SCHLESINGER

> After lunch, the Kennedy children were bedded down, the maids and houseman scuttled away, and silence reigned upstairs at the White House. During those hours, the Kennedy doors were closed. No telephone calls were allowed, no folders sent up, no interruptions from the staff. Nobody went upstairs, for any reason. . . . The household staff was attuned to the intimacy that actually existed between the young couple. . . . Many a morning . . . the valet would tiptoe into the room next door, and gently shake the president—so as not to awaken the president's wife.
>
> —J. B. WEST

Jackie was to always be extremely uncomfortable with public discussion of the extent of her marital intimacy. Their room was out-of-bounds to everyone except the children, George Thomas, and her maid Providencia Parades. Only when caught off guard did Jackie use her private nickname, Bunny, for him. Otherwise, he was always, "the president." When later, the chance to explain their intimacy arose in a friend's memoirs, she retorted that, "It is no reader's business whatever happened in a bedroom with me and Jack."

It came as no surprise to close friends that Jackie became pregnant in January 1963. A year later she frankly reflected on her marriage:

> I know my husband was devoted to me. I know he was proud of me. It took a very long time for us to work everything out, but we did, and we were about to have a real life together. I was going to campaign with him. I know I held a very special place for him—a unique place. . . .
>
> Jack was something special, and I know he saw something special in me too. . . . The three years we spent in the White House were really the happiest time for us.

PATRICK

IN EARLY SPRING 1963, JACKIE'S PEDIATRICIAN, JOHN WALSH, "ADVISED HER TO cancel all her official activities" in an attempt to remove any stress that might threaten a healthy birth. It meant forgoing a trip with the president to Ireland, Italy, and Germany in June, but before he left Jackie hosted two birthday parties for him. The first was in the West Wing with staff members, for which she provided a variety of gag gifts—a JFK doll in a rocking chair, a COMPLAINTS IGNORED desk plaque, and her own gift, a basket of "authentic antique White House grass" mowed that morning. The other party was on the presidential yacht with his family and old friends.

When the president returned from his state trip with a silver goblet presented to him by the citizens of New Ross, Ireland, his ancestral village, Jackie realized its significance and ordered it filled daily with flowers and placed in his office. He shared with her his emotional reactions to the land of his ancestors and two of her grandparents. She recalled:

> It wasn't just a sentimental journey. Ireland meant much more. . . . He had always been moved by its poetry and literature because it told of the tragedy and the desperate courage that he knew lay just under the surface of Irish life. The people of Ireland had faced famine and disease, and had fought against oppression, and died for independence, and all through the tragic story of Ireland. . . . They dreamed and sang and wrote and thought and were gay in the face of all their burdens. . . . His favorite song, his family came from Wexford, was, "We are the boys of Wexford, who fought with heart and hand, to burst and twain the gauling chain and free our native land."

With their lease on Glen Ora expiring, Jackie created a more permanent private home in Middleburg. Fifteen rooms on one floor, a glass wall measuring thirty-two feet, and complete with a bomb shelter, she named the house Wexford, and refused to have it photographed for publication:

> It's the only house Jack and I ever built together, and I designed it all myself. I don't want it to be exploited and photographed all over the place just because it was ours.

In the autumn of 1963, with their two children and new baby, the Kennedys would be spending most of their weekends at Wexford. Until then, Jackie would remain at Hyannis Port, continuing her work with Nancy Tuckerman as her new social secretary.

Nancy truly became her indispensable aide-de-camp. They were closer to each other over the years than any others. Nancy was devoted to Jackie, and with her through thick and thin, good and bad times, to the very, very end.

—LETITIA BALDRIGE

During the summer of 1963, she was writing daily and sending memos back and forth to her office regarding her continued plans for the restoration. She would be very upset if you didn't let her know what needed to be done.

—JIM KETCHUM

All summer, JFK spent weekends on the Cape and was increasingly nervous about Jackie's health:

On a Saturday morning of the weekend I was there [in July] he was quite concerned about her. . . . He asked if I would try to get hold of Dr. Walsh, who had come up to the Cape to be near the First Family. . . . I couldn't locate him. . . . [After] about an hour . . . Dr. Walsh did get the message and came right over. . . . The president was . . . very upset because of his concern about Jackie. . . . He said to Dr. Walsh, "I just hope that if you do go off for a walk for any period of time that you always tell someone where you are, how you can be reached immediately in case I do have to get in touch with you."

—JAMES A. REED, FRIEND AND TREASURY OFFICIAL

On August 7, from the Secret Service trailer at the back of the house at Squaw Island, I informed the president at the White House that Jackie was on her way to Otis [Air Force Base] Hospital. In a second conversation with him, I gave him a report from Dr. Walsh as preparations were being made to proceed with the emergency cesarean section.

"Mr. President, don't worry, Jackie will be all right."

"How about the baby?" his voice was anxious on the telephone. "Fifty-fifty, Mr. President," I replied. [He said,] "I'm coming up as fast as I can."

—JANET TRAVELL

He just kept sitting and staring out of the window, and obviously his thoughts were completely with her, and it was a very quiet trip—getting there as soon as possible—rushing to the hospital.

—Pamela Turnure

Jackie gave birth to a four-pound-ten-ounce son, Patrick Bouvier, just before one in the afternoon. He had trouble breathing, suffering from a lung ailment known as hydraline membrane, and was rushed to Children's Hospital in Boston.

I was with him at the hospital when he was holding Patrick's hand and the nurse said, "He's gone." And tears came into his eyes. . . . We went to Otis, where he was going to tell Jackie. He went in alone.

—Evelyn Lincoln, president's secretary

The family wanted the Mass of the Angels offered as part of the services. . . . The little chapel in the Archbishop's Residence accommodates about sixteen people. Only the members of the family were present. Jacqueline was too sick. . . . I wrote a special prayer that I gave to Jacqueline after I read it at the end of the mass. Then they all filed out, and for the second time I saw tears in the eyes of Jack Kennedy, and they were copious tears. He was the last of the family to leave the little chapel. I was behind him. The casket was there. It was in a white marble case. The president was so overwhelmed with grief that he literally put his arms around that casket as though he was carrying it out.

—Richard Cardinal Cushing

Jackie, still weak, had to remain in her room in the small, makeshift military hospital.

It was like living on a submarine because Nancy and I lived at the hospital with Mrs. Kennedy for the next several days . . . completely sealed off from the rest of the world. And it was the most uncanny feeling because you would look out the window and you would see the press out there. . . . Finally after the baby had died . . . things were setting into a pattern of just . . . waiting until she was strong enough to leave. . . . If she had said, "I cannot go through with it" [leaving the hospital with JFK in front of the press], then it would have been done some other way. But she said, "Yes, I can do it." And she did.

—Pam Turnure

Jackie thanked the doctors and staff and told them rather firmly, "I will be back next year. I will have another child." Some years later, when Schlesinger stated that President Kennedy "kept his family small," she corrected him, and in the process illustrated just how much they had considered Arabella and Patrick as their children, despite their short lives:

> He never wanted them all crowded together like Bobby and Ethel—so some children in the middle were miserable and the parents harassed. But he always wanted a baby coming along when its predecessor was growing up. That is why he was so glad when he learned that I was having Patrick. But he wished for five children. Before we were married he said that. And he had four children in seven years.

Jackie remained understandably depressed, and the president signed most of the condolence acknowledgments. "Most men don't care about children as much as women do, but he did," she later remarked. "He felt the loss of the baby in the house as much as I did."

> He did so much to protect Mrs. Kennedy at that time. . . . I didn't realize until after Mrs. Kennedy had come home that she hadn't realized how serious the boy was until he died. But he really protected her from all of this. He had a double concern—for her and then for the child.
>
> —PAM TURNURE

> Jack and Jackie were very close after Patrick's death. She hung onto him and he held her in his arms—something nobody ever saw at any other time because they were very private people.
>
> —BILL WALTON

> Chemistry is a very difficult thing to isolate, and whatever vagaries must have been sometimes very painful for Jackie, JFK really adored her, and was proud of her, and I had the feeling in '63 that they were extremely close and affectionate, after the death of the baby. Kennedy called me to say that Jackie hadn't heard anything from Adlai Stevenson, of whom she remained very fond. Kennedy asked me whether or not I might do something to encourage him to write. He had that kind of consideration about her.
>
> —ARTHUR SCHLESINGER

A month later, Jackie's mother noticed this closeness when they gathered to celebrate their tenth anniversary at Hammersmith Farm.

I remember his saying to me in the hospital in Boston that day, when Patrick was in the little incubator, . . . "Oh, nothing must happen to Patrick because I just can't bear to think of the effect it might have on Jackie." I remember, too, his saying to her at sometime—which she told me—"Jackie, we must not create an atmosphere of sadness in the White House because this would not be good for anyone—not for the country and not for the work we have to do." This made a profound impression on her. . . . She was wonderful and kept her chin up and went on.

I felt that they were closer. They'd certainly been through as much as people can go through together in ten years: tragedy and joy and their children's births and deaths and then Jack's illnesses and Jackie's cesarean operations, and then the campaigning and occupying the highest office in the world. I can't think of two people who had packed more into ten years of marriage than they had. And I felt that all their strains and stresses, which any sensitive people have in a marriage, had eased to a point where they were terribly close to each other. I almost can't think of any married couple I've ever known that had greater understanding of each other, in spite of Jackie's introvertedness, stiffness—I mean that it's difficult for her to show her feelings.

That night he brought up a whole lot of presents—really a wonderful collection—but he kept saying to her, "Now, you can only keep one; you have to choose." Some of them were pictures and some of them were antique Greek bracelets, and some of them were . . . Italian antique bracelets, ancient Greek stone heads, an extraordinary collection. . . . He kept saying to her, "Now, don't forget you can only keep one." I think perhaps she kept two.

—JANET LEE AUCHINCLOSS

Jackie's depression about Patrick's death, however, lingered, and a concerned JFK mentioned it to family and friends, which prompted an invitation from acquaintance Ari Onassis for a Greek island cruise on his yacht. Jackie accepted the offer with her sister Lee, who was a close friend of the Greek shipping magnate. The decision to take the trip had political implications. The most consistent criticism of the first lady had been that she traveled outside of America without her husband, and she had been picketed for vacationing in Italy. The most persistent myth about the Greek trip, however, was that Kennedy argued against his wife's going. In fact, in the privacy of the Oval Office, it was quite the opposite:

> And I had felt that perhaps even thought it might be good for her to get away, it was not the best choice to go out of the country at this time and I felt obliged to say this to the president. And I talked to some other people, and I talked to Nancy and to Kenny O'Donnell, and they thought it should be rediscussed before the plans were definitely decided upon. . . . I had something to drop off at Evelyn Lincoln's office. . . . The door was open as usual, and the president looked up and said, "Pam, do you have something for me?" and I just decided . . . I might as well say what I felt about this right now, and at that point Pierre and Kenny had come in from the other side of the president's office. They were both there when the president called me in and I made my little speech . . . and the president looked up and said, "Well, I think it will be good for Jackie, and that's what counts. I think it will be beneficial for her."
>
> I still felt I should say something more, and the men were beginning to chime in. They had been holding back all along and hadn't discussed this, and they said, "You know, you have an election year coming up, and it may not look right to have this sort of trip." But he said, "We will cross that bridge when we come to it, and that's final. I want her to go on the trip. It will be good for her, and she has been looking forward to it." And that was that.
>
> —PAM TURNURE

In Greece, when the yacht was docked, Jackie visited the museums and ancient sites she had missed in 1961, toured through Smyrna, Turkey, where Onassis showed his guests the places of his childhood, and stopped briefly in Istanbul to visit its famous Blue Mosque. She then accepted an earlier invitation of King Hassan and visited Morocco. Her sister recalled:

> At one point, Jackie forced me to sing "In an Old Dutch Garden Where the Tulips Grow" to the king's harem. We were waiting for His Majesty to arrive, and were being entertained by the ladies with endless glasses of mint tea. It was one moment of Jackie's humor I didn't share.
>
> —LEE RADZIWILL

Every day, the Kennedys spoke by phone, and JKF updated her on his activities, including a detailed account of the Nuclear Test Ban Treaty signing. Jackie returned home on October 17 so recovered that Kennedy personally phoned Onassis to thank him profusely for the hospitality shown to her. She even eagerly agreed to do some public speaking on the first trip of the president's re-election campaign, to Texas. In one of her letters to JFK from Greece, Jackie's longing for his company was evident:

> I miss you very much, which is nice, though it is a bit sad. But then I think of how lucky I am to be able to miss you. I know I always exaggerate everything, but . . . I realize here so much that I am having something you can never have—the absence of tension. I wish so much that I could give you that—so I give you everyday . . . I have to give.

THE LAST CAMPAIGN

The president had a commitment for some time to go to Texas, and I know that when Mrs. Kennedy came back she called several days later, upon her return, and said that she would be making the trip to Texas. And I don't know how she arrived at this decision, except that several days later I had a query from the *New York Times* about the fact that she was going on this trip—it was significant because it was the first domestic trip she had ever taken with the president . . . and they wanted to know what it meant. And I called her and asked, "How shall I answer this question?" So I wasn't sure whether one should get into political statements so early in the game, and she said, "Well, yes, say I am going out with my husband on this trip and that it will be the first of many that I hope to make with him, and if they ask about campaigning, say yes that I plan to campaign with him, and that I will do anything to help my husband be elected president again."

She was very concerned about one aspect of it because she wanted to be his helpmate—rather than be a predominant person in her own right. . . . On so many of the trips abroad the press was very interested in her wardrobe. . . . She was very much concerned about this trip not being played up this way. . . . She planned to buy no new things for this trip—she would take a couple of suits she had had in her wardrobe for two years and one short dress for cocktails and a day dress and a coat, and the whole thing was very, very simple.

I would say it was a particularly hectic trip. I understand, and I recall, that they did have some problems in organization between people in Washington and people in Texas. . . . We had less to work with until we actually got there

THE WHITE HOUSE
WASHINGTON

In this room lived John Fitzgerald Kennedy
with his wife Jacqueline — during the
two years ten months and 2 days
he was president of the United
States. January 20 1961 – November 22 1963

Inscription for mantel carving in room Jackie shared with the president, written by her at the time of his death, 1963.

than any trip I have ever been on with them. I mean, it wasn't until the last minute that everyone knew the motorcade route.

—PAM TURNURE

Mrs. Johnson had reported to her that the press in Texas seemed to be paying more attention to her impending arrival than to that of the president. She used this information to bolster her long-standing argument . . . that if she was indeed a political asset—and without ego she recognized herself as such—she could be of far greater help when employed politically with some discrimination. She had, on November 11, 1963, dispatched a memo. . . . "I guess if Pierre ends up putting me and the children on the cover of *Look* in a bubble bath, I'll have to put up with it."

—PIERRE SALINGER

The Kennedys arrived in Texas on late Thursday afternoon, November 21, stopping first in San Antonio, where she was presented with white cowgirl boots. She accepted them as if they were the French Legion of Honor. So instantly popular was she with the crowds that a political editorial in the *Chicago Sun-Times* suggested that Jackie might "win her husband this state's electoral vote." That night in Houston, accompanying the president and the Johnsons, she delivered a speech in Spanish at a Houston hotel to the League of United Latin-American citizens:

I'm very happy to be in the great state of Texas and I'm especially pleased to be with you, who are part of the great Spanish tradition, which has contributed so much to Texas. This tradition began a hundred years before my husband's state, Massachusetts, was settled, but it is a tradition that is today alive and vigorous. You are working for Texas and the United States. Thank you and *viva las Lulacs*!

Leaving the ballroom, she made another, impromptu speech in the lobby to a gathered group of Mexican employees, shaking every hand all the way to the elevator. Jackie felt exhilarated, she told an aide, because "I am needed." Kennedy asked Dave Powers about the crowd numbers compared with his 1962 Houston visit. About "a hundred thousand more," he replied. "You see," JFK told his wife, "you do help." That night, the president, vice president, and first lady assessed the day's speeches. A decade later, Jackie revealed the political tensions:

[Whether JFK would drop LBJ as running mate in 1964] would be brought up every now and then and was rather annoying. I don't think he had any intention of dropping Vice President Johnson. Vice President Johnson came to our hotel room in Houston the night before we went to Fort Worth. There was all of this about . . . [how Texas Governor] John Connally wouldn't ride in the car or Senator Yarborough wouldn't. . . . The point of the trip [was] to heal everything, to get everybody to ride in the same car. . . . I know [JFK] had always thought that Connally was very intelligent. . . . I know he was annoyed with him then. I remember asking him the night in Houston sort of what the trouble was. He said that John Connally wanted to show that he was independent and could run on his own and was making friends with a lot of—I think he might have said "Republican fat cats"—and he wanted to show that he didn't need Lyndon Johnson, or something, and that part of the trouble of the trip was him trying to show that he had his own constituency.

On Friday morning, November 22, the president was up and out early. Jackie was late in getting herself ready, dressing in pink, recalling in 1987 that "JFK picked out that suit."

People were asking "Where's Jackie?" . . . early in the morning. . . . In his speech he used the same gag that had gotten such a laugh in Paris, identifying himself as the man who came to Texas with Jackie Kennedy. Well, she was very much, from the standpoint of spectators anyway, almost the focus of that trip and was when we got over to Dallas, after those two quick speeches at Fort Worth. For some reason we flew over to Dallas instead of motorcading there. And I remember the president going the whole length of a chain-link fence over at the airport with Jackie at his side. . . . They . . . were turning to go back to get in the limousine, I asked Jackie how she liked campaigning. And she said, "It's wonderful, it's wonderful."

—CHARLES ROBERTS, REPORTER

Three times that day in Texas we were greeted with bouquets of yellow roses of Texas. Only in Dallas they gave me red roses. I remember thinking—how funny, red roses for me.

—JACQUELINE KENNEDY

He decided from the very beginning that he didn't want to be in a bubble top, and as a matter of fact, I had one conversation with him about it and he was concerned about Mrs. Kennedy—would it be taxing on her strength and if you go in a long motorcade obviously you are going to be windblown, and as she was doing her own hair, it would do much damage to the hair that it would be a problem, and he wanted her to look her best. We did discuss it, and I suggested the bubble top and just immediately he said, "No, that's semi-satisfactory, if you're going out to see the people, then they should be able to see you," and so I don't think it was ever considered by him at any point. It was just considered shortening in some way and varying the speed, but if the weather was good he would always have been in an open car. . . .

I don't think anybody had any qualms of anything serious happening. . . . I remember going in the motorcade and everyone saying, "Would you believe it, only the president could do this, imagine all the things they said about Dallas—there have never been crowds like this," and it was just fabulous—the reception—just marvelous.

—PAM TURNURE

Connally and his wife, Nellie, rode in the limousine with the Kennedys into Dallas.

There were such big crowds of such waving, nice, happy people. I certainly did have a feeling it was going well. There were, what, three motorcades I remember.

—JACQUELINE KENNEDY

The crowds were so enthusiastic and so loving, we didn't get to do much chatting because of the noise. But I was so pleased with our reception, I turned around in my seat and said, "Mr. President, you can't say Dallas doesn't love you." And just then the first shot rang out.

—NELLIE CONNALLY

"A PILLAR OF STRENGTH"

AT PARKLAND MEMORIAL HOSPITAL IN DALLAS, BEFORE THE EYES OF DOCTORS, nurses, policemen, and others, Jackie turned numb, immediately knowing that he was gone. Despite the fact that her husband had been murdered by gunshots just inches away from her, she pulled together, and went out of the hospital by his side, to Air Force One, where aides and Vice President Johnson waited.

> The casket was on one of these little rubber-tired dollies and Mrs. Kennedy was walking on the right side of it. . . . She was walking with her left hand on the casket and a completely glazed look on her face, obviously in shock. It was deathly still in that corridor as this casket was wheeled out. I had a feeling that if somebody had literally fired a pistol in front of her face that she would just have blinked. It seemed that she was absolutely out of this world.
>
> I saw the priest on the loading platform. In fact, Mrs. Kennedy stopped and talked to him for what seemed to me like minutes. . . . They put the bronze casket in the back door of the hearse. The curtains of it were drawn, and Mrs. Kennedy insisted on riding in the back of the hearse rather than in the front seat. Now Dr. Burkley was there, and he tried to talk her into getting into the front seat, riding, I guess it would have been, with him and the driver, but she wouldn't. She insisted on getting in the back. Jackie Kennedy, still wearing the raspberry-colored wool suit and matching pillbox hat in which she had started the day's campaigning—and still looking beautiful—walked slowly beside the casket, her right hand resting gently on it. A white-jacketed attendant quietly closed the rear door.
>
> —CHARLES ROBERTS

Before the plane left Dallas, LBJ was to be sworn in as president:

> At the moment of the swearing-in, Mr. Johnson said that we must wait for Mrs. Kennedy, and I remembered thinking, How can they ask her to do this? and then there she was. They went back and she said, "I will be ready in a moment," and she did it.
>
> —PAM TURNURE

As the flight home began, Jackie had only a brief moment of regret. "I should not have allowed him to come here. I didn't want him to come here. And he didn't want to come here. Why on earth did they make him come here?" Otherwise, aides found her calm remarkable:

> At one point, she turned to me and said, "Dave, you've known Jack all your life. What will you do now?" Imagine, concerned about me at a time like that.
>
> —DAVE POWERS

She was logical, as strong as I've ever seen a person. But she never cried. Never.

—GODFREY McHUGH, AIR FORCE AIDE

Robert Kennedy was at Andrews Air Force Base to meet Jackie as the plane arrived, and they headed to Bethesda Naval Hospital, where the autopsy was conducted. Told that Lee Harvey Oswald, an American Communist, had been apprehended as a suspected assassin, after having shot a Dallas policeman, her immediate response was rather political and, naturally, angry:

> He didn't even have the satisfaction of being killed for civil rights. It had to be some silly little Communist. It even robs his death of any meaning.

At the hospital waiting for Jackie were Nancy, the Auchinclosses, and Dr. Walsh:

> That first night she said, "I am going to walk behind the casket." Considering the emotional state she was in, she was thinking of all sorts of details and other people . . . were not expecting to hear it from her, and yet she was already thinking about how it must be done and getting the message to William Walton and Mr. West, to find out how Lincoln's funeral had been done. . . . Her sense of history came through on this occasion, and she knew it had to be the most fitting possible funeral.
>
> —PAM TURNURE

> I asked Jackie what I could do, and she asked me if I would spend the night at the White House. This touched me very much. I knew she didn't want to be alone. . . . She thought for a minute and then she said, "I think Miss Shaw [the children's nurse] . . . will have to judge how much the children have seen or heard or whether they are wondering."
>
> —JANET LEE AUCHINCLOSS

> It was 4:20 Saturday morning when Mrs. Kennedy came with the president's body [back to the White House]. . . . Many people feel that she is cold because during her appearances in public she was very composed, . . . but I personally saw her when she wasn't composed, and she was as any other woman would be who had lost her husband—probably even more so because of the terrific shock and the way in which she lost him. . . . [After a brief ser-

vice in the East Room] as she came around the corner from the hall to the elevator, our eyes met and there was a rapport there just for an instant. She was
crying very hard at the moment . . . and I knew no words were necessary.

—NELSON PIERCE

From her bedroom, Jackie handwrote lists of people to be invited to the
funeral, including the president's cousin in Ireland and Onassis in Greece, as
well as instructions for the funeral—the music, the choice of the smaller St.
Matthew's Church over a large one, the prayer and picture on the funeral card.
Some family members wanted the president buried at the plot in Brookline—but
her choice of Arlington National Cemetery prevailed. Barely twenty-four hours
after arriving from Dallas, Jackie was driven to the cemetery and chose a burial
site on a gentle slope—a site she first noticed in 1941. As she had ordered, army
engineers marked the site along a line to the Lincoln Memorial. Recalling the
Arc de Triomphe in Paris, she declared, "There's going to be an eternal flame."
Before a small mass for friends, family, and servants, Jackie did permit herself to
absorb the extent of the horror when she knelt to pray privately in the East
Room. A witness, an assistant to Sargent Shriver, recalled:

She takes the five steps to the casket and quickly kneels down, almost falling,
on the edge of the catafalque. Her hands hang loosely at her sides. She lays her
forehead against the side of the casket. She picks up the edge of the flag and
kisses it. Slowly she starts to rise. Then, without any warning, Mrs. Kennedy
begins crying. Her slender frame is rocked by sobs, and she slumps back
down. Her knees give way. Bobby Kennedy moves up quickly, puts one arm
around her waist. He stands there with her a moment and just lets her cry.

—DAVID PEARSON

Monday, November 25, was the funeral and burial. Besides the dignitaries
and heads of state gathered together for it, Jackie wanted many others there who
might easily have been overlooked.

I think we were the first Negroes to go to the bier at the White House when
they brought him back. We sat in the midst of the church at the funeral. . . .
We sat right next to de Gaulle and Haile Selassie, which was a little thing, but
it showed that Mrs. Kennedy had not forgotten.

—BELFORD LAWSON

> I think we [he and Robert Kennedy] had extraordinary respect for her inner strength and fortitude at the time of that walk beside her, and for her presence in the church. She was an extraordinarily powerful example for all the world, for all Americans, and for the family. While others were sort of trying to find themselves, to put this whole tragedy into some kind of context, she was a pillar of strength and resilience. It helped all the rest of us to sort of carry on.
>
> —SENATOR EDWARD M. KENNEDY

After the Arlington Cemetery burial, during which she lit the eternal flame, Jackie served as a surrogate president, receiving the visiting heads of state in the Red Room, representing the United States to these foreign leaders. In a private meeting with de Gaulle, Jackie gently discussed "this French . . . English thing," referring to increased hostility between those two nations' leaders. She then sought out Prince Philip, and brought him to de Gaulle for their first conversation of the day. She directly told Soviet Deputy Premier Mikoyan about Khrushchev. "I know he and my husband worked for a peaceful world, and now he and you must carry on my husband's work." She thanked former Colombian president Alberto Lleras Camargo for his early support of the Alliance for Progress, and warned Venezuelan president Betancourt, "He [JFK] feared for your life and for the whole future of Latin America if anything ever happened to you. How strange it is—I never thought anything like this could happen to him. Please be careful. You are so desperately needed now to make all your and his dreams come true, and to save the Western Hemisphere." After the state leaders left, she hosted her son's third birthday party.

In her closing days in the White House, Jackie gave gifts of JFK's small possessions to household staff and political aides and cleaned out the Oval Office. She successfully lobbied the new president to change the name of the space center from Cape Canaveral to Cape Kennedy and to support the Pennsylvania Avenue Redevelopment, the Historic Preservation Act, and the National Cultural Center—which he renamed the John F. Kennedy Center for the Performing Arts. She also wrote some extraordinary letters that revealed her thoughts, both personal and public, as she prepared to leave the world's most powerful pulpit. To Khrushchev she wrote about nuclear war:

> You and he [JFK] were adversaries, but you were allied in a determination that the world should not be blown up. You respected each other and

Jackie Kennedy, upon her return to the White House from Dallas and Bethesda Naval Hospital, November 23, 1963.

could deal with each other. I know that President Johnson will make every effort to establish the same relationship with you.

The danger that troubled my husband was that war might not be started so much by the big men as by the little ones. While big men know the needs for self-control and restraint, little men are sometimes moved more by fear and pride. If only in the future the big men can continue to make the little ones sit down and talk, before they start to fight.

In an insightful message to Richard Nixon, Jackie illustrated just how permanently the assassination changed her view of life, and the pursuit of power:

You two young men—colleagues in Congress—adversaries in 1960—and now look what happened—Whoever thought such a hideous thing could happen in this country—I know how you must feel—so closely missing the greatest prize—and now for you . . . the question comes up again—and you must commit all you and your family's hopes and efforts again—Just one thing I would say to you—if it does not work out as you have hoped for so long—please be consoled by what you already have—your life and your family—We never value life enough when we have it—and I would not have had Jack live his life any other way—though I know his death could have been prevented and I will never cease to torture myself with that—But if you do not win—please think of all that you have.

On December 6, Jackie asked to have the staff brought in to see her before she was called down for a ceremony in the East Room to watch the presentation of the Medal of Freedom, which she and JFK had redesigned.

She had all the staff up . . . the carpenters, the maids, the butlers—everyone in the house was invited up to say good-bye. . . . It was so wonderful seeing her smile—to be able to smile.

—NELSON PIERCE

I saw her the day she left. . . . She had put up a huge oil painting there on the north wall and the gold frame was badly scarred and the picture also had some scales. The canvas showed through. And she said, "Come up here and look at it. . . ." I . . . started . . . filling in the painting. . . . She wanted it to look real nice for Mrs. Johnson. So even though you know how she felt leaving the White House she sat over there and joked with me. . . . "Paint some Indians in the picture. . . ." I went along with it. I tried to cheer her up. I knew how she felt. So we kidded back and forth and when I got finished, she admired it very much—she was very nice. She said, "Now why don't you put your name down in the corner?". . . She was waiting for a signal for her to go downstairs. She talked to me real confidentially. I told her how much I enjoyed working with her, and she invited me to come to see her at the house and bring my wife. She said, "I'll be very lonely. You've worked with me and I think so much of you. I'd like to have you come and see me."

—JOSEPH KARITAS

After attending the East Room ceremony, but slipping away before its conclusion, Jacqueline Kennedy met her children, passed through the rose garden, and left the White House.

A year later, while writing to her of a routine matter, Lyndon Johnson

Jackie Kennedy leaves the White House, passing near the rose garden, with her daughter, Caroline, and son, John, December 1963.

ended with a thought that mirrored the bond that the world had now formed with her:

> Time goes by too swiftly, my dear Jackie. But the day never goes by without some tremor of a memory or some edge of a feeling that reminds me of all that you and I went through together.

SIX

The President's Widow

1963–1968

I said to myself—you must never forget Jack but you
mustn't be morbid.

—Jacqueline Kennedy

Jackie Kennedy at the ruins of Ankor Wat in Cambodia, 1967.

VERY MUCH ALONE

I think I have a tendency to go into a downward spiral of depression or isolation when I'm sad. To go out, to take a walk, to take a swim, that's very much what the Kennedys do. It's a salvation really.

—JACQUELINE KENNEDY

A week after the President's murder, Jackie spoke to journalist Theodore White, remarking on what she foresaw for her life without her husband:

I'm not going to be the Widow Kennedy—and make speeches like some people who talk about their family. When this is over I'm going to crawl into the deepest retirement. . . . I'm going to live in the place I lived with Jack. . . . That was the first thing I thought that night—where will I go? I wanted my old house back. . . . Then I thought—how can I go back there to that bedroom?

Jackie moved with her children to the loaned home of Governor Averell Harriman and several weeks later bought the house across the street, at 3017 N Street. For the moment, she distracted herself with Christmas and correspondence. Every day, Nancy Tuckerman and Pamela Turnure sent work folders by courier to her, and daily she sent back her handwritten responses.

The president had planned to give seventy-five books of Inaugural Addresses for Christmas, which he had specially bound for cabinet members and particular friends. She decided to inscribe and give them herself. The mail fluctuated for about a month between twenty to thirty or forty thousand each day. . . . She personally answered anybody who had sent a donation of over $1,000 to the Library, and then the heads of state [came] and she [saw] them.

—NANCY TUCKERMAN

During her first Christmas alone, Bobby Kennedy gave her a piece of Egyptian antiquity JFK had intended to give her. After the holidays, however, her grief set in deeply. As private as she was, Jackie opened up her emotions to cope with the loss. "Jack was the love of my life," she told Bill Walton. "No one will ever know a big a part of me died with him."

Jackie called me at home one evening soon after the funeral and asked me for some personal advice. We started on the most mundane subject. Gradually, she began talking, at first calmly and then emotionally, about her husband and his presidency. I felt an unutterable loneliness descending on her. I offered whatever help and solace I could, but there was an unreachable gulf between us, imposed by events. Worlds were closing in around her.

—CLARK CLIFFORD

When we all went skiing, she said, "There'll never be another Jack." There were escorts, companions, and another husband, but there was never another Jack for her.

—JOAN BRADEN

In the new year, Jackie explained to Pierre Salinger, "There's only one thing I can do in life now—save my children. They've got to grow up without thinking back at their father's murder. They've got to grow up intelligently, attuned to life in a very important way. And that's the way I want to live my life, too."

Right from the start, she wanted continuity in their life. In the White House, when Mrs. Kennedy was busy she would sometimes drop off John in the curator's office, and I began to tell him about the Russian folk character of Babayaga. When they moved to Georgetown, she asked me to come over and continue reading the story to him. Nancy Tuckerman was there and we all decided to get some dinner. Mrs. Kennedy went upstairs to say good night to the children. I said I didn't have any money. Nancy didn't either. So when Mrs. Kennedy returned, we told her. She said, "No problem." She went back upstairs, and from one of the children's banks got a huge fist of one-dollar bills! We decided to go to Billy Martin's pub. She had not been out in public at all, but people left her alone except the maître'd who boasted of their new Sam Rayburn Room and would she not like to see it? She smiled and made up some excuse as to why she really didn't want to see the Sam Rayburn Room, but after dinner it was time to pay the bill. Remember, she was clutching the money. She said, "Jim, I'm going to put my hand under the table, and you put your hand under the table, and I'm going to give you the money and you pay the bill." I'm reaching under, and of course, she dropped the money. The next thing you know, I'm underneath the table of Jackie Kennedy, on my hands and knees gathering crumbled dollar bills. Everyone was just staring open-eyed, and she was just loving it. She really laughed, which was so good for her. To this day, I'm still trying to figure out whether she was trying to call attention to who was really paying for this or just wanted to laugh, even briefly, after just six weeks.

—JIM KETCHUM

As the winter wore on, Jackie began to focus on the next direction of her life, even briefly considering going back to work in some unofficial capacity:

I don't want to be ambassador to France or Mexico. President Johnson said I could have anything I wanted. I would like to work for someone, but . . . one is expecting someone to come home every weekend, but no one [is]. . . .

I will tell you one thing. They will never drag me out like a little old widow like they did Mrs. Wilson when President Wilson died. I will never be used that way. . . . I don't want to go out on a Kennedy driveway to a Kennedy airport to visit a Kennedy school. . . . I'm not going around accepting plaques. I don't want medals for Jack. I don't want to be seen by crowds. The first time I minded the crowd was when I went out with the Irish Mafia to the grave.

Admitting that "I was really living in my own shell of grief," Jackie turned down many invitations to state dinners and White House preservation committee meetings offered by the Johnsons. "It was just too painful for me to go back to that place," she recalled. "Even driving around Washington I'd try to drive a way where I wouldn't see the White House." She was certain of one thing: she did not want to become a political figure.

Once she got out of the White House, she closed that door shut. About ten days after the assassination, LBJ told Jackie, "I want to make you ambassador to France." She said, "No." If she wanted to keep some kind of a government link after she had been in the White House, if she really wanted to remain a public figure on her own, she would have accepted that job. But this is the end of it. Except for projects in memorial to the president, that was it for her.

—PIERRE SALINGER

IN HIS MEMORY

THROUGHOUT THE SPRING OF 1964, PLANNING PROPOSED OFFICIAL MEMORIALS to JFK became an outlet for her creative energy and executive ability. She even approved a Dallas plan to build a memorial plaza near the site of the assassination. It was, however, her vision for the John F. Kennedy Presidential Library that made her days as busy as they had been with the White House restoration. Though a presidential library is traditionally a museum and archive administered by the National Archives, the planning, fund-raising, site location, and building ultimately rested on her decisions. The effort briefly brought out the writer in Jackie again, with a lengthy magazine piece in *Life* she wrote elaborating on the items she chose for the traveling exhibit, and plans for the museum:

I wanted people to see the rather personal side of the president, so I have parted with some of our greatest treasures, the pictures, objects and books, which we always kept at home. . . .

He gave me so many beautiful pieces of sculpture, which he went and picked out himself. . . . There is a Roman Imperial head of a young satyr, which he brought me from Rome. I thought if this were shown in a case next to some carved shore birds from Cape Cod, which I gave to him and which he loved and kept in his office, it would show people a side of him that was rarely seen. . . . I have added some books which he always kept in the Oval Room in the White House. He had them when we were married and they, too, give an insight to what he really loved.

In January, Jackie formally addressed the nation on television from the attorney general's office, acknowledging the hundreds of thousands of letters written to her, which would become part of the archives of the library: two months later, on JFK's birthday, she delivered a similar message to the peoples of Europe:

> We want this library to be . . . a place which can keep alive all the things he stood for. . . .
>
> Many people in many countries have written to me, saying that he gave them new confidence in America, and in their own ability to solve their own problems. . . . The deep desire to inspire people, to take an active part in the life of their country . . . attracts our best people to political life. . . . We should all do something to right the wrongs we see and not just complain about them. We owe that to our country. . . . [It] will suffer if we don't serve it. . . . That's why we're working to build the library. . . . His office will be there. . . . You can hear every speech he made, and movies. You can see all the manuscripts of his speeches and how he changed them.

In the late spring, she began gathering building ideas.

> Jackie . . . went around the country a lot, looking at libraries, and cultural centers, and at drawings and scale models, talking with architects, trying to plan what should be done.
>
> —ROSE KENNEDY

After meeting with an advisory panel of internationally recognized architects to discuss the sort of designer and creation that might best capture the spirit of Kennedy, Jackie visited the individual architects to explore their ideas.

> The day Mrs. Kennedy came to my office, I told her: I have no big concert halls to show you, no Lincoln Centers. My work is unglamorous—slum-clearance

projects. . . . She didn't say much, but she kept asking "Why? Why? Why?" about what I'd done.

—I. M. PEI, ARCHITECT

In describing his way of choosing materials specific to the location of a site, she recalled:

> He didn't seem to have just one way to solve a problem. He seemed to approach each commission thinking only of it and then develop a way to make something beautiful. This building was going to be complicated. I thought I.M.'s temperament was right. He was like a wonderful hunting dog when you slip the leash. I don't care if he hasn't done much. I just knew he was the one. I marshaled all these rational reasons to pick I.M., but it was really an emotional decision. He was so full of promise, like Jack; they were born in the same year. I decided it would be fun to take a great leap with him. A presidential library is by nature static, but the way I.M. described this one involved you so in his excitement. It sounded wonderful.

It was originally intended for an area adjacent to Harvard, but local residents felt it would bring congestion, and Jackie feared the opposition "could have kept it in the courts for twenty years." The project began to drag. When someone thought the museum could be located in unused areas of the planned Kennedy Center, she retorted, "Are your proposing that we put the Kennedy Library in a basement?" While the site was debated, collecting was not forestalled:

> Jackie joined in the search. She could put her finger on everything. Most of the pictures I have, I either took or Jackie sent me or she took. . . . I call them Jackie Specials. Rose saved everything. She still had Jack's and Joe's uniforms, report cards. I used to go down to Cape Cod and spend hours. Rose thought I was winterizing the house. [Jackie said of mildewing photographs,] "Save them, Dave. Bring them to the library." A lot would be dead and buried if Rose's attic hadn't been winterized.

—DAVE POWERS

Of equal importance to Jacqueline Kennedy as the archive and museum was establishing some forum to perpetuate what she considered JFK's most significant legacy—a call to public service. The director of what would first be the

Institute of Politics, then Kennedy School of Government at Harvard, recalled her involvement throughout the organization's growing pains:

> I had initial credibility with her only because I had done a report on an Anglo-American conference—which she read! The president had read it and gave it to her, saying, "If you want to know what my life is like, read this." I don't think she was apolitical at all.
>
> Mrs. Kennedy was at the heart of wanting something more than the museum and archive—which was all the government would support—intimately connected with the president's memory, which would engage undergraduate students but in a nonacademic way. She wanted it to be like Boulevard St. Michel, students sitting around engaged in lots of intense conversations.
>
> Before the institute formally opened, I told her that we'd have to start experimentally, and it would take ten years for a pattern to emerge. She seemed shocked that things would move in such slow agony. We created an advisory committee and she served on it, came to every meeting, and made her views felt. She wanted to help do for other students what she felt part of an undergraduate experience had done for Kennedy—get them interested in politics. She was very enthusiastic about the study groups and internships. She wanted to be heard. She thought that a graduate school was bound to be stuffy and fall under the influence of Harvard. . . . I think she had gotten from her father-in-law a very skeptical view of Harvard. Bobby Kennedy had different ambitions than she did for the character of the memorial. He wanted it to make a big national impact. A Kennedy school could do that. The institute by itself couldn't. She was less interested in big impact—and skeptical about what that meant—than she was in exciting undergraduates and doing things for them that these damn academics wouldn't do.
>
> She remained a good adviser who kept coming to meetings, always asking what we were doing for undergraduates, and what they were doing for themselves. She was conscious of making sure it had to be bipartisan. What she cared about was that we had lively people who would stimulate the students, regardless of affiliation. The institute would never have happened without her vision.
>
> —PROFESSOR RICHARD NEUSTADT,
> FIRST DIRECTOR OF THE INSTITUTE OF POLITICS

Ultimately, Jackie's persistence about student involvement became a permanent part of the institute, which was made evident early on in the planning stages.

After my own stint at the Kennedy Institute, I had the opportunity to watch Jacqueline Kennedy on the advisory committee. . . . [She] always asked to be seated with student members . . . asking them what they thought worthwhile in the institute . . . and what . . . should be done to make it more useful to a wider range of young people. More than anyone else in the room, she was the one prodding staff members to extend . . . into the community to involve young people less privileged than the typical Harvard student. She had the knack for putting young people at ease, so that once they overcame their initial shyness in her presence, they would really talk to her.

—DAVID S. BRODER, COLUMNIST, POLITICAL COMMENTATOR

SUMMERTIME 1964

Jim Fosburgh and his wife asked me to come for a weekend in the summer of 1964 at their house, in Katonah, New York, with Jackie, this being one of her first weekends away from Washington after the assassination. We were sitting around the pool, and the conversation lagged, and I said, "Let's all tell what our Walter Mitty is, we all have a Walter Mitty." Jackie said something so fasci-

Jackie Kennedy at a meeting of the board of the Kennedy School of Government at Harvard University, 1966.

nating. She said, "I'd like to be a bird." I understood completely. She wanted to be in a different element, away from the earth, up in the sky, not attached to all the problems, flying free. She had a poetic mind, and it was very revealing.

We were later both changing for a swim, and we sat there on a bench in the changing room. And she went over the last three minutes in that car in Dallas, over and over and over again. And she wondered, "What could I have done? How could I have changed it?"

—KITTY CARLISLE HART

During her first summer alone at Hyannis Port, it became evident that Jackie was regaining her balance between solitude and companionship:

We would both go off alone and do what we enjoyed. For me it was music and reading, for her painting and reading. The rest of the Kennedy family was all off doing things together. And with great glee, she said to me, "Joan, they think we're weird! Weird! We're the weird ducks!" She said the word *weird* in the funniest way. She just made you laugh. But she did love to spend time alone, unlike the rest of the family. She would even go walk down the beach by herself, not in conversation with anyone, just in her own thoughts.

When she painted, she said she liked to listen to chamber music, not symphonies or concerto music, but chamber music, because it was more subdued and allowed her to intently concentrate without distraction.

She often took me water-skiing with her. The Secret Service agent would drive the boat, and I would be the one getting her signals—go faster, go beyond the wake. And she'd stay on those water skis for a good hour, then drop off, and I'd get on while she rested up. After that, she went out again! Then, we'd both swim for about a mile from the breakwater back to the shore. She was an incredible swimmer, and in great shape. And she always used flippers when she went swimming because she said, "If you wear flippers, it's a great way to trim your thighs!"

—JOAN BENNETT KENNEDY

Jackie recalled how the Kennedys' strength helped in her recovery:

They all have a humor that's my favorite kind, a little self-mocking, a little sense of the ridiculous, and in times of sadness a wildly wicked humor of irreverence. They have been such a great help to me. If I ever feel sorry for myself, which is a most fatal thing, I think of [Rose]. I've seen her cry just twice. . . . Once her voice began to sort of break and she had to stop. Then she took my hand and squeezed it and said, "Nobody's ever going to have to feel sorry for me."

Bobby Kennedy spent intense private time with Jackie, talking through the assassination, providing strength, advice, and protection. He became a surrogate father to her children. In late July, he organized a surprise party for her thirty-fifth birthday. Her appreciation was boundless, and in his attempts to draw her out, she began a deeper political tutelage:

> One of the things she used to say about her husband was that he was really most interested in the political process, that he loved the idea of making forces move, pitting one against the other. Bobby was the opposite, without patience with that stuff. He was the one that she said she would put her hand in the fire for. And she really didn't care about this larger political world of ins and outs. Her political sensibilities became more like Bobby's.
> —FRED PAPERT, FRIEND AND RFK AIDE

Jackie's political role reemerged that summer as family conversation focused on the 1964 Senate and presidential elections. She offered to publicly support Pierre Salinger in his race for the California Senate seat and gave a rare newspaper interview discussing how "valued his advice and counsel on all major matters" had been. When she met Fred Harris, who was also running for a Senate seat, Jackie excitedly told him how much she disliked his opponent, Bud Wilkinson, who had served as head of JFK's physical fitness program, because he had used that post to launch a right-wing campaign against Harris. "Of course Jack and Bobby were gaga over him because Wilkinson was this sports symbol," she later recalled, "the winning coach of the University of Oklahoma as the great white hope." Then, with comedic timing, she reenacted how she would slip JFK official-looking memos, forged as if they came from other advisers, against Wilkinson.

In preparation for the 1964 Democratic Convention, Jackie began playing a role similar to the one she had in 1960, providing Bobby with literary allusions for his speeches, from *Romeo and Juliet* to Aeschylus. As soon as she gave him a copy of *The Greek Way* by Edith Hamilton, he began "reading that and underlining things," she recalled. When Bobby despaired and considered dropping out of politics, it was a moving and strong letter from her that convinced him to stay. He successfully made a run for the U.S. Senate seat from New York later that year.

After a cruise of Yugoslavia's Dalmatian coast, Jackie attended a reception with Lady Bird Johnson at the 1964 Democratic Convention, held in Atlantic City, for five thousand delegates, but she refused to be further drawn into appearances during the event:

> We were on the plane leaving for Newport after the reception. We waited and waited. Jackie finally asked what was taking so long. It was Air Force One, and President Johnson wanted her to come out on the runway and greet him. She understood, but she didn't want to be used for any political purpose by anyone. It went back and forth by radio, from plane to plane. Finally, LBJ got on the radio and spoke to her. She was polite, but she said no.
>
> —JAMIE AUCHINCLOSS

That election day, Jackie chose not to vote. As she explained:

> I know that [LBJ] was hurt that I didn't vote in 1964. People in my own family told me I should vote. I said, "I'm not going to vote." This is very emotional, but . . . I'd never voted until I was married to Jack. I guess my first vote was probably for him for senator. . . . Then this vote would have been—he would have been alive for that vote. And I thought, I'm not going to vote for any[one] because this vote would have been his. Of course, I would have voted for President Johnson. It wasn't that at all. It was some emotional thing, that [JFK] would have been alive. They were all rather cross at me. Not cross, but they'd say, "Now please, why don't you? It will just make trouble."

Later that month, the memorial essay she had written in the summer appeared in *Look*:

> I should have known that it was asking too much to dream that I might have grown old with him. It is nearly a year since he has been gone.
>
> On so many days—his birthday, an anniversary, watching his children running to the sea—I have thought, "But this day last year was his last to see that.". . . Soon the final day will come around again . . . expected this

time.... Learning to accept what was unthinkable when he was alive changes you. I don't think there is any consolation. What was lost cannot be replaced.... Now I think that I should have known that he was magic all along. I did know it—but I should have guessed that it could not last. I should have known that it was asking too much to dream that I might have grown old with him and see our children grow up together.... Now he is a legend when he would have preferred to be a man. I must believe that he does not share our suffering now.

In the fall, Jackie made a break with the past, leaving Washington. Through Pam Turnure she said that "the change in environment to New York from Georgetown, and its many memories, will be more beneficial to her and her children."

You could never be bored when you were with Jackie, because you never quite knew what to expect from her. She had this love of intrigue that often led to some sort of conspiratorial act. For instance, in 1964, when she decided to move from Washington to New York and we went apartment hunting, to avoid publicity she came up with the idea that I would play the part of the prospective buyer while she'd come along disguised as the children's nanny!

Going back to our childhood days, she always loved New York and everything about it—the museums, the parks, the people. She was always drawn back to New York.

NANCY TUCKERMAN

TEN-FORTY

*I*N SEPTEMBER OF 1964, JACKIE PURCHASED HER COOPERATIVE APARTMENT AT 1040 Fifth Avenue. She never called it her "building." It was always "ten-forty." It was always home. She chose it because of its access to Central Park for exercise for herself and the children.

The apartment was very much a kind of English style, and so one felt as if one were going into a drawing room in London, old comfortable stuff, an ambience of total comfort.

—ARTHUR SCHLESINGER

Located on the fifteenth floor of a pre-World War I building, it was to become the home where she would live longest. There were fourteen rooms, including five bedrooms. As one stepped off the elevator, there was a long hall. Immediately to the right was a large living room which ran parallel to Fifth Avenue, and fenced terraces where she placed large crabapple trees in blue wood box planters. Near a window, Jackie would often watercolor or sketch, or use her high-resolution telescope to watch people in Central Park. The furniture was the same from the White House and Senate years, a mix of French antiques and contemporary pieces. The color was subdued, always in off-whites. There was a familiar terra-cotta bust of a small child, which she had kept on her White House bedroom mantelpiece and before that on one in her Georgetown living room, and which she later included in the background of her White House portrait.

She made the dining room, in the northwest corner, into the coziest room, later with red walls, and always hundreds of books, a piano, and television. It had a view of the George Washington Bridge, and a map with pins pointing out the various places where the president had visited, for the children's knowledge. An unchanging white kitchen was tucked in a corner of the apartment.

Scattered through the rooms were a mix of fine artwork—drawings, pastels, watercolors and oils—and sentimental objects like a soda bottle with seashells glued on it crafted by her children, to a leather-bound collection of Winston Churchill's writings that had been given to the president. Marta Sgubin, initially the children's' governess, eventually ran the household.

> In her apartment in New York, the only indication of [the presidency] was an important bureau plat she had placed prominently in her drawing room that displayed a number of the president's papers and favorite objects. It was a simple—but dramatic—testimonial.
>
> —ALBERT HADLEY, INTERIOR DESIGNER

Her own room was located in the southwest corner of the apartment, initially decorated in pale green and beige silk, with a baldachino of curtains above the bed as she had in the White House, filled bookshelves, framed Indian Rajput paintings, and at one time a small silver-framed photograph of JFK on her dresser. From the windows there, she could overlook the Metropolitan Museum of Art. At home, she continued to write lengthy, expressive personal letters, on what would become her trademark stationery of pale

Jackie Kennedy with Ambassador Sol Linowitz and Roger Stevens for meeting on the Kennedy Center of the Performing Arts, in the living room of her home at 1040 Fifth Avenue, overlooking the Central Park reservoir, 1965.

blue with white lettering of 1040 FIFTH AVENUE, or a scallop shell, when she was away from New York.

With Nancy Tuckerman and Pamela Turnure working in an office nearby, the other familiar faces that became part of Jackie's daily routine were the Secret Service detail guarding her and the children. One of them rescued Jackie from drowning in a cold and strong current in Ireland. Eventually, the men became like family. She later told Thomas T. Hendrick, special assistant to the secretary of the treasury, Secret Service detail, that she had long prayed for the day when she could be freed from their protection, because it was "brutal in its intrusion." The many threats, however, posed to her children in New York—even in her presence—made her feel "irresponsible" in wanting to be rid of the guards. She turned to and depended on them.

Continuing the family routine of winter weekends in the country, Jackie leased a home in the hunt country of Peapack, New Jersey, later purchasing a rambling, yellow house with white trim—converted from a sheep barn, with a meadow and a hill.

Jackie bought the house down the dirt road from our family. We had nine children, so our house was always a bit chaotic and noisy, but when they came out on the weekends, John and Caroline could slip unnoticed into the pack of kids. They were at home here. Even their ponies were at home in our stable. The children would play. Jackie would ride. It was close to a normal life. . . . For years we've had a parade on Easter Sunday. Everyone has five minutes to create a hat for the parade. Jackie always joined in. Once she dashed to the attic, found an old lampshade, turned it upside down, and led the parade of children around the lawn and into, as tradition dictates, the children's playhouse. Every year we counted to see how many people could squeeze into "Pooh's Corner," like clowns in a Volkswagen.

—Peggy McDonnell, friend

Triangle of Friendship

Many years after they were grown, Jackie spoke about how she dealt with her children's being in the spotlight, to a new friend facing a similar ordeal with her daughter:

One of the things we talked a lot about was the effect of the press on children, in ways that aren't always obvious, and adults around children in these roles who cater, or play up, protect, or give them all sorts of benefits, whether they earned them or not. She told me about how once the Secret Service intervened when her son encountered some bullies in the park. Obviously, she didn't want her children endangered, but when it came to ordinary give-and-take with kids, she wanted them to handle their own problems.

She also talked about how she would often say to her children, "Just remember who you are and remember how proud your father was and would have been, and never forget that." She gave that constant kind of instilling of family pride and belief that you're a valuable person, and that even if other people are writing silly stories about you, you don't have to let that affect you, you can keep your head up high and keep going.

—Hillary Rodham Clinton

While it was obvious to the children that being trailed by photographers or visiting former President Herbert Hoover didn't happen to other children, Jackie refused to let their recognition interfere with her raising them as she wanted. She asked them to invite friends over, helped with their homework, took them to ballet, theater, and museums.

At a certain point, after the children had attended Catholic schools, Jackie transferred them to Collegiate and the Brearley, nonsectarian institutions where they mixed with children of varied racial and religious backgrounds. On the rare nights when she was going out, Jackie made certain that she was home for the children as they went to sleep, but she spent almost every evening with them at home. She discussed them in a 1967 interview with Bob Considine and Frank Conniff:

> I don't want the children to be just two kids living on Fifth Avenue and going to nice schools. There's so much else in the world, outside this sanctuary we live in. . . . I want them to know about how the rest of the world lives, but also I want to be able to give them some kind of sanctuary when they need it, some place to take them into when things happen to them that do not necessarily happen to other children.

Jackie also took them on trips that focused on their missing parent or let them meet "people who knew Jack well." In 1965, they all took part in the ceremony at Runnymede in England where Queen Elizabeth dedicated a park area to President Kennedy, and Jackie's speech quoted Sir Walter Scott and Britons Raymond Asquith and David Cecil. In 1966, they spent Easter in Argentina with the Carcano family, just as JFK had, and a year later they made a "sentimental" trip to Ireland, visiting their relatives in Dunganstown. In the summer of 1965, she took her children to live in relative seclusion on Hawaii for two months and remembered the sojourn for years, fondly remarking, "I had forgotten and my children have never know what it is like to discover a new place unwatched and unnoticed." The increased intrusions into her family life troubled Jackie. She recalled:

> The strangest stories that haven't a word of truth in them, great long analytical pieces [are] written by people [I] never met. . . . I guess they have to make a living, but what's left of a person's privacy or a child's right to privacy? . . . Why is it so important to do a story to give our address, or the name of the children's school, times of classes?

She anticipated press coverage when making a public appearance, but when everything she did was imbued with political consequence, it left her frustrated. She made an obvious statement by refusing to stay at the Lake Placid Club because of its anti-Semitic policy. On a trip to Spain, however, during which she was criticized for watching a bullfight, praised for donning an Andalusian outfit, and dubbed ambassador-at-large, she was embarrassed by the ludicrous claim of a Spanish diplomat who proclaimed that "the ties between our nations are better for her visit."

Scrutinized wherever she went, Jackie most looked forward to summer, when she found genuine refuge in familiar places:

> When she came back to Hammersmith in summer, Jackie was always drawn to the bay. She went down alone and talked of her teenage years there, how it had been a refuge to her in those years. In the 1960s, as she began to recover from Jack's murder, she was able to start remembering happy times there with him.
>
> —Yusha Auchincloss

WASHINGTON

THE FORMER FIRST LADY ASSIDUOUSLY AVOIDED WASHINGTON. WHEN LADY Bird Johnson renamed the East Garden of the White House "The Jacqueline Kennedy Garden," Jackie panicked about returning, and asked her mother to attend the dedication in her stead, recalling, "I just couldn't go back to that place." On December 2, 1964, President Johnson turned the first spadeful of dirt on the site of the Kennedy Center for the Performing Arts. Although she was not there, nor would attend any board events in Washington, she hosted meetings at 1040, and made her feelings known.

*Jackie Kennedy, daughter Caroline, and brother Jamie
celebrating Thanksgiving at home, 1967.*

She wanted a grand entrance to the Kennedy Center, with full, oval steps spilling out onto the Potomac and fountains—but it was too expensive to redesign. A film theater, bike racks outside, outreach to the black community, large brass planters, and ample rehearsal space were things she approved and were all incorporated.

—JOAN BRADEN

The one event that brought her back to Washington was the completion of her husband's grave site. In the sleet of early morning darkness, she silently watched both Patrick and Arabella interred with JFK as his brothers and LBJ stood behind her. The site reflected her design concept, and after asking Ted Sorenson to gather several of the late president's quotations, she chose which ones were to be engraved in the stone that cradled it.

She wanted me to present a design based on studies of the graves of the different presidents and how they resembled the character of the time. She didn't want some towering monument. It is a simple design. I don't recall her being overly emotional or depressed. She focused on it calmly. She approved the design, but she wanted every member of the family treated as though they were the client, asking me to make a presentation to each of them for their individual approval. Jackie said, "Take your time. Be patient. Don't worry. Keep going." Finally, toward the end of the summer, I said, "Come on out and see the model." I remember specifically Jackie loving trees, and how they could protect the grave site. I wanted it all open. So, we put them on the side, and we kept the hill open.

I took it for granted, and am sure that she knew, that there was a place for her. She knew that the nation revered her, and she was conscious about it. Not that she was looking forward to it! It was not a subject that we would talk about every day.

—JOHN CARL WARNECKE

Jackie tried to focus on the events and people that brought her happier memories. Remembering how Pablo Casals had played for her at the White House, she warmly wrote him a birthday letter. Recalling the kindness of Nina Khrushchev in 1961, she wrote her a generous sympathy letter when Nikita died. Jackie encouraged the late president's friends and staff to record their memories in oral histories for the Kennedy Library. She wanted Jack Kennedy's life celebrated on his birthday, not his murder recalled on his death anniversary, and she refused to see films or programs pondering the details of the assassination. Nor did she read William Manchester's *The Death of a President,* for which she granted a lengthy interview about "private things" and, amid negative publicity, demanded later that they be removed. "The worst thing in my life was trying to get all those things of Mr. Manchester's out of his book," she later recalled.

Concerning the many assassination conspiracy theories that began to circulate, she separated her understanding of the public's need to know from her personal view that all such theories were ultimately futile. In 1964, she provided a long and detailed account of the murder, as she recalled it, for the Warren Commission, but she saw no value in dissecting the ambitions or motives of those who served on it. In 1981, she recalled:

> To tell you the truth, everything that happened that caused the Warren Commission to exist—you know, I don't think I really sat and thought, "Hmm. Let me look at the makeup of the Warren Commission." Somehow I had this feeling of, what did it matter what they found out? They could never bring back the person who was gone. Obviously, I knew it had to be done.

THE CITY

> When she first moved to New York, and we were planning on going to dinner, I might get a call from Nancy saying, "Jackie isn't feeling well today." I'd see Robert Kennedy later in the day and say, Jackie is indisposed. He'd get on the phone and say, "Jackie you get yourself feeling up! Don't just sit around there and mope!" He was very good in keeping up her morale and spirits when she might get into a depression.
>
> —ROSWELL GILPATRIC

Gradually, Jackie began to participate more in a social life, drawing herself into the more artistic circles of New York.

> A lot of the old guard in New York, the Social Register, to her were extremely boring. She found the theater and artistic crowds much more stimulating and exciting. Jackie had had to survive within a restricted frame for so long. She was a very liberal woman.
>
> —LETITIA BALDRIGE

In New York, Jackie went to the performances of Maurice Chevalier's one-man show, Maria Callas singing *Tosca*, and Ballets Africains, but among the performing arts, she became a most avid theatergoer, taking in a wide variety of works including *Indians*, *Two Gentlemen of Verona*, *Fiddler on the Roof*, *Hair*, *The Boys in the Band*, *Rosencrantz and Guildenstern Are Dead*, as well as numerous experimental repertory theater productions, and intellectual modernist dramas. She became particularly close to directors Alan Jay Lerner and Mike Nichols, and Oliver Smith, a renowned set designer, often visiting Smith's Brooklyn home and painting from an easel.

> She seemed to most enjoy the works of Tennessee Williams and other southern gothic playwrights. Her senses were always working. She really delved into a subject with great depth, pursuing its study singularly. She was more interested in artists and their motivations for doing something rather than just the result. She looked for the mental reasoning for the way a subject was treated.
>
> —PAMELA HARRIMAN

Jackie also lent her name to preservation fights, not always successfully, as in the case of the old Metropolitan Opera House. In an open letter to the press, she stated:

> I cannot believe that one Opera House . . . is enough for a great city like New York. So many different types of productions—ballet, Shakespeare, repertory theater—could use the Old Met that its operation would not be competitive with the Lincoln Center House. . . . Is another office building as valuable as an historic building which can provide a setting for artists of the future?

While she never served in any official capacity at the Metropolitan Museum of Art, Jackie took an active interest in its exhibits and collections:

> She had no ambition to be part of the power structure of the Metropolitan Museum, or that New York circuit. She was really more involved in projects for Jack's memory, not Rembrandt's. She wasn't a social climber because she was there, and didn't want to be there. She wanted peace. She adored art, and knew a lot about it, insistently asking questions to learn more. She was never particularly excited about nor had the upper-class devotion to Impressionism. She

adored Gauguin and Van Gogh because they were a little bit later. When the Temple of Dendur was given by Egypt, she initially wanted it in Washington as an appropriate monument to her husband. She wanted it outdoors, without any covering. Perhaps she was right, because it's used as a setting for glitzy parties now at the Metropolitan Museum of Art.

—TOM HOVING, FORMER DIRECTOR, METROPOLITAN MUSEUM

Jackie herself had chosen the Temple of Dendur when, in memorium to President Kennedy, the Egyptian president had offered one of the small displaced temples she had helped to save.

Jackie said that she always loved the temple because she could look out and see it from her Fifth Avenue apartment, especially at night, when it is dramatically lit up.

—ASHTON HAWKINS, EXECUTIVE VICE PRESIDENT,
METROPOLITAN MUSEUM TRUSTEES

Furthermore, Jackie helped establish the Met's Film and Television Office, "being instrumental in getting corporate, foundation, and private support" for it, said Hawkins, and later became honorary chairman of the museum's Costume Institute when it was revived under the curatorial imagination of her friend Diana Vreeland. She would also donate many pieces of her couture to the collection anonymously, wishing the focus to be on the construction of the item, not on her.

Jackie also began to entertain in New York, her first large event being a dance party at The Sign of the Dove for the Kenneth Galbraiths. Besides inviting relatives and longtime political and social friends, she also invited artists, illustrators, playwrights, and producers, and she even tried dancing the watusi and frug, telling famous instructor "Killer Joe" Piro, "I'd like to do them well too."

Jackie went to enormous efforts. . . . It was just an evening of pure fun. Time had passed, and this was an expression of her enjoying herself again.

—JOHN KENNETH GALBRAITH

By 1966, Jackie appeared to be happier than at any time in three years—whether exploring Coney Island to sample its famous hot dogs or, as Oliver Smith recalled, "gamboling like a kitten" in a Boston snowstorm after bolting out wearing a bandanna. She encouraged her many friends in Europe and Asia to contact her when they were in New York. Among them was Ari Onassis. Often there for business, he kept an apartment at the Pierre Hotel, down the avenue from her. Although they did not dine out publicly, he was frequently invited to small dinners at 1040. Wherever she now went, and with whom, became news not only in the New York media but also in the national and international press. When she first appeared in the mod miniskirt of the late 1960s, for example, it was actually printed in many papers as a legitimate news story. One survey showed that magazine sales went up 5 percent every time Jackie's name or face appeared on the cover.

I remember going to the opera with her once. I don't remember the opera, but I do remember that while we were sitting in a box, the public curiosity about her was absolutely extraordinary. She said she wanted to go to the ladies' room. We walked out from behind the box and this enormous crowd followed her— into the ladies' room!

—GEORGE PLIMPTON

THE VIETNAM WAR

THROUGH HER READING, HER TRAVELS ABROAD, AND SEEING THE ANTIWAR rallies and marches in New York City, Jackie began to develop strong reactions against the Vietnam War. As Bobby Kennedy increased his criticism of LBJ's Vietnam policy, Jackie sent her brother-in-law an acerbic piece by William Graham Sumner attacking countries that conquered other lands "in the name of civilization." She began also to confront those in power who engineered the policy:

We had been discussing the work of Gabriela Mistral, a Chilean poet who won the Nobel Prize, who wrote some beautiful poetry—Jackie had a wide and deep knowledge of modern poetry—when she suddenly exploded about Vietnam. She began punching me in the chest and yelling, "Stop the killing, stop the killing!" She understood the cold war, the containment policy that we had in place since George Kennan wrote that famous article in *Foreign Policy*. She read it. She knew the threat of potential Communist aggression. She'd seen the Soviet Union take Poland, Hungary, and Czechoslovakia. She'd lived though the pressure on Berlin in August of 1961, which she knew was much more dangerous than most people understood. She was quite aware of the threat of further Communist aggression whether it be from the Soviet Union or China. At the same time, she was absolutely overwhelmed by the tragedy of Vietnam. She had an acute sensitivity to the tragedy of American deaths and its tearing apart of American society. She had that feeling about the veterans, and the tragedy for American families—and Vietnamese.

—ROBERT MCNAMARA

Jackie was fascinated by Asian culture and sought to learn more about the history of the people who were enmeshed in the war. Through her correspondence with André Malraux, who had once done an archaeological dig in Cambodia, her interest was reignited.

I knew of her great interest in seeing the Cambodian archaeological sites, so I helped to arrange her trip there. I called Averell Harriman, who was then in a subcabinet post at the State Department, and worked with him in making it happen.

—ROBERT MCNAMARA

Cambodia's Prince Sihanouk had broken off diplomatic relations with the United States in July of 1966 because of its Vietnam policy. When Harriman learned of Jackie's trip, he spoke with State Department officials who agreed that American public relations could be improved with Cambodia by her visit, but that no speeches, or visits, to South Vietnam should be sanctioned.

Jackie was on a subtle, probing mission camouflaged as a tourist trip . . . to pave the way for further diplomatic exchanges between Phnom Penh and Washington. . . . It took the chill out of Cambodian-American relations and by doing so, opened the door to an improvement.

—MARVIN KALB, REPORTER COVERING CAMBODIAN TRIP

In November 1967 she began her trip to Cambodia and Thailand. The highlight of her first three days in Cambodia came near the small town of Siemreap, about 140 miles north of Phnom Penh, as she explored the Angkor ruins of the ancient Khymer Empire, guided in French by an expert, and later lunching under the massive jungle banyan trees. Despite the broken relations with Cambodia, American flags were flown in honor of her visit to the capital, named after Sihanouk. In dedicating an avenue named for JFK, she delivered a speech suggesting the United States' interest in having Cambodia as an ally against North Vietnam, saying, "By your commemoration of his name you have shown that you recognize his dedication to peace and understanding between all peoples."

When she was less than two hundred miles from the fighting in South Vietnam, Jackie learned that two American civilians had been captured there by the Vietcong. On her last day with Sihanouk, Jackie pleaded with him to ask the Vietcong for a promise that American POWs would not be mistreated. The prince made no commitment, but this did not stop her from making a second inquiry. She asked about Douglas Ramsey, a civilian official of the U.S. Agency for International Development, who had been taken near Saigon in 1966 and held as prisoner. Sihanouk responded publicly in a general press statement aimed at the U.S. government:

> Mrs. Kennedy and her party are certainly very interested in the destiny of your prisoners, and I told her that one thing America has to do would be to accept the solution I propose. That is, to accept the principle of your withdrawal from Vietnam and, before all, to end the bombing of Hanoi and North Vietnam. Her visit has produced a lessening of tension between our two countries . . . Cambodia can appreciate fully the charm of America so far as her ablest representative is concerned. . . . The visit is a very great contribution to a moral and sentimental rapprochement between—I do not say our two governments—but our two peoples.
>
> —PRINCE SIHANOUK

Upon her return, Jackie's reaction to the war began to emerge more definitively to others beyond her family and close friends.

> Harvard had its explosion of student uprisings in the spring of 1969, and the Institute of Politics, being an undergraduate institution with a strong connection to the Establishment, was in a defensive posture. That happened to be the year that Vernon Jordan was a fellow, and he made this little building a center for the blacks on campus, and the white radicals weren't going to dare to touch it. She got quite charged by that and she liked the students rising up.

She wasn't horrified by their questioning the Establishment. She wanted to know why more of the real radicals weren't engaged and involved in the Institute of Politics. We'd say look at this advisory committee of Establishment people—they are who the radicals were fighting against. She knew that but wished there was a way to make the Institute more of a radical center than it could be, given the circumstances.

I never heard her express conservative worries about whether the Establishment would survive, or wonder, "Are these kids going to burn down everything that I care about?" I caught a gleam in her eye when Bob McNamara precipitated the first riot in Harvard's modern history in 1966, when he came up to give some talks for the Institute. At the next advisory committee meeting she was amused, and she liked the idea that the Institute had gotten involved in controversy. The fact that it was a good friend of hers made it more interesting.

What worried her about the Kennedy School was that it was too Establishment and status quo, "TMBS," which stood for too many blue suits.

—RICHARD NEUSTADT

Without a son old enough to be drafted, many people assumed that Jackie Kennedy was sheltered from the effects of Vietnam. In fact, she came closer to it than most of those Americans who only saw the carnage on television.

It was during the Vietnam War, and they were flying the soldiers straight from the battlefield to the veterans' hospital in Queens. I was on the board of the Red Cross at the time, and they asked if I could bring someone out there to help with the wounded soldiers. I asked Jackie if she would go, and she said yes. Well, I had no idea that these very young men, teenagers, were just thirty-six hours away from the battlefield. I worried—you know how shy she was. They were missing limbs, some of them. Row after row, panicked or stunned, in bandages. Some of them were dying—in fact, some of them were dying as we spoke to them.

And Jackie just went from bed to bed, and she talked with them. I don't know how she did it, but, somehow, someway, Jackie seemed to calm them, and comfort them. No hanging back. I just followed in her wake, because she was doing it all herself. She just knew what to say, and what to do. No fear, hesitation, or anxiety. She cared a great deal about these poor souls.

—KITTY CARLISLE HART

Shortly afterward, Vivian Crespi expressed her surprise to Jackie about how fully recovered she seemed to be from the assassination's trauma. Jackie responded:

If you get out into the world, and move around a bit, you begin to see that there are people who have been through much worse things than I have.

1968

Shortly after reading some books on the Yucatán Peninsula lent to her by Roswell Gilpatric in early 1968, Jackie initiated a trip to Mexico with him, to see some of the archaeological digs there. They investigated sites at Chichén Itzá Uxmal, and Palenque with Brazilian friends, one of whom photographed the excavations while Jackie took notes.

Jackie kept a detailed journal. The idea was to put these pieces together as a chronicle. All during our travels, by plane, by car, Jackie was scribbling away. In Palenque, which is the most impressive of the Mayan centers, we were with an archaeologist, and Jackie spent all evening talking about Mayan culture. She was very intense, bought a lot of books, catalogues, and guides—and voraciously read them. She wanted to experience the ruins by moonlight on horseback, to get the feeling of the past, and even walked into the water to get close to them. It was essential to her nature. When she got interested in a subject, she thoroughly immersed herself.

—Roswell Gilpatric

Jackie—focused on her own writing for the first time since 1953—decided to adapt her Yucatán notes into a magazine story and book and turn the proceeds toward an educational project in the region. Thrilled to be working on something that could turn into a long-term project for her, she could not know then how suddenly her life would again be uprooted. In Mexico, she was abruptly descended upon by reporters wanting her reaction to Bobby Kennedy's announcement that he was going to run for president. Jackie stated, "I will wholeheartedly support his position and will always be with him." Privately, she predicted to Arthur Schlesinger:

Do you know what I think will happen to Bobby? The same thing that happened to Jack. . . . There is so much hatred in this country, and more people hate Bobby than hated Jack. . . . I've told Bobby this, but he isn't fatal-istic, like me.

Jackie was at 1040 when she heard that civil rights leader Martin Luther King Jr. had been assassinated, and she decided to attend his funeral in Atlanta. Arriving the night before, she went directly to Coretta King, telling her, "I want you to know that I came because I know what is going through your heart and mind now," and instantly struck a bond with nine-year-old Martin Luther King III, later inviting him to vacation with her family. The next day, prior to the funeral service, Jackie returned to see Mrs. King and sign the guest book, telling her:

> Your husband was one of the greatest and most inspiring leaders that any of us has known. I share your grief in this hour of sorrow but his death will help to free us from the violence and tragedy which hate often produces. He will always be remembered as one of our nation's martyred greats.

Mrs. King was moved by Jackie's presence and statement:

> She came to my house . . . [and] she came back to my bedroom . . . and I thanked her for coming and also for what her family and her husband had meant to us. . . . I told her that I felt very close to her family for this rea-son . . . and I said, "for our people." She said something about how strong I was and how much she admired me. I said the same thing back to her because I did feel that way. Then she said to me, "And you're such a good speaker. You speak so well."
>
> —CORETTA SCOTT KING

Jackie, in turn, was struck by the funeral ceremony.

> I'll tell you who else understands death—people of the black churches. I remember at the funeral of Martin Luther King. I was looking at those faces, and I realized that they know death. They see it all the time and they're ready for it.

Two weeks after the King murder, with the media's instant focus on racism in America, Jackie spoke almost bitterly of it all with Bobby Kennedy. "Of course people feel guilty for a moment. But they hate feeling guilty. They can't stand it for very long. Then they turn." Several weeks later, she received a phone call in the middle of the night:

> We had gone out to a fund-raiser that night. I came home about eleven-thirty. I woke up in the early morning hours, turned on the radio, and heard about the shooting of Bobby Kennedy. So I called Jackie, and she asked me to come right up, as soon as possible, to 1040. I got there at about five in the morning. She acted calm but was obviously extremely tense, and I could see emotionally quite disturbed. She asked me if I could help arrange for her to fly out to Los Angeles. She had some hope. It appeared then that Bobby could perhaps recover. I called up Tom Watson, head of IBM, a personal friend. I knew he had a number of planes at his disposal.
>
> —ROSWELL GILPATRIC

> When [we] got [to Los Angeles], Chuck Spalding was in the car riding into town with us. Jackie said, "Chuck, what's the story? I want it straight from the shoulder." And Chuck said, "Well, Jackie, he's dying." So then we knew that it was all over.
>
> —THOMAS J. WATSON, PRESIDENT IBM

> His death was such a blow. I think she had a prop just taken from under her completely. She had to turn to somebody who could give her security. She so desperately needed security.
>
> —ROSWELL GILPATRIC

Ari Onassis flew to Los Angeles to comfort Jackie, then flew back to New York to attend the funeral in the city's Saint Patrick's Cathedral. At the end of the mass, she encountered a reminder of November 1963, a sympathetic Lady Bird Johnson.

> I called her name and put out my hand. She looked at me as if from a great distance, as though I were an apparition.
>
> —LADY BIRD JOHNSON

On the train trip to Washington, for the burial at Arlington National Cemetery, family, friends, colleagues, and journalists spiritedly remembered

Jackie Kennedy, Reverend Ralph Abernathy, and sister Lee Radziwill at funeral service of Robert F. Kennedy, St. Patrick's Cathedral, New York, 1968.

Bobby's life, among them a longtime supporter, Maurice Tempelsman, a businessman who had first met JFK in the 1950s when he arranged a meeting for the senator with African leaders. Throughout the trip, however, Jackie was dazed, steeling herself for the return to Arlington.

Back home, she was more broken than ever. This murder not only ended the hope that Bobby Kennedy had given to her life after Dallas, but it also provoked panic attacks about the increasingly violent nature of America and threats made to her and her children. When a friend asked her if she had ever been in danger while visiting Cambodia, Jackie responded sharply.

"It's safer there than here."

SKORPIOS

NINETEEN WEEKS FROM THE DAY THAT ROBERT KENNEDY WAS KILLED, ON October 17, Nancy Tuckerman issued a statement to the press:

> Mrs. Hugh D. Auchincloss has asked me to tell you that her daughter, Mrs. John F. Kennedy, is planning to marry Aristotle Onassis sometime next week. No place or date has been set for the moment.

While Jackie had decided to definitely accept Onassis's May marriage proposal after Bobby Kennedy's murder, her decision to hold the wedding was sudden. She had confided her plan to a very few friends. Her mother was so unprepared to attend the ceremony in Greece that she had to make a desperate search for her misplaced passport, a situation finally resolved by the U.S. passport agency's granting of a special clearance. Jackie admitted to Roswell Gilpatric, "I would have told you before I left, but then everything happened so much more quickly than I'd planned."

Jackie and Onassis had become closer in the summer, as he comforted her, and she came to learn more about him as a person. Onassis was born in Smyrna, Turkey, on January 20, 1906, to an Anatolian Greek family; he and his sister, Artemis, grew up in a wealthy household. Their father, Socrates, was a successful tobacco merchant, and after their mother died when Ari was just six, their father remarried, giving them two half-sisters, Metrope and Calirrohe. By Ari's teenage years, however, the Onassis family experienced catastrophic changes. As a young child he had already been the victim of bigotry as a Christian living under the tyranny of a Turkish sultan, and despite the family's wealth, their race barred them from social acceptance, not unlike what the Irish Catholic Kennedy family was experiencing at the same time in Boston. Turkish intolerance, however, proved more brutal. The family was placed in prisons and work camps, and Onassis saw three of his uncles hanged.

After fleeing to Argentina in the squalor of a steamer hold, Ari worked as a dishwasher, construction worker, telephone operator, and cigarette peddler, all the while reading about business and industry. Eventually, he would be able to converse in French, German, English, and Spanish, become an armchair expert on Greek and British history, and learn enough about portrait art to make his own purchases of priceless pieces, including El Greco's *Madonna and Child*. He invested his money and lived modestly. During World War II, he lived in New York, which became his base of operations as he amassed a tremendous fortune in the shipping business. His marriage to Tina Livanos gave him two children—Alexander, born in 1948, and Christina in 1950—but Onassis began an affair with Maria Callas, and his wife divorced him in 1960.

The first time Jackie and Onassis were publicly seen together was at the 1967 dedication of the aircraft carrier *John F. Kennedy* in Newport News, Virginia. After the ceremony, as friends gathered around her, Jackie was surprised when she suddenly glimpsed him, then called out, "Ari, I didn't know you were here!" She was impressed that he had come from New York without having first made his presence known to her, or even intending to be able to speak with her.

Throughout 1968 they saw each other frequently. In May, she joined him for a two-week Caribbean cruise, and it was then that he asked her to marry him. She didn't decide right away.

> She told me in the late spring before she married that she felt she could really count on Onassis, to be there for her and for her children. That he was extremely protective of her, that he truly worried about her well-being. He could afford to build the buffers she then needed to ensure some degree of privacy from the public eye.
>
> —ROSWELL GILPATRIC

In July, Jackie brought Onassis to meet her family in Newport.

> When Jackie was marrying him, my father and stepmother called and asked if I knew anything about Onassis. I didn't and couldn't imagine it. Jackie had never mentioned marrying him. I can now see the reason. In Greece, she had a completely different lifestyle. She wanted to be on her own. I don't think we could ever understand but we tried because we loved her.
>
> —YUSHA AUCHINCLOSS

> Onassis came to Newport with his sister Artemis, and his daughter, Christina, about two weeks after the assassination of Robert Kennedy, and I was there that weekend and was assigned to chaperon or do whatever Christina wanted to do. I found her the most difficult person I think I've ever met, sad, spoiled, willful. As I've gotten older, I have more sympathy for her, and realize that she was under tremendous stress with her father, and feared whatever was going to be his new life. Ari was quite nice to me and certainly made a big effort to be nice to my mother. I don't know whether he suffered from insomnia, but he would stay up quite late at night, listening to Chopin and Tchaikovsky. He'd also be on the telephone much through the night, and he seemed to virtually never write anything down. He had a phenomenal memory. With his shipping interests, there was always some part of the world that was in daylight office hours, and so he communicated with them. My mother was impressed with his small tape recorder, and at the end of the visit, he gave it to her with the tapes

he was listening to, and she warmed up to him quite a bit, but kept saying, "No, no, no, you shouldn't part with this," which was rather amusing because, of course, Onassis could pick up another one!

—JAMIE AUCHINCLOSS

In September, Jackie twice took Onassis to visit Rose Kennedy. More than that of any other family member, her blessing was perhaps the most important to Jackie.

I had known Aristotle Onassis for some years. I used to see him here and there when I was traveling in Europe. We would be at some of the parties and receptions and be having lunch or dinner at some of the same restaurants, so we . . . became friendly acquaintances. . . . He was quietly companionable, easy to talk with, intelligent, with a sense of humor and a fund of good anecdotes to tell. I liked him. He was pleasant, interesting, and, to use a word of Greek origin, charismatic. Even so, when Jean [Kennedy Smith] called me one morning in October 1968 and said Jackie was going to marry him—and would be calling me later in the day to tell me about it—I was completely surprised. In fact, I was rather stunned. And then perplexed. I thought of the difference in their ages. I thought of the difference in religion, he being Greek Orthodox; and the fact he had been divorced; and I wondered whether this could be a valid marriage in the eyes of the Church. I thought of Caroline and John Jr. and whether they could learn to accept Onassis in the role of stepfather. . . . There were many things on my mind—my thoughts were awhirl—but I began trying to sort them out, give the various factors some order of priority.

And, with contemplation, it seemed to me the first basic fact was that Jackie deserved a full life, a happy future. Jack had been gone five years, thus, she had had plenty of time to think things over. She was not a person who would jump rashly into anything as important as this, so she must have her own very good reasons. I decided I ought to put my doubts aside and give Jackie all the emotional support I could in what, as I realized, was bound to be a time of stress for her in the weeks and months ahead. When she called I told her to make her plans as she chose to do, and to go ahead with them with my loving good wishes.

—ROSE KENNEDY

She of all people was the one who encouraged me. Who said "He's a good man" and "Don't worry, dear." She's been extraordinarily generous. I was married to her son and I have his children, but she was the one who was saying, if this is what you think is best, go ahead.

—JACQUELINE KENNEDY

On the evening of October 20, the wedding took place in the tiny whitewashed stone Chapel of the Little Virgin, nearly one century old, on the 350-acre Onassis island, Skorpios, on Greece's west coast, in the Ionian Sea. To appease the press, Jackie let a corps of them cover their entrance to and departure from the chapel. As she told them:

We know you understand that even though people may be well known, they still hold in their hearts the emotions of a simple person for the moments that are the most important of those we know on earth—birth, marriage, and death. We wish our wedding to be a private moment in the little chapel among the cypresses of Skorpios with only members of the family present—five of them little children. If you will give us these moments, we will gladly give you all the cooperation possible for you to take the pictures you need.

Jackie walked from the yacht through the gardens in a rain mist, dressed in a short white lace dress and hair ribbon, to the candle-lit chapel, its interior lined with gardenia trees. The Orthodox ceremony, with Byzantine hymns, had the couple kissing a gold-covered New Testament, drinking red wine from a chalice in symbolic oneness, and walking around the altar, holding hands in the Dance of Isaiah. As they emerged into a driving rain, the twenty-one guests threw white rose petals. At the yacht reception, Janet toasted Ari, saying "I know my daughter is going to find peace and happiness with you." There was dancing, pink champagne, and cake, which the couple cut with an antique knife.

He was a very dynamic person, a source of refuge and protection for her and her children. I think she felt safe with him, and after 1968 she had been fearful for their safety.

—SENATOR EDWARD M. KENNEDY

Jackie Kennedy Onassis and Aristotle Onassis emerging from a Greek Orthodox chapel, follow-ing their wedding ceremony on his island, Skorpios, in Greece, 1968.

Although she did later tell Roswell Gilpatric that she had taken to heart the critical reactions to her remarriage, for herself, she had no regrets about her decision. As she later stated:

Aristotle Onassis rescued me at a moment when my life was engulfed with shadows. He meant a lot to me. He brought me into a world where one could find both happiness and love.

SEVEN

Mrs. Onassis
1968–1975

I think I'm more of a private person. I really don't like to call attention to anything.
—JACKIE ONASSIS

Jackie Kennedy Onassis at African Art exhibit,
National Gallery of Art, 1973.

REMARRIAGE

*I*T WAS A RELEASE," JACKIE LATER REFLECTED ON HER MARRIAGE TO ONASSIS,
"freedom from the oppressive obsession with me and the children." Paradoxically, it was also a desperately needed security.

Her marriage to Jack was different from her marriage to Onassis. One didn't
have anything to do with the other. Her first marriage was in innocent youth.
By the time she married Onassis—the years had gone by with much sadness.
In a sense, although he was Greek, he was really isolated from the whole

world. He roamed the seas of the earth, a lord unto himself. Imagine being able to slip into that, away from the real world after so much sadness.

—PAMELA HARRIMAN

He was a diamond in the rough who enjoyed the power of his extraordinary money and the convenience of ships and an airline. He offered her just about anything she could want. That's terrific if you've been through hell, and you come back to your apartment, and somebody has flown over from Greece to be there to comfort you.

—LETITIA BALDRIGE

She didn't need money. She needed to escape for sanity. I went out to a Martha Graham performance with her one night. Some strange woman came up to her and said Jackie killed her husband. It was ghastly, really a horrible way to live, putting up with this every day. I told her she should leave the country and never come back. She absolutely would not. She felt a very strong obligation to Jack and to bring up their children in the United States. So after she remarried, she was always commuting back to America every two weeks. The marriage was probably a mistake, and might not have gone on forever had he lived. She understood him, but he didn't really understand her completely.

—VIVIAN CRESPI

After the onslaught of public rebuke, Jackie began to get support from unexpected sources. One telegram she received stated, "All the happiness in the world magnificent Jacqueline STOP Wish my name were Aristotle Onassis instead of Maurice Chevalier." Lady Bird Johnson wrote that "this complete break with the past might be good." In thanking Jackie for the "extraordinary consideration" of telling him about the marriage beforehand, Thomas Hendricks of the Secret Service wished her well for the "wonderful new adventure on which you are embarked." Cousin Edie Beale wrote letters to both Jackie and Ari, encouraging them not to worry about what other people thought about their marriage. The public statement that was the most personally important to her came from Cardinal Cushing. In recalling how he had promised JFK to guide her if anything should happen to him, Cushing added:

My advice to people is to stop criticizing the poor woman. She has had an enormous amount of sadness in her life and deserves what happiness she can find. . . . Time advanced. She wanted to get married. She selected her own partner in marriage some months ago. She came to me after others had advised her against her marriage. Her mind and heart were set upon Mr. Onassis. I could not nor would I presume to change her thinking. I said she could marry anyone she wished. . . . Once again I appeal for Jacqueline, for her children whom President Kennedy committed to me, for a little more charity on the part of those who are condemning her.

—RICHARD CARDINAL CUSHING

The frankest public defense, however, came from her sister, in a 1969 interview:

Americans can't understand a man like Onassis. If my sister's new husband had been blond, young, rich, and Anglo-Saxon, most Americans would have been much happier. . . . He's an outstanding man. Not only as a financier, but also as a person . . . active, great vitality, very brilliant, up-to-date . . . amusing . . . a fascinating way with women. He surrounds them with attention. He makes sure that they feel admired and desired. He takes note of their slightest whim. He interests himself in them—exclusively and profoundly. . . . My sister needs a man . . . who can protect her from the curiosity of the world. She's tired of having to exercise such enormous control over herself, not to be able to move without all of her gestures being judged and all her steps being traced, not to be able to live like other people. I think she's rather tired of being a public personality and a part of the political life. Politics has never been her dominant interest. Not at all. Nevertheless, in the past she knew how to assume public responsibilities quite well, it seems to me. She did it proudly and with honor. But it isn't fair that she should have to continue to force her nature. My sister is very jealous of her private life, very timid.

Had she married just anybody, she'd probably have remained exposed to the curiosity of the world. She loves Onassis. Onassis is rich enough to offer her a good life and powerful enough to protect her privacy.

—LEE RADZIWILL

ARI

THE TRANSITION FROM MRS. KENNEDY TO MRS. ONASSIS BECAME EASIER FOR Jackie as she arranged dinners where Ari could get to know her friends. "I like seeing all these politicians dealing with Ari's squiggly name," she joked.

Frequently they dined at his favorite New York restaurants—from Chinatown storefronts to French haute cuisine spots uptown.

I remember a dinner Jackie and Onassis and I had in Greenwich Village. We talked about reliving the Greek legend of the golden apple, which was rolled out onto the floor at Olympus with the words "To the fairest" on it. Three goddesses began squabbling over it—Hera, the wife of Zeus; Athena, the goddess of mischief; and Aphrodite, the goddess of love. Zeus finally decided that Paris, an honest shepherd of oxen, a mortal, should be the judge. He found himself confronted by these goddesses trying to bribe him. Hera offered him riches. Athena offered him a palace. And Aphrodite offered him Helen of Troy. I was going to portray Paris and get a French villa. Ari said no, it should be on his yacht. Then we would have three contemporary goddesses come and spend a week, and at the end of it, the *Ladies' Home Journal* would offer the golden apple, and I would write about being with these three women. We had this marvelous supper deciding who these goddesses would be. Then I added, "You must realize, Ari, that Jackie is the Helen of Troy in this story." And Jackie was there, giggling away.

—GEORGE PLIMPTON

I remember going to a dinner when she was married to Onassis. She insisted that I sit next to him because she said, "No one else will argue with him except you. He won't be bored." He was like a steamroller, saying things like "the Greek civilization was the greatest because the sun rises in the east!" Now, what does that have to do with it? I essentially responded. And had a similar attitude about female roles. So we fervently argued. But she wanted him to be part of things, amused, stimulated. She said, "If you knew him, you would like him very much."

—GLORIA STEINEM

After she married Onassis, I would see her for lunch. Often when I came to pick her up, say at about a quarter to one, Onassis would just be coming in! He had been out all night, going around to some Greek nightclubs! But, I think he did attempt to lead a normal married life for a while. I remember one of the dinners she gave. Mrs. Auchincloss was there with Rose Kennedy. Onassis and I were assigned to play bridge with them! He was going crazy!

—ROSWELL GILPATRIC

The Onassis children had been raised in a radically different manner from Jackie's. They had no home life—teenager Christina, for example, lived in a New York hotel suite. Their parents did not make them feel emotionally secure, and as a substitute the Onassis children were lavished with gifts and grew accustomed to receiving everything they asked for. Alexander was particularly open in his hostility toward any woman whom he feared would replace his mother as "Mrs. Onassis"—Jackie included. Briefly, however, Christina found companionship with Jackie, who tried talking with the chronically depressed young woman to help her self-esteem, and even encouraged her in a romance with Peter Goulandris, whose family Jackie had long known. In 1971 Christina remarked publicly, "Maria Callas never liked me very much, but Jackie is my stepmother and great friend."

Jackie doted on Ari, sketching portraits of him, buying mod neckties to offset his somber suits, and a cigar cutter so he wouldn't bite off his cigar tips. She even convinced him to permit her and Nancy Tuckerman, who worked in public relations at his Olympic Airlines, to improve the stewardesses' uniforms by having Pierre Cardin design attractive sleeveless uniforms. After her first flight with stewardesses wearing them, she realized the uniforms had to go: Greek women had different underarm habits than American women.

The most unpleasant aspect of the marriage in its first years was the unrelenting gossip about it, though Onassis took delight in responding—"We enjoy these rumors more than the people who invent them." Over the years, he had developed a self-deprecatory humor about such things—but then, so had Jackie.

> We met for dinner at Le Côte Basque. Ari had just arrived by plane from Europe and had seen some very revealing photographs of Jackie changing bathing suits on a beach in Skorpios. "I really don't like to see pictures of my wife's behind in cheap, Italian magazines," said Ari quite irate. Jackie smiled sweetly and said, "But, Ari, they're saving yours for their Christmas issue."
>
> —VIVIAN CRESPI

LIFE IN GREECE

SINCE HER 1961 VISIT TO GREECE, JACKIE HAD LOVED ITS CULTURE AND STUDIED its history and mythology. Her beliefs on "what I feel about being Greek" arose even in her mythological view of JFK, when she disputed Arthur Schlesinger's idea that Jack Kennedy was like a Roman. In 1965 she had written him why she felt JFK's "desperate defiance of fate" made him like an ancient Greek warrior and marked her ideas on how "Greeks fought the gods":

> There is a conflict in the hearts and minds of the Greeks. Greeks have esteem and respect for the gods; yet the Greek was the first to write and proclaim that Man was the measure of all things. This conflict with the gods is the essence of the Greek tragedy and a key to the Greek character. The Greeks are mystics. This mysticism can be traced to the influence of the sea—the boundlessness and mystery of the sea respond to the yearning of the Greeks for a supernatural rapport with divinity. The Greeks are curious and it is this curiosity that inspired a search and a thirst for knowledge and the Socratic contribution to the world that virtue is knowledge.

Often it seemed the Greeks better understood Jackie. "The trouble with me is that I'm an outsider," she said during her life in Greece, "and that's a very hard thing to be in American life."

> One day we were relaxing at the beach in Greece. We were lying in the sun . . . drinking wine in our bikinis. And she turned to me. "Do you realize how lucky we are, Vivi?" she said. "To have gotten out of that world we came from. That narrow world of Newport. All that horrible anti-Semitism and bigotry? Going every day to that club with the same kinds of people. Don't you feel sorry for them? You and I have taken such a big bite out of life."
> —VIVIAN CRESPI

Jackie never moved to Greece, nor did the couple ever permanently settle together in one place, owing to the nomadic nature of his global business. Even when she was on Skorpios, he was rarely there for more than several days at a time. During business trips to New York, Onassis would stay at 1040, but otherwise lived at his Pierre Hotel suite, maintaining a nonresident status for tax benefits. When he built Olympic Towers on Fifth Avenue and leased an apartment there, his wife, as a citizen, was the official leaseholder. Onassis explained their marriage of distances:

> Jackie loves traveling, sightseeing, long walks, mountain climbing, skiing, and literally hundreds of things that are just not to my liking. If we were together, she would probably get nervous always seeing me bringing up the rear! I know Jackie would eventually give up her activities to please me and just stay with

me, but then, that wouldn't really be Jackie. I don't want that to happen. When I do see her, she enthusiastically tells me what she has been doing. I have found that the longer the separation between us is, the happier we are to meet again. She asks what I have been doing during our separation, and her interest in my life doesn't weaken as it could if we were seeing each other every day.

Jackie is often at the other end of the world with her children—whom I should say I love very much. But they need time to get used to me, and I want to give them that time. They need time to understand that their mother has remarried and that I want to be their friend, and not replace their father, whom I admired so much. A father cannot be replaced, especially one like John Kennedy. I only desire that they consider me a best friend. That is another reason why I believe it is a good idea that Jackie has time alone with her children.

—ARISTOTLE ONASSIS

Onassis also owned an Avenue Foch apartment in Paris, and when Jackie was in town, their favorite place was a corner table at Maxim's restaurant. With headquarters in Athens, he also had a home in the suburb Gylfada. But Skorpios captivated her the most, understandably:

It was an absolutely fantastic place. The warm water was a color that is often mentioned in Greek mythology as wine colored, a deep purple that wasn't blue, the clearest, most beautiful water. It was like a lake. There were various places on the island where you could swim or have a tea or eat dinner or lunch. Each site was perfect at a different time of the day. The sun was everywhere, the setting sun, the rising sun, shining on the other islands in the distance, it was factored into the relationship of these incredible spaces to the environment. The place was covered with beautiful flowers. There was a whole little stable of miniature horses that Onassis liked. There was this kind of invisible world of people who were making up beds, and cleaning, and cooking. The yacht was extraordinary, and it was the biggest damn thing. Each room was named after a different Greek island, and the furnishings and the appointments in each of the rooms came from the island that it was named after—the wood, the stone, the art. There was a whole part of the island set aside for a marvelous variety of herbs and fruit and vegetables. The fresh fish was bought from the locals at the market. You could take a boat right over to the mainland, and one could go and just tool around just in the little village and market there.

—KARL KATZ, FRIEND, CURATOR, ARCHAEOLOGIST

Jackie imported cherry tomato plants, blueberry bushes, and Florida tropical plants. In the mornings, she clipped orchids, roses, and tulips, making dozens of bouquets for the yacht and house, and recorded her redesign of flower beds in watercolor plates. She took long hikes through the hills heavily forested with pine trees. She decorated the main house, which was on the island's highest cliff, primarily with native wicker. Jackie embraced native customs, speaking Greek, dancing the *surtaki*, even preparing stuffed grape leaves. One holiday season, she brought the Auchinclosses there for a traditional celebration, and wore a native Corfu costume.

> Onassis was certainly a proud Greek. As a result, his wife became tremendously interested in educating herself in Greek history, literature, and art—and remained so.
>
> —KARL KATZ

Jackie became familiar with the corners of the small country—searching Athens for antiques and old books on Greek art; attending with Alexis Miotis, the Greek National Theater director, classical performances at Apitdeivros, the fourth century B.C. stage; going to mass at Corfu's Saint Francis Church; exploring Onassis's favorite island, Ithaka. In 1970, while going through the old flea

Jackie Kennedy Onassis with Ari Onassis at their favorite corner table at Maxim's restaurant in Paris, 1970.

market on Pandrossov Street, at the foot of the Acropolis, she met artisan and poet Stavros Melissinos, who sold sandals crafted after those in ancient carvings. He told her the history of the street and that it was to be demolished owing to a scheduled archaeological dig.

> I explained to Mrs. Onassis that it would be good to see more of the old city's walls and other buildings, but that we, also, are making history, and that it would be a pity if this street, which has its own character, were destroyed. Two days later I received a telephone call from the Ministry of Public Works saying that the street will stay. . . . Mrs. Onassis intervened. She said a word in the right place. They had already put the crosses on the pavements showing that this part was to come down, and then nothing more happened.
>
> —STAVROS MELISSINOS, SANDAL MAKER AND POET

Jackie relished sharing her pleasure in being in Greece with her friends and family, inviting them to Skorpios. In an interview with Steve M. L. Aronson, Peter Beard recalled a summer there:

> She was like a dormitory roommate . . . completely casual. Great meals, fantastic picnics. It was lush—nonstop Dom Pérignon and OJ. She water-skied, swam. . . . Everything she [did] was voracious. She was reading Anaïs Nin's diaries . . . at length, and laughing all the way. . . . Jackie was on top of everything. She liked Richard Lindner's [paintings] very much. She wanted to meet Francis Bacon. . . . She was a real artist herself. I once won a $2,000 bet with Ari staying underwater for more than four minutes—Jackie was the timekeeper. She did a very beautiful watercolor that night and gave it to me, and everybody signed it—it looks exactly like the way I look underwater and it shows her writing the minutes on my back as the time ticked by. She did fantastic scrapbooks, too—huge ones. She gave me the enormous diary book that I laid out all my dead-elephant photos in. . . . One night Ari told me why Jackie had married him: "For the privacy."
>
> —PETER BEARD

Jackie's most cherished guest was Rose Kennedy, who visited three times in the first year of the marriage—once just after her husband died—and joined their first anniversary party at 1040.

Jackie sent me an album of photos taken while I was in Greece and wrote amusing captions under them. One . . . of me going to church . . . she captioned, "Demure like Heidi with a kerchief on her head." Along with the album she sent a letter that quite overwhelmed me, with her really heartwarming expressions of the pleasure all of them shared in my visit at New Year's. And how utterly unexpected was life's chain of events—that she and I, after all our experiences together, should now start to share new experiences in an extremely different environment and atmosphere, and it all happened so unexpectedly. I [was] thrilled by her assurances of welcome . . . and to know that all enjoy having me with them, including Ari and his relatives. . . . He was very congenial, considerate, a perfect host . . . . It seems to be a good marriage. Jackie has often quoted the words in the biblical Book of Ruth in which Ruth declares to her mother-in-law, Naomi: "Whither thou goest, I will go."

—ROSE KENNEDY

FORMER FIRST LADY

ALTHOUGH SHE WAS MRS. ARISTOTLE ONASSIS, JACKIE RETAINED THE PUBLIC status of former first lady and fulfilled duties as such, including her posing at 1040 for her commissioned White House portrait by Aaron Shikler. In his studio, she watched the process with fascination.

She loved poking around. . . . Perhaps it had something to do with her own feeling for painting and painting materials. . . . At some point . . . a government arts official wrote Jackie questioning whether I should be allowed to paint her without some kind of official aesthetic criticism. Washington wanted to put in its two cents' worth. Jackie showed me the letter and her reply. . . ."Let the artist alone. Don't look over his shoulder."

—AARON SHIKLER

Although Jackie spoke frequently with her former White House staff about scholarly research on the mansion, when Pat Nixon asked her about the traditional public ceremony for her portrait's unveiling, Jackie said the "thought of returning" to the home she and her children had left "under such traumatic conditions" was something she "did not have the courage to go through." Instead, the Nixons arranged a private visit for the family on February 3, 1971, to view the painting of herself and one of JFK, and dine together. Pat Nixon showed her the recently redecorated state rooms and Jackie was particularly impressed with the Blue Room, remarking, "I never intended for Boudin's work to remain in the White House forever. Every family should put its own imprint there. I think it looks lovely." The visit went well, Jackie thanking Pat Nixon:

> Can you imagine the gift you gave me to return to the White House privately with my little ones while they are still young enough to rediscover their childhood—with you both as guides—and with your daughters. . . . Thank you with all my heart. A day I always dreaded turned out to be one of the most precious ones I have spent with my children.

Jackie also came away with an appreciation of the Nixons:

> Jackie was very impressed with Pat Nixon during that visit. She told my mother how warm and gentle and understanding she was, how she asked good questions of the children and developed a rapport. She was fascinated by Nixon and said he had an extremely brilliant mind, a fascinating character with a lot of complexity. And a good writer. She later said she felt terribly for him, with Watergate, and that he had wanted the presidency so much and that it was really ironic but sad how it ended.
>
> —JAMIE AUCHINCLOSS

A year later, Jackie returned to the capital again, making her first public appearance there since the 1963 funeral, for her first glimpse of the new Kennedy Center. In 1971, she wrote of it:

> The existence of the Center will be justified only by the artistic quality of what goes on within the great halls and by the impact this artistic life has on the nation. . . . It must not be a shrine, resplendent but lifeless. It must be rather a working place, alive with ideas and experiment, attracting the most vital of our artists, drawing alert and demanding audiences into its great halls . . . a living part of the artistic future of our nation and the world.

At the time of her return, Jackie visited the graves of Bobby Kennedy and her husband. Despite her remarriage, she continued to attend many Kennedy family events, and remained close to particular members such as Senator Ted

Kennedy. When she learned of the Chappaquiddick accident, Jackie made the poignant request of asking him to serve as Caroline's godfather, since Bobby Kennedy had served in that capacity:

> It was a special trust and it was her way of saying that she wanted Caroline to remain close to her father's family. It meant a great deal and so did the support she gave me at the time.
>
> —SENATOR EDWARD M. KENNEDY

Although she had largely recovered from the assassination, Jackie was still threatened by the strangers who rushed her, particularly photographer Ron Galella, who harassed her from Europe to America until she obtained a court order keeping him at a distance. With the onslaught of 1970s terrorism—hijackings and hostages being taken—Jackie, however, felt an even more pressing threat to her and her children's safety. Still, she hated the idea of having to be protected "by objects of death," as she referred to firearms, stating:

> The very sickness that causes such means to be necessary repulses me the most about it all. Guns have cost us all so very, very much. It's so sad that anyone—even the police—have to even carry guns, much less ever have to use them. I wonder if there will ever be a time when the guns of the world will be nothing more than antiques—reminders to future generations of what the world was like back in the 1960s or 1970s.

Rarely did Jackie state her opinions publicly on issues like gun control, but she was willing to help old friends running for office, and her unsolicited financial support for George McGovern's 1972 presidential campaign toward the end of the race, when funds were needed for television advertising, did become public knowledge. She surprised everyone by enthusiastically agreeing to do her first political radio spots since 1960, on behalf of John Glenn's race for the U.S. Senate seat from Ohio. Even when old friend Helen Bowdoin's husband, Republican Sy Spaulding, was running for Massachusetts attorney general in 1974, Jackie impulsively agreed to support him:

> Then Jackie thought a second. She said, "Well, the only problem is that if I come out for one Republican, then *all* the other Republicans will ask me to!"
>
> —HELEN BOWDOIN SPAULDING

Jackie Kennedy Onassis visiting in 1972 the gravesite of President Kennedy for the first time since 1965.

ALEXANDER

O<small>N THEIR FOURTH ANNIVERSARY, IN</small> 1972, J<small>ACKIE AND</small> A<small>RI INVITED SOME SIXTY</small> friends and family, including Rose Kennedy, to celebrate with them at his favorite New York club, El Morocco:

> I cannot explain why I was glad to see her again, giving a party like that. It told me that she was still herself, after all the years that had passed, and that she still wants fresh flowers and the pink tables. Not many women I have known have been driven back upon themselves as she had. It is a long and hard journey none of us need envy. She is a survivor, someone who has shown that the world couldn't finish her off.
>
> —G<small>LORIA</small> E<small>MERSON</small>, <small>FRIEND AND WRITER</small>

In three months time, however, Jackie's serene life was suddenly broken with another tragedy. On January 22, 1973, at his father's urging, Alexander Onassis was training the personal aviator of Ari in his hydroplane when it crashed. She flew to Alexander's side in Athens, bringing with her a leading neurosurgeon, but Ari's son died shortly thereafter. The loss changed Onassis forever:

They had a falling out when Ari's personality changed. Greeks are very fate oriented, and he felt that it was a curse that Alexander had died and that he was responsible, making him go into the helicopter business when he didn't want to. So, he felt responsible, and he had suffered—a lot of people say—a minor nervous breakdown. He unfairly blamed her, and maybe wasn't conscious of that. So, it became inevitable for that marriage not to work.

—Letitia Baldrige

I saw the biggest fights between them you could ever imagine. He would blow up all the time—tantrums about everything. Yelling and screaming at her.

—Peter Beard

Jackie told me over the phone that everything went wrong right after the son's death. Mr. Onassis really lost his mind when his son died in that airplane crash. It wasn't anything to do with her, it was that tragedy. Jackie said there had been an argument and he just went out in his airplane recklessly. Onassis was no longer interested in life. He became a perfect horror to live with.

—Edie Beale

Just months after the death, Ari rapidly declined with myasthenia gravis, a muscular disintegration. Intending to keep him engaged in activity, Jackie tried to save him from his despair by arranging getaways through 1973 and 1974 to Egypt, Mexico, Spain, and the Caribbean.

I got a call from her saying, "I really need your help. Ari's son just got killed. And we're going to go on a Caribbean cruise and he's in such a bad mood. And I need someone like you to get him back in a decent mood, to talk to him."

—Pierre Salinger

She asked me to have dinner with them and said, "Bring along one of your pretty girlfriends for him." So I did, but I did it for Jackie because she was desperately trying to keep him going. I didn't always hear good things about him from Jackie at the end.

—Yusha Auchincloss

I was with her and Ari down at Loel and Gloria Guinness's in Acapulco the winter after Alexander Onassis was killed in the air crash. When it was midnight and the fireworks began, Ari started to sob. Jackie put her arms around him, just like the *Pietà*, and held him. She let him cling to her for what seemed like ten minutes. It was so touching because he was not kind to her. But she stuck by him in this awful time when he was mourning so terribly.

—ELEANOR LAMBERT

It was during a trip with Ari to Iran that Jackie gave what was perhaps the most public statement she ever made about herself, in an interview with Maryam Kharazmi of the English-language newspaper *Kayhan International*. While she did sheepishly admit, "I do love to live in style"—her spending having become a matter of public discussion and bone of contention with Ari—she also addressed what she believed were more misconceptions about her:

I get afraid of reporters when they come to me in a crowd. I don't like crowds because I don't like impersonal masses. They remind me of swarms of locusts.

The truth of the matter is that I am a very shy person. People take my diffidence for arrogance and my withdrawal from publicity as a sign, supposedly, that I am looking down on the rest of mankind. I am today what I was yesterday, and with luck, what I will be tomorrow.

Why do people always try to see me through the different names I have had at different times? People often forget that I was Jacqueline Bouvier before being Mrs. Kennedy or Mrs. Onassis. Throughout my life I have always tried to remain true to myself. This I will continue to do as long as I live. I am a woman above everything else. I love children and I think seeing one's children grow up is the most delightful thing any women can think about.

I have been through a lot and I have suffered a great deal, as you know. But I have had lots of happy moments as well. I have come to the conclusion that we must not expect too much from life. We must give to life at least as much as we receive from it. Every moment one lives is different from the other, the good, the bad, the hardship, the joy, the tragedy, love and happiness are all interwoven into one single indescribable whole that is called life.

One must not dwell on only the tragedies that life holds for us all, just as a person must not just think of only the happiness and greatness that they've experienced in life. If you separate the happiness and the sadness from each other, then neither is an accurate account of what life is truly like. Life is made up of both the good and the bad—and they cannot be separated from each other. It is a mistake to try to do that.

"BEING PRESENT"

She stacked the library of the *Christina* with the works of new authors—poetry, nonfiction, art books, everything. Often she would disappear for two hours and read. But she wanted to do more. Once she said to me at the opening of an exhibit of my work, "I wish I could do what you're doing—but I can't."

—PETER BEARD

Jackie had become restless with her own isolation even before Onassis become ill. In later suggesting that columnist Aileen Mehle write a book, Jackie reflected on the world of New York society women. "Write about them, their lives, their ambitions, their lies. Write how nothing really is the way it seems. How these women who seem to have it all, are really desperate and trapped." For herself, Jackie had been quietly exploring creative venues:

In the spring and early summer of 1971, she worked as a volunteer teacher's aide at a shelter for ghetto children on East 112th Street in Spanish Harlem, run by New York Catholic Charities, which cares for the children of drug addicts.

—GLORIA EMERSON, FRIEND AND WRITER

She also conceived of an enterprise for the Bedford-Stuyvesant Project, a self-help effort for the underprivileged of that Brooklyn neighborhood.

She believed that out of the African culture a designer could find inspiration . . . that could be utilized onto fabric. There was a designer who did work with traditional African symbols and patterns. Jackie liked them and engaged a friend of hers in manufacturing into helping this entrepreneur develop a business of hand-printed, hand-blocked African designs on cloth. What resulted was very good, in bright colors. She then organized a Metropolitan Museum of Art exhibit preview and provided the best publicity by using the cloth as curtains, tablecloths, and napkins in her own apartment, and having it all photographed there for magazines and newspapers. The material sold very well.

She was the spark plug that connected the two—the African-American design-er and the manufacturer.

—JOHN DOAR, FIRST DIRECTOR OF THE
BEDFORD-STUYVESANT PROJECT

Archaeological dig work remained a leading fascination for her. When she explored a Brooklyn Museum exhibit on Egyptian antiquities with Andy Warhol, for example, he was amazed at her detailed knowledge of the artifacts in the vitrines. Archaeology led her to Karl Katz, the Met's chairman for exhibi-tions, loans, and special projects. Katz hoped to do an exhibition on the excava-tion of Thera, on the island of Santorini, a site where she had worked. Jackie tried to facilitate the loan from Greece, but the frescoes were too fragile to move. For the Met, she later did help arrange one of the first loans of Greek material to the United States.

In 1973, Jackie was asked by a friend, producer Karen Lerner, to work on an NBC documentary on Angkor Wat and Venice. Earlier, when asked to narrate a piece on the Sistine Chapel, Jackie cringed. "The only time I ever appeared on television was when I took the camera around the White House after the renova-tions. I was so awful I decided never to do it again." This time, she was eager to try again, but Onassis protested—"Greek wives don't work."

I remember Ari saying to me, "Grace Kelly was a working girl when she mar-ried a prince and became a princess. You want to take my wife, whom I con-sider a princess, who was the wife of a head of state, and turn her into a working girl?" Ari had a marvelous ability with words that influenced her. She was totally devoted to him.

—LUCY JARVIS, FRIEND AND TELEVISION PRODUCER

Although Jackie conceded to him on the documentary after some heated discussion, Ari supported her writing the afterword to Peter Beard's book *Longing for Darkness: Kamante's Tales from Out of Africa*, about the friendship between Nairobian Kamante Gatura and Isak Dinesen. In part, it read:

Peter Beard recalls the immediacy [Dinesen's] philosophy can have for the young people of today—who are so persistently idealistic, so ready to be martyrs. This book can help them; show them that they had allies in an ear-lier time, who knew that courage was endurance as well as abandon. Today, everything is about to happen. But "about" can mean a generation, not the next six months. That is where the courage of endurance comes in. Black people, here as well as in Africa, know what endurance means. Isak and Thomas Dinesen knew too.

How contemporary Isak Dinesen is; her prescience of how man would destroy his environment, her belief that his only hope was to get in tune with it again. It seems to me that so many of the movements of today, ecology, anti-materialism, communal living—they were all in *Out of Africa*. She was one of the first white people to feel that "black is beautiful." She was the first to see how all the dark forces of time, evolution, nature were being disrupted in Africa. . . . This book is a work of love—of a love that a young man, young enough to be her grandson, was struck with when he first read *Out of Africa*. That book changed his life. He went in search of that Africa she knew. He saved its memories, her memories for us.

Before it is too late?

At the end of 1974, as the new International Center of Photography was being organized with the help of Karl Katz, he encouraged Jackie to visit its executive director, photographer Cornell Capa. What resulted was a lengthy January 13, 1975, *New Yorker* article titled "Being Present." It was Jackie's first reporting piece since 1953:

"The Center will be concentrating on photography as a means of communication rather than as art," Mr. Katz told us. . . . We walked into a circular, marble-floored entrance hall. A young girl with long hair and glasses sat at a table, talking into a telephone cradled on one shoulder, and filling envelopes with both hands. As she talked, a second phone kept ringing. She greeted Mr. Katz with a smile, and we headed up a broad marble stairway. On the second floor, we emerged into a long high-ceilinged, wood-panelled room with a fireplace at one end and a handsome parquet floor. . . . There we found a young man holding a metal rod . . . Bhupendra Karia, an Indian photographer, who had been working with Cornell Capa for two years and is now the Center's associate director. As we stood talking, Mr. Capa walked in—a sturdy man of fifty-six, with bushy gray hair, bushy eyebrows, and a smiling face. "There you are," he said. "The baby is about to be born. We will make it for the opening. Come. . . ." Capa . . . led us upstairs. . . . We both sat down in director's chairs of red canvas, drawn up to a Formica-topped table. . . . Mr. Capa explained [that] [s]ome of the leading photographers would come here once a week and conduct seminars. . . . "I became concerned. . . . All their negatives, all their life's work—I could save them. But what happens with the other photographers? The family puts their photographs in the attic, and one day they get thrown out. All the history of the twentieth century will be in photographs—more than in words.". . . Downstairs, in the entrance hall, the long-haired young girl was still simultaneously talking on the telephone and filling envelopes. A bearded young man was squatting on the floor beside her with another telephone and an open telephone book. He was introduced to us as David Kutz. He said, "Today a telephone operator, tomorrow an electrician, next day a carpenter, maybe one day a photographer.". . . The [Henri] Cartier-Bresson exhibition was being hung. On a wall between two windows was a 1954 photograph of young Russians dancing in a club under giant posters of Lenin and Stalin. . . . Cartier-Bresson had recently given an interview to *Le Monde* in which he stated that painting, not photography, had always been his obsession. . . . [Capa] smiled, "The whole thing is so French: love, hate, respect, misrespect, answers, re-answers. So now we have these vibrations crossing the ocean. . . ." We went into the library and sat down on a folding chair. The room was dark and empty. Cartier-Bresson slides flicked on and off a screen, and Cartier-Bresson spoke, in almost unaccented English: "Sometimes, like in this picture in Greece, well, I saw the frame of the whole thing and I waited for somebody to pass. . . . That is why it develops a great anxiety in this profession . . . always waiting. What is going to happen?. . . You have to be yourself and you have to forget yourself. . . . And poetry is the essence of everything. . . . The world is being created every minute and the world is falling to pieces every minute. . . . It is these tensions I am always moved by. . . . I love life. I love human beings. I hate people also. . . . It's a way of saying, 'Yes! Yes! Yes!'"

That same month Jackie actively pursued another passion for the first time in almost as many years as her reporting.

The phone rang in my office. The chairman of the Preservation Committee answered it and said, "There's some woman on the line who wants to volunteer and she says she's Jackie Onassis. Do you want to take the call?" And I said, yes. And it really was Jackie! She asked what was happening with the fight to save Grand Central Station against the threat of its owner, Penn Central Railroad, to destroy it and sell the valuable property for an office tower. She'd heard all about it, and wanted to be helpful. She said she wasn't working. I tried to ask for something modest, and told her we were having a press conference, and perhaps she could just appear—but I realized she was a very busy woman, and we'd give her notice ahead of time, and some dates to choose from. And she said, simply, no problem, she was going to be in town for a couple of weeks. I said, "That's great. I'm sure you would like to see our statement, and someone on your staff can review it." And she said, no, she'd read it and that she didn't have a staff. She established right there in the initial conversation how her relationship would always be—direct, active, and available. At the press conference, we set up a table and Congressman Ed Koch took my chair in order to be photographed beside her. Luckily I didn't break them up. He became mayor.

—KENT BARWICK, FRIEND,
PRESIDENT MUNICIPAL ARTS SOCIETY

As 1975 began, it was obvious that Jackie's life had grown apart from Onassis. A week after her Grand Central press conference, a call to 1040 came from Athens. Ari had collapsed.

A SECOND WIDOWHOOD

FOR FIVE WEEKS, JACQUELINE ONASSIS LITERALLY COMMUTED BETWEEN HER children and her husband, from New York to Paris, where Ari was hospitalized and underwent gallbladder surgery on February 16. Despite his apparent recuperation, he had lost the will to live, even letting his business slump throughout 1974, a result of not only market spirals but also his lack of interest.

He lost his zest for living and for fights. And with that, life became not worth living. He just gave up in the end.

—COSTA GRATSOS, ONASSIS CONFIDANT

On March 13, just as Jackie arrived back home, she called her sister-in-law Artemis, and was assured that he was doing as well as could be expected. Four days later she again was assured that he was fine. Late that same evening, however, he suddenly declined. Jackie was called. She was packing to return immediately to Paris when she was called again and told that Ari had died.

Jackie Kennedy Onassis with sisters-in-law Artemis and Metrope leaving American Hospital chapel following the death of Aristotle Onassis, Paris, 1975.

Jackie asked Valentino to create a black dress for her, having worn a white one designed by him for her wedding to Ari, and with her mother, children, and Ted Kennedy, attended the Skorpios funeral and burial in the chapel where she had married. When the press began speculating on inheritance disputes and whether Ari had intended to divorce her, she retorted, "I'll answer with something my husband often told me. Throughout the world people love fairy-tales and especially those related to the rich. You must learn to understand and accept this."

Christina, who was "distressed at the distorted stories," also said "rumors of intended divorce are untrue," and that "based on mutual friendship and respect there are no financial or other disputes."

Once I was visiting Jackie in her New York apartment, after Ari Onassis died, when all the papers were full of stories about a fight between Jackie and Christina Onassis. Christina unexpectedly dropped in, and I tried to excuse myself. But Jackie said, "Oh, no, stay and we'll all have a good time." She and

Christina sat there, telling stories about Ari and laughing together. They certainly were not fighting.

—MARC RIBOUD, FRIEND AND PHOTOGRAPHER

On April 24, Jackie went with Christina to a Skorpios memorial service, and three months later joined Artemis in dedicating a new wing at a summer camp to Ari's memory. She influenced Ari in his bequest of a full half of his estate to the Alexander Onassis Foundation, by having it help finance artists. On the first anniversary of his death, she took part in a Skorpios memorial service, her last visit there. She attended Christina's first wedding, and after her stepdaughter's attempted suicide, Jackie discreetly asked her own doctor to see if he could assist the young woman. Jackie insisted on fondly remembering her life with Onassis. When she once heard friends talking about him, she joined in:

Do you remember how he used to love to roam around the city at all hours of the night because of his insomnia? Remember that night he ran into you on Park Avenue at 2 A.M. and brought you home for a drink and came into my bedroom, so happy that he had found someone he knew I liked?

In Greece, others likewise recalled Jackie:

Jackie helped make Skorpios, which was rather neglected until her arrival, an Eden. Ari, strangely, resented her for it. . . . Nothing she could do was right, but his staff thought she was heaven-sent. After Ari died, I visited the island, and the maid who looked after me asked, "Do you know Mrs. Onassis?" I said that I did. She said, "Will you please tell her that all of us here on Skorpios love her very much and miss her. We wished she could be here forever."

—AILEEN MEHLE, COLUMNIST AND FRIEND

EIGHT

The Editor

1975–1984

Like everybody else, I have to work my way up to an office with a window.

—Jacqueline Bouvier Onassis

New York newspaper cartoon of Jackie Kennedy Onassis as editor, 1975.

BACK TO WORK

SPENDING PART OF THE SUMMER IN HYANNIS AFTER SHE HAD LOST JACK Kennedy had helped Jackie to redirect her life. In 1975, after Ari's death, she returned there, visiting Rose Kennedy, with whom she swam daily. She reflected:

> Sometimes I think that time heals things and you forget certain things. I mean, I can't remember Jack's voice exactly anymore but I still can't stand to look at pictures of him. . . . When I came back everything just hit me, because this was the only house where we really lived, where we had our children, where every little pickle jar I had found in some little country lane on the Cape was placed, and nothing's changed since we were in it and all of the memories came before my eyes. After I had looked around and unpacked . . . the first thing I did was walk over to see [Rose]. And we were sitting and talking about a lot of things, and I said, "It really hits, doesn't it?" That evening she called me and said, would I like to take a little walk

around nine-thirty because she didn't want me to be here and alone and be sad. And I found myself becoming so happy here.

That summer, Jackie was reflecting on her life in Greece, deep into her reading of the Greek poets Seferis and Cafavy. That autumn, however, it was also literature that spurred her, upon her return to New York in September, to enter the workforce. In 1950, through George Plimpton, she had met another writer of the fledgling *Paris Review*, Tom Guinzberg, now the president of Viking Press publishing house. He offered her a job as an editor, not just for her love of literature but also because of her "range of contacts." In the second week of September, for the first time in twenty-two years, Jackie showed up for work. With her multimillion-dollar inheritance from Onassis, it was obvious that she didn't become "consulting editor" and go to the office four days a week because she needed the $10,000 salary. It was rather to utilize her skills and knowledge. Ultimately, it would provide her with a stronger sense of self than she had ever had.

As far as her entering a profession at the age of forty-six without previous publishing experience was concerned, she told reporters:

> I expect to be learning the ropes at first. You sit in at editorial conferences, you discuss general things, maybe you're assigned to a special project of your own. Really, I expect to be doing what my employer tells me to do. Part of an editor's job [is that] you keep asking everyone—friends, authors, agents, experts; anyone with access to a particular world—if they know of a person who should be published or a subject that should be treated.

Jackie worked on books of personal interest—one on Lincoln daguerreotypes, a novel about Sally Hemings, Jefferson's mistress—and collegial efforts, establishing a rapport with co-workers, one of whom recalled her on the kitchen floor opening a huge bag of coffee and making pots for the staff. Beyond comradery, however, editing provided immediate creative satisfaction.

> I think she got enormous intellectual stimulation from it. Part of the joy of publishing is that every book brings to it a different sensibility. She had intellectual curiosity in that she had a great interest in things classical but also everything contemporary. She loved gossip—fascinated by people's living arrangements. Even books that weren't bought led her down new paths. After breakfast we once went to see a Met exhibit to turn it into a possible book pro-

ject and another time to the New York Public Library's rare books room, looking at a handwritten medieval manuscript. It helped to quench her unrelenting desire to observe new things.

—LISA DREW, FRIEND AND PUBLISHING EDITOR

She came into her own. When she was with Ari, she put aside parts of herself to pursue his interests. I sensed a change in her . . . very much more like the girl I first knew, who had a great sense of fun and enthusiasm. It must [have been] an electrifying, extraordinary thing for her to be on her own—she was always somewhat diminished by the men around her. Not that she was any less, but, for God's sake, one husband was the president of the United States, and the other was an enormously wealthy, powerful man.

—GEORGE PLIMPTON

Jackie herself later explained what working did for her, and her public comfort in the role:

What I like about being an editor is that it expands your knowledge and heightens your discrimination. Each book takes you down another path. Hopefully, some of them move people and some of them do some good. . . . I don't get questioned about my salary or why I work. I've never felt that kind of resentment. Perhaps the people who resent my working say it to everyone else—but not to me. I think that people who work themselves have respect for the work of others.

Call the Darkness Light, a novel by Nancy Zaroulis, was a project to which Jackie was particularly devoted. In discussing it, she revealed her new awareness of the women's market:

It's the story of a girl working in the mills of Lowell, Massachusetts, in the nineteenth century. The manuscript seemed to weigh about twenty pounds, and I thought: My God, it will just depress everyone. But once I started to read it, I couldn't put it down. I realized that the story would illuminate a period of American history and the lives of a whole group of women.

During a 1965 dinner, when a male admirer of JFK went on some about the late president's virtues, with Jackie referred to only as his appendage, she afterward told a friend, "For God's sake, the way the man talked you'd think I never even existed. Maybe we should import the Indian custom of women throwing themselves on their husband's funeral pyres!" At the time, it was a rare admission for a woman who spent the first half of her adult life depending on men and largely removed from the problems that many working women faced. In fact, in 1969, when a *Newsweek* editor mentioned how women reporters there were fighting for equal pay for equal work, Jackie had responded, "I don't go for all that. I had no trouble finding a position in journalism as a photographer." Her perspective changed once she went to work. As she recalled in 1979:

> What has been sad for many women of my generation is that they weren't supposed to work if they had families. There they were, with the highest education, and what were they to do when the children were grown—watch the raindrops coming down the windowpane? Leave their fine minds unexercised? Of course women should work if they want to. You have to do something you enjoy. That is the definition of happiness: "complete use of one's faculties along the lines leading to excellence in a life affording them scope." It applies to women as well as to men. We can't all reach it, but we can try to reach it to some degree.

At a fund-raiser for Radcliffe College's Schlesinger Library on the History of Women, Jackie quipped, "We'll know we have arrived when Harvard men start saying that they graduated from Radcliffe!" She even granted an interview to *Ms.* magazine.

> The change in consciousness about women affected her as it did everybody. She did the *Ms.* interview and agreed to be on the cover because it treated her as a person, instead of talking about her husbands. She asked me to remove references to them from the interview. She said, "It has helped me to be taken seriously as an editor, for my own abilities." She read and like *Ms.* magazine, made regular contributions of $1,000 to the Ms. Foundation, supported the Equal Rights Amendment, and was pro-choice but did so privately, not wanting to be dragged into the political arena. She never mentioned reading *The Feminine Mystique*, but it was more her style to read Kate Millett. She never mentioned the Miss America Pageant, but I think she disapproved of beauty contests on aesthetic grounds if nothing else.
>
> She supported the women around her. She once told me a story about a rel-

ative who was too young but getting married to a much older man. Jackie took it upon herself to educate her about many things having to do with sex and all kinds of things, because this woman was very sheltered. Jackie practiced feminism by being herself and helping other women be themselves. She became secure enough to do so. To like other women you have to first like yourself, and not feel competitive. She continued to mean something to women in general because she didn't continue to play the role of widow, politically or socially. When she went to work, she essentially did what she would have done if she had never been married and was on her own.

—GLORIA STEINEM

Jackie's closest friends felt that after she went to work, she began to outgrow some of her deep insecurities. This maturity became apparent even to colleagues outside of publishing.

It always struck me how at home Jackie was with outrageous conversations and how much of a New York sensibility she had. By the time I began working with her in 1975 she never tried to act out some part. She came to meetings relaxed, wearing slacks and sunglasses. People didn't expect to recognize "Jackie Kennedy" that way. She was out all over the city, exploring.

—KENT BARWICK

THE MUNICIPAL ARTS SOCIETY

We planned a lighting ceremony of Grand Central Station to bring more attention to it when we realized that the ceremony was scheduled for the first night of the Democratic Convention, which was being held in New York. Nobody would cover it, all the reporters being at the convention. I called around and was asked, "Who is going to pull this switch?" I said—Jackie! Here it is, opening convention night, and there was a huge crowd of reporters covering Jackie as she pulled the switch and the lights went on. She made the cover of the *New York Times* and every other paper the next morning.

—FRED PAPERT, FRIEND, FIRST PRESIDENT OF M.A.S.

Jackie's initial 1975 effort for Grand Central developed into a full commitment to the Municipal Arts Society. She became a board trustee and even signed the lease for their headquarters in the restored Villard Houses, in a public ceremony. The fight to stop Penn Central from tearing down Grand Central Station persisted: the New York supreme court said the station's landmark designation prevented Penn Central from selling the land and paying its debts, but the appellate division overturned the decision. It came down to a public relations battle. Jackie lent herself to everything from rallies to concerts, but her headlining a delegation on an April 1978 "Landmark Express" train to Washington, D.C., where the Municipal Arts Society was appealing its case before the Supreme Court, thrust her into world headlines. At each train stop along the way, the mayors of the cities, the media, and citizens crowded the stations to hear Jackie. Kent Barwick recalled that when a public relations aide tried to protect her from a horde of photographers, she balked: Jackie knew that the success of the effort depended on publicity about her.

When we got to Washington's Union Station, two terrific people, Joan Mondale and Pat Moynihan, came to greet the train. The station was mobbed with reporters. Mondale could have been a Girl Scout and Moynihan a porter. Everybody went right to Jackie.

—FRED PAPERT

After that trip to Washington, the reaction to Jackie and Grand Central took on mammoth proportions. The public relations people built on this with her, and she agreed to do a press conference in our conference room. On all the walls were these huge photographs of Grand Central Station. Dozens of journalists from the Midwest and all over the country attended, to talk to her. The fight for Grand Central had become a national issue. People would send us money and letters of support from all over—because of Jackie. Here was the Municipal Arts Society, eighty-three years old with members that tended to be society types. It hadn't been a populist organization. Jackie changed all that. It was the right time. People were touched by the idea of saving this building. Jackie gave it legitimacy. What she did was somehow tap people's feelings about what was happening to the country's historic buildings.

I was in a small upstate New York town and met this schoolteacher. I only told her I was from New York and she said, "What about Mrs. O-nay-ziz? Is she going to save Grand Central Station?" In this forgotten village, in the corner coffee shop, someone had picked up on Jackie and Grand Central. It was a change in the direction of the country.

—KENT BARWICK

When the decision came down upholding the landmark status, it set a national precedent. One of the councils asked Justice Powell about it. He said, "The justices were very impressed with the public interest in this issue." That public interest had been generated by Jackie.

—FRED PAPERT

While attending an M.A.S. event at the Isamu Noguchi Garden Museum in Astoria, New York, Jackie mused, "I'd have liked to study architecture. Not to be an architect but to know how to build a building." Indeed, her interest in architecture was no passing fancy. Kent Barwick noted that she considered "air and light" to be elements that made buildings "works of art," and that age alone wasn't a reason to preserve a structure. When the 1952 blue glass Lever House was threatened, her appreciation of modern architecture prompted Jackie to lobby City Comptroller Harrison Goldin, who was on the Board of Estimates, which was predicted to vote against saving it.

Goldin wanted his picture with her. They stepped outside, and the City Hall paparazzi took a picture when Jackie suddenly decided to kiss Goldin. And he voted to save Lever House.

—KENT BARWICK

Jackie also joined the board of the Forty-second Street Development Corporation, to revitalize the corridor running through Times Square and the once glorious theater district.

Forty-second Street had been the city's brightest memory—and had generated jobs and taxes. Much of what success we did have in renewing it was attributable to Jackie's planning instincts and political reflexes. We had a largely inaccessible mayor's office. She called, and we got a meeting with anyone we wanted—and at the meetings these guys would alert the press. It was never a surprise to her that she had this power. She carefully chose the causes she would use it for, and the right moment to apply it, permitting her to sustain that power in New York City.

It's reasonable to assume that any public-spirited person would have an interest in their environment, and this city was Jackie's environment. She never used that fancy word *urban planning*. She felt that a private interest in reasonable projects was more effective than trying to be a global force, that the

Jackie Kennedy Onassis with Fred Papert(to her left), Kent Barwick, and Harry Helmsley, at lease signing for Municipal Arts Society, 1977, woman unidentified.

bigger the goal the smaller the chance of pulling it off. To be a thinker, a master planner and speaker—with a gentle voice and tough, pragmatic heart—you didn't want to stand between Jackie and whatever her goal was.

She liked the idea of a trolley running between the east and west ends of Forty-second Street, with one end being a grand river boulevard, stringing together all these urban wonders to become a destination within itself. Others pushed for something grander, and it became a transit study, and a computer model showed it at $400 million. She knew nobody would be interested in that. She was one who felt we needed to focus on the small project that could be done immediately, and if it were successful, we could start extending. She also helped to edit the corporation's pamphlets, financial guidelines, and general information for the public. She always came to our ceremonies. At one where we began to crack the sidewalk for some construction, Jackie suddenly put on this hard hat and the cameras went off. Despite the area being run-down, she always came to meetings on Forty-second Street, and felt hopeful with the development on Theater Row. She came to the theater and a restaurant down here. The maître d' had a Maurice Chevalier accent and made her laugh. And, of course, they could speak French.

—Fred Papert, chair of Forty-second Street
Development Corporation

EXPLORING NEW WORLDS

Despite her commitments in New York, Jackie remained an avid globetrotter. The cold war had long prevented her from going to the Soviet Union, but in 1977 an editorial project—and détente—got her there. Diana Vreeland was organizing one of her Costume Institute exhibits at the Met, "In the Russian Style," on the court dress of czarist Russia, and Jackie was planning an accompanying book. Her Soviet Union trip—on which she was accompanied by the Met's director, Thomas Hoving—was, she said "an example of publishing that literally took you into the world."

She was really intent on gathering everything for the exhibition and book. On the flight there, she talked about the items she wanted, asked what the museum staffs were like and whether they were Communist Party stooges.

When she got onto something, she was inexorable. She wanted the costumes of the late Czar Nicholas and Czarina Alexandra, and she just either absolutely hammered them or stepped back and then nudged. It was still a huge political issue, the czar's murder. She asked about the costume at the highest levels of the Ministry of Culture, and they gave us the old "we'll look into it." She did a marvelous book and the exhibit was sensational, but she felt another half million would have come if she could have obtained those costumes. They finally gave her a sleigh of Nicholas and Alexandra's, and led her to a large trunk with Alexandra's costumes. They didn't let her take it, but she did get to try on the czarina's white coat!

She particularly liked Russian art influenced by the French, and at the St. Petersburg Museum she loved what the Russians used to call "rich, peasants' art," these scenes of beautiful landscapes and people. In the Hermitage, she was quite taken with this huge gallery of beautiful portraits of a series of ministers nobody had ever heard of. She was also most fascinated with the way the Russians painted portraits on tapestries. She was interested in what she'd never seen.

Jackie Kennedy Onassis trying on the fur coat of Russian Czarina Alexandra in museum storage room, Moscow, Russia.

She adored Pavlovsk, one of the retreats that was restored after the Nazis burned it, right back to the hairbrushes at the right place on the tables. She gave star treatment to the people doing the work, impressed with their dedication and the excellent work. What really got to her was the fact that this czarist place was one of the first to be restored after the war. She talked of the continuity of people caring enough to restore what had been destroyed.

—TOM HOVING

At a press conference for "In the Russian Style," Jackie joked about the costumes, saying, "You love to see it, the way you love to see *Gone With the Wind*. But wouldn't you rather wear your blue jeans than wander around in a hoop skirt?" She also discussed another Russian project.

Editing *The Firebird and Other Russian Fairytales* for Viking meant working with a Russian translator and doing research in the New York Public Library's Slavonic room. I love doing illustrated books—a great art book can reveal a whole world to the reader. This was a rediscovery of the work of Boris Zvorykin, a member of Diaghilev's circle. He was a master of decorative art, yet virtually forgotten.

Some years later, editing also brought her back to India, and while there she facilitated loans of historic court costumes, art, and antiquities for the Met's India Festival exhibitions, and the collaborative publication of Naveen Patnaik's *A Second Paradise: Indian Courtly Life, 1590–1947*, which she edited. As she did whenever she traveled, Jackie conducted intricate research. Patnaik's sister, Gita Mehta, who would also have an editor in Jackie, observed:

> [She was] really an extraordinary, nineteenth-century type of editor. I watched her do *A Second Paradise*. . . . Jackie sent Naveen pages of research material annotated by herself. It was obscure research. I know as a writer that to have that kind of attention by a commissioning editor is quite rare.
>
> —GITA MEHTA, FRIEND AND AUTHOR

> She never pretended to be a great scholar, but on almost every topic of mutual interest that came up, she just happened to know the right thing to read. When my wife and I were leaving for India for the first time, she made no promises. But within a couple of hours a shopping bag was brought round to our door. In it were more than two hundred photocopied passages from rare nineteenth-century books on India, each marked in her own hand.
>
> —JOHN RUSSELL, FRIEND AND ART CRITIC

Jackie's work eventually brought her into the American Southwest, which she had avoided since the assassination. Working on a book with JFK's former interior secretary, Stewart Udall, in his native New Mexico, she reveled in the beauty there, inspecting mesas and Indian villages, and taking in the evening pastel skies. In the late 1970s, Jackie also made her first trip to Israel. Accompanied by President Ephraim Katzir and Nahum Goldman, who was former president of the World Jewish Congress, she attended the dedication of the museum of the Jewish Diaspora in Tel Aviv on May 15, 1978. It was Karl Katz who escorted her to the Mideast.

> I took her through the old city of Jerusalem and to archaeological sites that I had excavated like Gath and Caeserea. She really loved the Diaspora Museum,

which I conceptually designed, and we also went to the place I helped build, The Israel Museum, where she was very interested in the archaeology of the Bible. She visited an Israeli kibbutz and talked to the students in a class. It was a whirlwind week. She was always asking questions. You never ran out of questions with Jackie. She was very moved by the combination of the young-ness and the antiquity of Israel as a country. She certainly knew the Bible—both the Old and New Testaments—remarkably well. You didn't have to clue her in that this is where David hid from Saul, or where Joshua stopped the sun, or whatever happened. One of the most touching moments came when we visited the John F. Kennedy Memorial Forest, and she planted a tree there. Did it affect her? Well, she never did anything without a complete sense of fullness.

—KARL KATZ

A year later, in October 1979, Jackie went to China, joined there by Tom Hoving and his wife. Having taken a course in Chinese art, she also was consid-ering a book on the topic.

She was a little frightened of China. It was quite rugged. The Chinese offi-cials made it clear that she had to have their so-called luxury and insisted that she be in the limo, but it was old and in bad shape. The rest of us trav-eled in an air-conditioned bus, and she wanted to be back on the bus with the gang. They grabbed her to see "special things," like the Great Wall and the tombs, which we saw. When she got free, it was delightful. We went down the Li River and saw these dried ocean formations that had been painted realistically in the eighth century, but were like a surrealistic fantasy. We were pulled along in a barge by a diesel tug so we couldn't hear any engine sound—which made it all the more like A.D. 800. There were other tourists on the boat, and one woman would say to another, "That's Jackie!" Even in A.D. 800 China on the Li River, they knew Jackie! In Peking for the opening of the Fragrant Hill Hotel by I. M. Pei there was horrible sabotage going on by the hired work gangs. When Jackie asked what I thought, I said I was going to write that this hotel will never open. She got really mad at me. She said, "It just couldn't be true. It must just be a mistake." She never could understand that people could have that kind of dedicated, blind evil. She still had a sunny view of the world.

—TOM HOVING

PUBLIC DUTY

*T*HE MORE COMMITTED JACKIE BECAME TO HER OWN WORK AS AN EDITOR, THE less she obligated herself to public duty as a former first lady. She chose carefully which events to attend—an L.A. fund-raiser for a youth center in the Watts ghetto, a Bicentennial concert in Washington with Gerald and Betty Ford—and writing offers to accept—for the *Paris Review*'s anniversary issue she submitted her memories of the "slight expatriates all, determined that our lives would not be mundane." She refused political offers, however, including one to serve as New York cultural affairs commissioner.

> She avoided anything partisan because it would drag her into a gutter fight, which she knew could diminish her credibility and ultimately her ability to help in the projects she cared about. Jackie felt that the idea of celebrities telling us what to think was often misguided. She also knew that most public problems aren't solved with black-and-white solutions, but gray.
>
> —FRED PAPERT

The personalities of presidential candidates, however, always captured her fascination.

> In 1976, I was a delegate to the UN, and she said she believed strongly in the idea of the United Nations, and that the American delegation was in need of good representatives. She followed the 1976 presidential race closely, but not early on, and consequently she didn't know enough about Jimmy Carter to be enthusiastic about his candidacy. She was uncertain as to what she should do for him. She wanted to know about him, and asked me very detailed and rather intellectual questions on the issues and his stand, as well as on his record in Georgia as governor, and whether he was strong enough and good enough to be president.
>
> —GEORGE MCGOVERN

Jackie accepted an invitation to attend the Democratic National Convention in 1976—her first since 1956—in New York, and watched as Jimmy Carter was nominated and delivered his acceptance speech. Her presence at Madison Square Garden caused a surprise uproar.

> Democratic Party Chairman Bob Strauss dramatically pointed out Jacqueline Onassis in the VVIP boxes. There were cheers across Thirty-third Street in the

NBC control room. She spread awe in her path and chaos in her wake. Photographers charged the Missouri delegation like a strobe light brigade—they just happened to be seated directly in front of the VVIP section.

—RICHARD REEVES, AUTHOR OF CONVENTION

During the primaries, Jackie contributed $25,000 to her brother-in-law Sargent Shriver. Four years later, on November 7, she made what would be her last public appearance with eighty-nine-year-old Rose Kennedy in Boston's Faneuil Hall, as her brother-in-law Ted Kennedy announced his candidacy for president. In what would also be her last stint at campaigning, Jackie campaigned for Kennedy in 1980 on the campus of Boston's Regis College and at a St. Louis reception. She once again made speeches in Spanish, in Puerto Rico and New York's Spanish Harlem. To the familiar sounds of bouzouki music at a Greek-American fund-raiser, she quipped, "I'm homesick!" Worried about Ted's being unable to defeat the incumbent Carter for the nomination, Jackie asked former JFK advisers to gather at 1040 to discuss how he might best withdraw his bid. Still, it was Ted Kennedy's personal safety and health that most concerned her.

She was loyal and supportive, but also concerned for my welfare. . . . She told me to make time in the campaign for my family and to set aside time to get needed rest, and she was right.

—SENATOR EDWARD M. KENNEDY

The idea of Ted's becoming president two decades after his brother prompted speculation about a second Kennedy administration. When it became the premise of a questionable novel, however, Jackie was thrust yet again into the news. It began with a 1977 lunch with Nancy Tuckerman, who was now working at Doubleday publishing company, and another friend, editor Lisa Drew.

Several days before we met, I'd heard that in the middle of February, Viking had purchased a novel which I had turned down at Doubleday, by Jeffrey Archer, called *Shall We Tell the President*. The premise was an attempted assassination of Ted Kennedy. I was appalled and told the English agent it was totally tasteless, and I wouldn't have anything to do with it. With Jackie being at Viking, and their buying it—I was dumbfounded. At our lunch, I said to her offhandedly, "How about this Jeffrey Archer book that Viking bought?" And she said, "Who's Jeffrey Archer? I don't know anything about it. What's it about?" I said, "It's a political thriller, and Ted Kennedy's a character, and I thought they might have mentioned it to you." She said, "I don't know anything about it." And I thought—leave that alone. Six months later, Viking published *Shall We Tell the President.* Among other negative reviews was one by John Leonard in the *New York Times*, which said in the very last sentence, that "anyone associated with the publication of this book should be ashamed of herself."

All hell broke loose. Newspapers began calling Viking and asking "How could she have done this!" She wouldn't take the calls, but Tom Guinzburg said she was completely aware of the book from the beginning, and approved it, and that Viking wouldn't have bought it if she hadn't. And, the truth of the matter is, she first heard about it from me—after they'd bought it.

Jackie called me at home that night and said, "I don't know what to do, but I think I'm going to quit. Nancy said you were quite outraged," and I said, "Well, I'm quite outraged because frankly, a week or so after Viking bought the book, I mentioned this to you at lunch, and you'd never heard of it." And she said, "Oh, is that the book you mentioned?" I said, "Yes." And she responded, "I went to Tom Guinzburg after our lunch, and I said I just had lunch with Lisa Drew, and what is this book by some guy named Archer that's about Ted Kennedy. He said, 'Don't you worry about it. It's not anything that you're going to have anything to do with.' So, I thought, fine. I'd known Tom a long time, and I thought he was looking out for my interests with respect to this, so I paid no attention. Now, here he is on the front page of the *New York Times*

Jackie Kennedy Onassis campaigning in Spanish Harlem for New York presidential primary election for brother-in-law Ted Kennedy's presidential race, 1980.

saying that I knew all about exactly what happens in this book, and I didn't know about it at all! I didn't realize that was the book!" She felt awful. About two hours later, Nancy called and said, "She's resigning, and sending a hand-written letter to Tom Guinzburg by messenger tonight."

I wrote her a note saying that while the events of the last week had been distressing, I hope it didn't color her view of publishing as an industry. Many of her colleagues, in and out of Viking, already knew of the contributions she had made, and I hoped her absence from publishing would be temporary. Shortly thereafter, she invited me to her apartment for lunch. We talked about Doubleday. She gently raised the question about working there. I said it would be a safe haven. Nancy was there, and she had known John Sargeant, the CEO. She felt there were enough people there to protect her, that it was safe to risk exposure one more time. I asked her later why it took her a few months to decide. She said, "I just really wanted to be careful. I'd made some mistakes in my life by reacting too quickly, and I really wanted to be sure I was doing the right thing."

—LISA DREW

DOUBLEDAY

IN FEBRUARY 1978, JACKIE REPORTED TO DOUBLEDAY'S OFFICES THREE BLOCKS north of Grand Central Station. She was named associate editor in the large publishing house.

She was sometimes painfully shy with strangers, not given to small talk, and certainly aware of people's nervous excitement at meeting her. About two months after she came to Doubleday she said, "It's always interested me how you were so comfortable with me from the first time we met because most people aren't, and I'm very aware of trying to put them at their ease, but that's hard for me too." I said, "I feel quite schizophrenic about you because when I see television retrospectives I don't think of Mrs. John F. Kennedy as the person I know." Once people got over those first months of feeling awkward, she just fit in and everyone treated her as a colleague. It was the first time in her life that people just took her for who she was, which she loved. To those outside who might describe a project, I'd say, "That isn't for me, but why don't you send it to Jackie Onassis?" They raised their eyebrows, as if she were a dilettante dabbling in this field. But it didn't take long before they began to realize she was bright and serious, and got involved with her authors. Much was made in the press about the fact that she got her own coffee and did her own photocopying. It wasn't a big deal within the company, but it was written about as if a miracle had occurred. It amused everybody there how people outside were so dazzled by this celebrity. Brighter, funnier, nicer than many, yes, but she was just another person.

—LISA DREW

Jackie kept her office spare, brown-bagged her lunch, joined in company picnics in Central Park and holiday parties, and sat on the concrete stairwell during fire drills. Life there was routine.

She didn't have a computer in her office. It was never beneath Jacqueline Onassis to always make her own phone calls. She always greeted her own guests. If you typed a note for her to sign, she wanted the salutation and closing left blank so she could personalize it. As often as not, she wrote her letters by hand. She understood the importance of personal written communication. She avoided putting distance between herself and those she had business with.

—BRUCE TRACY, EDITORIAL ASSISTANT, FRIEND

Few outsiders realized that Jackie was a real professional who cared about the book for itself, who did arduous line edits on all of her books, knowing she didn't have to, that copy editors and proofreaders would pick it up. She had a good ear for a well-wrought sentence. With that exquisitely refined aesthetic sense, she wanted everything done right. The art director, Peter Kruzan, did a lot of her books, and she would tell him, "This is what I want. Back to the drawing board until it was right." In choosing photographs, she would get down on the floor, squat Indian style, spread the pictures around her, and laboriously agonize over the final illustrations. She loved the pursuit of the project. She loved when she knew she was closing in on it. She would rub her hands together and say, "Hot spit," which is one of my fond memories of her.

—SCOTT MOYERS, EDITORIAL ASSISTANT, FRIEND

Jackie's list of titles varied wildly: photography books, biographies that ranged from Czar Nicholas II to Jean Harlow; memoirs of World War II Poland and of postwar Paris; children's books by Carly Simon; collections of Civil War courting letters and of *Rolling Stone* articles; a series of Olivier Bernier books on Louis XIV, Marie Antoinette, and Napoleon. One book, *Men and History*, by Don Cook, focused on ten historic leaders, two of whom she had known—de Gaulle and Adenauer.

> This is classic Jackie. Naguib Mahfouz had been published in the United States in a very small way for the American University in Cairo Press, and his work was virtually unavailable. She was reading Mahfouz in French. She loved it so much that she successfully lobbied for Doubleday to do *The Cairo Trilogy—Palace Walk*, *Palace of Desire*, and *Sugar Street*—for which he's probably best known. His novels have a nineteenth-century feel, a huge cast of characters, about class strife, politics, East meeting West, on a grand canvas. It had a lasting effect—Mahfouz recently did his twentieth book for Doubleday, and represents a huge chunk of its backlist. Jackie made it a whole cottage industry, from her vision. This played itself out in a very permanent way, like the Bill Moyers series on healing. She did many wonderful books that made a splash, and delighted people, and books that did well for Doubleday. She also did a high percentage of books that will be around forever.
>
> —SCOTT MOYERS

Jackie even searched for potential authors in newspapers and on television. After seeing actor George Hamilton on the *Merv Griffin Show*, Jackie asked Lisa Drew to send him a note about an autobiography he mentioned that he was thinking of writing and express her own interest in acquiring it. Hamilton then told a gossip columnist about it, saying it "made my week."

> She got the proposal in, and in her report noted that the ghostwriter present-ed George Hamilton as an historically important figure whose saga crossed the seven seas, spanning cultures and continents. Jackie said, "Hhm. He's George Hamilton—not quite Alexander the Great." She once tore a story out of a gossip column that read: "Dolly Parton has been bitten by the writing bug, and her first tome is tentatively titled *Wildflowers*. Says Big D, 'It's sort of exaggerated with a little bit of truth, a little bit of humor, and a little bit of dirty stuff, to make it sell.'" Jackie laughed at that. "Well," she said, "it sounds like another cultural watershed."
>
> —LISA DREW

Dealing with celebrity authors wasn't always easy for Jackie, and she once joked about the ulcer one such author would give her. After completing the complicated negotiations on Michael Jackson's book, she joked to Lisa Drew, "Is there anybody else that you'd like me to try and get? Because people do sometimes take my phone calls." Drew said Barbra Streisand. Not particularly a fan, Jackie still arranged a meeting with her in Los Angeles. Then she heard nothing from the star.

> About a year later, after I had left Doubleday for another job, Jackie called to say, "I got a message that Barbra Streisand called, but I wasn't here." An hour later she called me up laughing, and said, "Well, I've talked to Barbra." And I said, "Well, what? What?" And she said, "She isn't interested in doing a book at all. She wanted the name of a good libel lawyer. I told her I didn't have one because I don't sue for libel."
>
> —LISA DREW

THE LIBRARY

FOR DOUBLEDAY, JACKIE WILLINGLY APPEARED AT BOOK PARTIES, KNOWING HER marquee value to getting a book off the ground. The only other institution for which she gave such carte blanche remained the Kennedy Library and Museum. As late as 1975, it was still in the planning stage

But at a meeting that year, Jackie voted to settle on a site at Dorchester's Columbia Point. "I'm so glad. It has gone on long enough. The death agony can't last forever," she remarked. "You do the best you can, and then the hell with it." Jackie oversaw the landscaping, including dune grass because, as she said, "I think the president was a wind man." She considered ornamental rocks, but noted that high tide made them look "like little hippopotamus ears." Jackie knew where everything belonged—and noticed when asphalt was being placed where she wanted trees.

> She was not at all above giving very direct criticism when warranted. She called one of I. M. Pei's guys out and pointed to the asphalt. She nearly ate the guy for lunch.
>
> —CHARLES DALY, DIRECTOR OF THE JFKL FOUNDATION

The library was dedicated and opened in 1979, but the big news came when Jimmy Carter kissed her.

> She said to me later with a wry smile. "Isn't that strange the way we hardly know each other, and the president kissed me? I suppose he thought it was

droit du seigneur." That was an old feudal right of the lord of the manor to have his way with the serfs' wives!

—ARTHUR SCHLESINGER

Jackie's earlier successful efforts to have Ernest Hemingway's papers donated to the library was complemented with the creation of a research room, and at its dedication she granted a rare interview. She attended a five-day Hemingway conference there and recommended an annual one.

After the museum was refurbished in 1993, she called to ask if we could walk through it together. "You've got it just right," she said. She knew I cared deeply about the president's legacy, and when I went to the library foundation, she gave me a signed copy of her painting of the nineteenth-century White House. She was a perfect combination of being kind and tough.

—CHARLES DALY

Annually, Jackie attended the library's foundation dinner, and she returned to Washington for a special library fund-raiser at Ted Kennedy's home, where she met President and Mrs. Reagan. Jackie made herself available to Nancy Reagan for advice and support—especially during one crisis:

She was very kind to me when my husband was shot, and we didn't know whether he was going to live. . . . She wrote a very sweet, sensitive note and called me. She couldn't have been nicer at a time when I really needed it.

—NANCY REAGAN

PICTURES

CENTRAL TO THE KENNEDY LIBRARY'S EXHIBITS WERE ITS PHOTO DISPLAYS. Jackie was familiar with the collection, and adamantly barred from release images that she felt were unflattering. She had long cultivated her eye for the well-composed picture:

An accomplished photographer, she owned a simple camera and a little tripod, no gadgets. Confused by techniques, she often asked me, "Should I use Tri-x for this job?" Or "What kind of lighting should be used?" She appreciated photography as a creative medium.

—JACQUES LOWE

Jackie still maintained volumes of scrapbooks, jammed with personal photos of family and friends from throughout her life, including her latest horse, Frank:

> It's not true that she hated being photographed. She loved being photographed on Frank or with our team, or in front of her house. She had her own camera and she was always getting Jimmy Mason, who was in charge of her horses, to take pictures.
>
> —CHARLES WHITEHOUSE, FRIEND

Many of Jackie's signature works as an editor were photography books. One photographer whose work she reintroduced was Eugene Atget. When the International Center of Photography, of which she was a board member, planned an exhibit of his work of French gardens, Jackie decided to do a companion Doubleday book.

> That book was not only quite beautiful, and the pieces well chosen, but within the community of photographers and historians, it revived an entire rediscovery of his work.
>
> —JOHN SARGENT

Jackie herself wrote the book's introduction in some of her most beautiful published prose:

President Jimmy Carter kisses Jackie Kennedy Onassis at the dedication ceremony of the John F. Kennedy Presidential Library, 1980; with John and Caroline Kennedy.

Jackie Kennedy Onassis after attending conference on Ernest Hemingway, with Norman Mailer, John F. Kennedy Library, late 1980s.

To be able to look at the French garden through the eyes of Eugene Atget is one of the great gifts that artist has left us. . . . His prints lie in buckram boxes and cardboard folders in museums' stacks or on collectors' shelves, hang on dealers' walls, or are pasted matter-of-factly into the topographical albums of government archives. To see them together at last is unforgettable. His images communicate beauty, emotion, and history in powerful harmony. Each element illuminates and reinforces the other as we follow the self-effacing, obsessed photographer on his rounds winter, summer, spring, and fall, through the gardens of Versailles, Sceaux, St.-Cloud, the Tuileries, and the Luxembourg. He will find an allée of trees, a statue, and return to photograph it again and again, in different seasons, different years, different light. As we look at the iconography of architecture, sculpture, and fountains recorded by the honesty of Atget's vision, the ancient mysteries of the places return to haunt us. We are taken by his poetry. His conquest of us, like that of his own visible world, is complete. . . . His passionate persistence was echoed a half century later by George Duhamel at the Academie Française: "In the present disorder of the world, to conserve is to create.". . . . Atget was at ease with beauty wherever he found it, in the damp city streets, among scraps of old ironwork, or on the surface glass of a shop window. But one feels that it was in the parks and gardens, recording with his camera what William H. Fox Talbot called "the injuries of time," to the marble, stone, and old trees, that he made his most soaring discoveries of beauty. It is not just the fading romance of something about to disappear that he gives us, but rather a new statement now framed within his photograph that transcends the evocative beauty of the gardens themselves. . . . .

In the noble sweep of the vistas of Versailles, with the sun-touched decorations everywhere, Atget seized the political as well as the aesthetic triumph of that glorious despotic creation. . . . Atget's photographs of St.-Cloud have in close-up a sensuality and in long view a stark architectural quality. The château is gone; burned and vandalized in the disastrous events of 1870–71. . . . His views of the park and waterworks convey the accumulation of history at this loveliest of sites, the palace erased, heroic balustrades framing the emptiness he found.

Sceaux's visual coherence was made possible by its neglect. By 1900 "the injuries of time" had made it a mirage of history that can hardly be believed. Could the intrigues of the Duchesse du Maine, the malicious smile of Voltaire have quivered here, in this image that seems a wild Greek island with terme and tree torn by wind, in this one which shows a sorcerer's wood? The wildness has been largely corrected now by careful civic restoration, so that Atget's record of Sceaux at its greatest moment of decay is a unique historical documentation. In the city parks we feel Atget's humanity. He photographs with tenderness and melancholy. In the Tuileries, the park chair, as French as the croissant, lies overturned beside a leering faun. . . . We find these photographs troubling because we can connect to them. . . . Our grandfathers sit in black serge suits along the paths laid out by kings and queens.

As she was wandering through the International Center of Photography during an installation, Jackie came across television reporter Norma Quarrels, and agreed to do an impromptu interview about the center. She named one particular picture, of Neapolitan mothers and their children during World War II, as her favorite, and when Quarrels asked her about her own work, she replied, "I took pictures of my children when they were young." "Why did you stop?"

asked Quarrels, waiting for a momentous scoop. Jackie merely shrugged and laughed. "They grew up!"

> She had an ambivalent feeling about photography because of the paparazzi. I remember going out with her, and at the end of the evening, there was always this mess, this barrage of people. We went to the opening of a film once, on Broadway, and got separated. Photographers just got in the center and I was pushed away. It was violent, and truly frightening for her.
>
> —KARL KATZ

The most disturbing case was the unrelenting harassment of Jackie by Ron Gallela. The photographer's intrusions compromised not only her privacy but also her safety. In one instance, he chased her into a four-lane street, where she was nearly hit by traffic. She took him back to court, stating:

> I used to go to Hyannis at the beginning of every summer. That began to be gradually intolerable to me with this surveillance. I said to him, "Don't get that close to me." I was extremely agitated, upset, desperate in a way. I thought Galella was going to start pursuing me all over again. By the time I went to bed I was just upset.

Overseas, the problem continued—at least in some countries:

> In Russia, what she liked about communism was that no one took her photograph unless they asked her permission. They would come and say, "Is it all right, yes? Photo-graf?" She'd say, "No, thank you. I'm too tired." They'd say, "Okay." She adored that. Red Square was jammed with people, but they left huge spaces around her. One brave person would finally dart in and say, "Are you—?" And she would say, "No. But I'm told I look remarkably like her."
>
> —TOM HOVING

Jackie was instantly recognizable, but those often photographed with her were not. By 1982, however, one man had become a familiar presence. In 1976, a magazine mentioned that she had dined with "Max Tempelsman," a "New York jeweler." In fact, he was a pioneer of the diamond industry, and a Kennedy friend since the 1950s. And he was not Max. He was Maurice.

I went down with my son to see Irene Worth do her one-woman show on Edith Wharton at the Public Theater. And there, alone in the lobby, were Maurice and Jackie. We went over to have some coffee. My son was carrying a violin case—and a guitar. This interested Jackie. "What are you doing with two such different instruments?" He told her that after the show he was going to a square dance at the World Trade Center. This got her going. "A square dance—in New York City, and at the World Trade Center? Tell me!" For fifteen minutes, she kept asking questions—who would be there, what kind of music did they play, and so forth. She loved contrasts like that. It was a wonderful example of her cross-interests and affectionate way with people. She loved New York, New York loved her, she belonged to us and we belonged to her.

—SCHUYLER CHAPIN, FRIEND

To get to work, Jackie headed out from 1040 by taxi or foot, depending on the weather. Like others in publishing, she often took writers to the Four Seasons, or her favorite, the Russian Tea Room, for lunch. If she were on the run, she would often grab a cheeseburger on a swivel seat at a coffee shop diner. She never tired of trying New York's many restaurants.

I brought her to this French restaurant that she had never been to or heard about. While there, a group of rather attractive Frenchmen sent a bottle of wine to "Madame la Presidente!" She loved that, and called it "the only place in New York where nobody speaks English."

—VIVIAN CRESPI

Jackie's evenings were almost exclusively at home alone, but when she did go out publicly, it was only for causes of institutions or organizations of which she was a member, like the Literary Lions at the New York Public Library. For an evening event, she might hire a driver, but on a daily basis, she took cabs around town. She had an easy rapport with New York cabbies, once treating one and herself to hot dogs on a street corner. On another occasion, while in a cab going up Third Avenue, the song "You Light up My Life," sung by Debbie Boone, came on the radio. Jackie began singing along, in her impersonation of Boone. The cabbie looked into his mirror, realized who was singing, and almost swerved off the street. She loved their small talk with her:

A taxi driver took me to the office. He said, "Lady, you work, and you don't *have* to?" I said yes. He turned around and said, "I think that's great!"

Jackie was a familiar neighbor in the Upper East Side. Nearly every day, she jogged around the Central Park reservoir, and she contributed to the Central Park Conservancy.

> Whenever she'd set out for the park at dusk on a winter's evening, I'd warn her of all the horrible things that could happen to her, and true to form, she never paid any attention. By her nature she was fearless, and I think experience had taught her to trust fate.
>
> —NANCY TUCKERMAN

When Jackie bought fruit at a Korean grocer's or magazines from the newsstand, or ran into the Gap for a T-shirt, she often knew the managers and clerks and chatted with them about their lives. She even contributed her favorite lamb recipe to her butcher when he wrote a cookbook.

> I'll never forget the time Jackie was here and I found a prowler under the stairs. Afterward I was shaking. She was wonderful. She put her arms around me and calmed me down. "Don't get excited," she said. "And don't drink that coffee, because it will just make you more nervous." She couldn't have been more concerned.
>
> —MARGIT SIMON, FORMER OWNER OF
> ELLEN'S CHOCOLATIERS

> What she always, always did was treat me, the shopkeeper, as an equal. Not a friend, but an equal. Which, I believe, is as it should be. The sense of respect is what helps to demystify all the rest of it for me.
>
> —LEON LOBEL, BUTCHER

> She would usually stop after mass to exchange pleasantries with the priests.
> —REVEREND GEORGE BARDES, PASTOR,
> ST. THOMAS MORE CATHOLIC CHURCH

As much as she enjoyed the theater, particularly the performances of a small French repertory company, Jackie was frequently in the city's movie houses,

Jackie Kennedy Onassis being serenaded by musicians after dining in Little Italy, New York, 1980s.

often arranging to link up with friends in the powder room. In film, like every-thing else, Jackie had an eclectic taste:

> When the movie *Tootsie* first came out, she was dying to go see it. I told her that it was impossible, it had opened just a day or so before. And she said, ridiculous, so we went. When we went to get tickets the man in the booth said, "I'm sorry, Mrs. Onassis, Mrs. Crespi, we are all sold out. We don't have any seats left." And then Jackie said to him, "But couldn't we just sit in the aisle?" And I said no to her, and she said, "Now don't be so difficult!" Well then, there we were, Jackie and I watching *Tootsie*, sitting on the floor in the aisle of the movie theater. Once I sat through a sordid and depressing film of Mr. Fassbinder with her. The boys looked like girls, and vice versa, there were incestuous relationships, everyone was hideous. Leaving, she said to me, "Didn't you find it fascinating? One must see all sides of life."
>
> —VIVIAN CRESPI

Jackie enjoyed the documentary film *Grey Gardens* about her aunt and cousin, the witty, enchanting Beales, affectionately remarking, "I should think Mr. Fellini might finally offer them a contract!" The "great Fellini," as she called him, was perhaps the filmmaker whose work she most loved. In 1965, she had hosted a dinner for him and his wife at 1040, before the New York premier of *Juliet of the Spirits*, but twenty years later, she had a chance to dine alone with him and a friend. "When I knew he was coming for dinner," she said, "I watched all his films and read practically all the books written about him." Her single favorite image, she revealingly said, was "the blue peacock in the snowstorm," a magical scene from *Amarcord* of the bird descending in an Italian village square in winter.

It proved easier for Jackie to dine with Fellini than with the famously elusive Greta Garbo. A mutual friend arranged a dinner for the two of them to meet again—Garbo had once dined at the White House—but the actress nervously got up to leave before Jackie arrived. Jackie would occasionally spot her in Manhattan and watch her with fascination.

> She was always excited to see Garbo, and to update me. "I saw her today again! Just walking along by herself," Jackie would say. "She's so mysterious!"
>
> —NANCY TUCKERMAN

Jackie Kennedy Onassis jogging around reservoir later named for her, Central Park, New York, 1980s.

What drew Jackie to Martha's Vineyard? The lure of its extraordinary beauty and privacy. That particularly large tract of land she had embraces many different kinds of terrain. Jackie loved it when she first saw its oceanfront dunes, ponds, farmland, and, of course, the ocean itself. It was big enough to be completely private, and the Vineyard did not have a history for her. The locals loved and admired her, but ensured her privacy. She could walk around through the villages. People didn't gawk or impose on her. If someone was invited to go along on Maurice's boat, they were delighted to come, but nobody asked to go. Her home had the feel of serenity, of the open air, and the view of the ocean and the lawns from everywhere. There was a graciousness of large rooms with lots of books in the bookcases, and a sense of pastel color, which went with the landscape outside. Always a feel of summer.

—ROSE STYRON, FRIEND AND WRITER

In 1981, Jackie purchased several hundred acres of land in Gay Head, the southern tip of Martha's Vineyard, off of Cape Cod. On one of the two ponds on her property, Squibnocket Pond, she kayaked alone or with her son, or

Jackie Kennedy Onassis rowing boat near Red Gate Farm, her house on Martha's Vineyard, Massachusetts, 1980s.

bird-watched with binoculars. Designed by Hugh Newell Jacobsen, the floor of the main house was 3,100 square feet with nineteen rooms in a series of small connected saltboxes, windows looking out at the sea, and fireplaces throughout.

> I got a call from her when she was up at the Kennedy compound in Hyannis Port, saying that she had laid the house out from my floor plans in sand on the beach, so that she could walk from room to room, to visualize the spaces. She put stones down where the windows were. . . .
>
> She was wonderful to work with, extremely attentive. Like most clients, she didn't completely understand blueprints, so . . . when we talked about the eleven-foot height of a room, I told her where to find a store with that measurement in Edgartown. She wanted to feel the spaces. She liked little surprises of design. I liked her dedication to the problems, how it addressed the land, light, views, progress of spaces within. We worked closely together, first going around the Vineyard and looking at the houses that had survived time. The site is out on the Atlantic, you can hear the ocean roaring like a lion. . . . It was home. The whole concept was how she could have a real base for her children and herself. More than any other client I've ever had, she wanted to participate, rather than just trust in blind faith.
>
> —HUGH NEWELL JACOBSEN, ARCHITECT

In her kitchen, where she often had morning coffee, sat, and chatted with the housekeeper, Jackie had a huge restaurant-style stove and hung cork boards pinned with family pictures taken by her throughout the years. Scattered throughout were primitive nineteenth-century farm furniture and gray-blue stoneware crockery, evoking an old, rustic feel. She named the site Red Gate Farm, but affectionately called it "my wonderful little house." She lived there from July to September, usually in solitude. Even during Hurricane Bob, which destroyed much of the New England coast, she found inspiration.

> We had no electricity or plumbing for six days. A hurricane would really be a good background for a novel, the way people all behave differently in the midst of disaster. Some panic, some get nasty, others are brave. We had to live by candlelight. It's hard to read by candlelight. How did Thomas Jefferson get through reading all that stuff?

Upon Jackie's return from her first summer at Red Gate Farm, she began her sixth year at Doubleday. Earlier that year, when she found "sixth anniversary" flowers from Lisa Drew blooming on her desk, Jackie compared their brightness and freshness to her emotions about how working had changed her, and how she anticipated having more adventures with her colleagues that always ended in laughter.

Indeed, it had begun, she said proudly, "the happiest time of my life."

NINE

Matriarch
1984–1993

Well, I think my biggest achievement is that, after going
through a rather difficult time, I consider myself compar-
atively sane.

—Jacqueline Kennedy Onassis

Jackie Kennedy Onassis speaking to children visitors at the John F. Kennedy Library, 1993.

M. T.

They were truly affectionate. When they looked at each other you could see they were terribly in love. But it was a love also offering great serenity.

—YOLANDE CLERGUE, FRIEND

Of the three primary relationships in Jackie's life, her lengthiest was her most private. Maurice Tempelsman avoided being photographed and did all he could to preserve their privacy. She often referred to him simply as M.T. and never felt the need to talk about their relationship.

They were naturally together. Most people put her on a pedestal, but with Maurice it was different. He didn't regard her as a trophy.

—TONY COELHO, FRIEND, AND FORMER CONGRESSMAN

For those of us who cared about Mrs. Onassis, it was comforting—it was terrific—to know she was with somebody who was a good, generous, and gentle man.

—ROGER WILKINS, FRIEND AND
KENNEDY ADMINISTRATION OFFICIAL

Born a month after Jackie, in Antwerp, Belgium, Tempelsman was raised in an Orthodox Jewish family. The family escaped Belgium just before the Nazi invasion there, leaving everything they had known, and moved to a refugee neighborhood in New York. Maurice went to work with his father in the diamond merchant business and was unable to complete his formal education. In 1950 he began serving as liaison between the African diamond mining industry and the American government, which stockpiled the stones for military and industrial use. He later became a sightholder, which allowed him to make direct purchases from the DeBeers diamond cartel.

With his ties to Africa, Tempelsman had to be sensitive to the political changes of the emerging nations, and was on personal terms with many in the various camps of the independence movements—black and white—and an important business figure in countries including Zaire, Botswana, Ghana, and Angola. He chaired the African-American Institute, strongly supported South African democracy, and underwrote Nelson Mandela's first American visit.

> They were a well-matched and distinguished couple. And she respected and admired him and held him in great affection.
> —VIVIAN LOWERY DERRYCK, FRIEND

Tempelsman studied poetry, literature, and Mediterranean and mideastern history, and collected Turkish and Greek antiquities and African art as an authority. With Jackie, he shared a devotion to theater and ballet. Between themselves they spoke French and shared a similar wit.

> I went to see my granddaughter at school on a grandfather's day and there was Maurice. We went to watch the children at their game period. Mine was playing cards, and at the denouement of the game, my granddaughter laid down all her cards—and the game was over. Maurice came over to me, poker-faced. "Do you think we could take her to Las Vegas?"
> —SCHUYLER CHAPIN

Maurice was single when his friendship with Jackie developed into a deeper commitment. In 1984, by the tenets of his faith, he and his wife obtained a mutually amicable "get," a divorce in the Orthodox Jewish religion, difficult to obtain and similar to an annulment. His three children and six grandchildren became close to Jackie, as he did likewise with her family. When he suffered a heart attack and recuperated in the hospital, Jackie was the one who took charge until he recovered. During this time, she revealed to her old friend Vivian Crespi—who had been a friend of both JFK and Onassis—just how vital this extremely private man had become to her life.

Maurice gave her a complete peace of mind. Husbands did not always treat her the way she deserved. Maurice, however, worshiped the ground she walked on. He did not dominate her, she did not dominate him. They were equals. They did things for each other. They worked together. Maurice brought a deep and lasting happiness that was integrated into her everyday life without fanfare and was most helpful in assisting her to avoid publicity, which she so disliked. I had never seen her that happy or relaxed with anyone.

—VIVIAN CRESPI

JACKIE'S COTTAGE

BY 1986, JACKIE HAD BEGUN TO FREQUENTLY RETURN TO THE WASHINGTON area as she resumed foxhunting in Middleburg, Virginia. Although she was a different person from the young first lady who had spent much of her time there, her return renewed her friendships there with Eve Fout and Charles Whitehouse.

The team event is a competition we have here in the fall. She was champion, overall. She would come down in the fall for a month, starting the last weekend in October, to make the team event, and stay through Thanksgiving. Then she would come back again in March. She said it was an exciting affirmation of life to cross beautiful country, out in the fresh air.

—EVE FOUT

There's a man here who is paralyzed from the neck down. He crashed right in front of Jackie one day. The horse stepped in a hole. That made the danger vivid for her. She also had falls from time to time. But that added to the zest of it too. She was an accomplished cross-country rider. When we did team events, she would lead, partly because her big gray horse, Frank, pulled if he was behind and was a bold jumper. She had great confidence in him and would ride boldly over a course of about thirty jumps in four miles.

—CHARLES WHITEHOUSE

Jackie Kennedy Onassis, Charles Whitehouse, and friend with prize ribbons following team riding event, Middleburg, Virginia, early 1990s.

Jackie initially stayed in the Red Fox Inn, then rented a cottage less than a mile from the home where she had lived with JFK. Her place was described as "country cozy, with lots of chintz," and she wrote that she would "subsist on Lean Cuisine and candy bars. . . . My horses live in greatest luxury but my cabin is not famous for gourmet delights."

> She loved the solitude. I would have thought that she would need a cat or a dog. She worked on letters, did her editing, chatted with friends on the phone. The men at the stable helped take care of her riding clothes, polishing her boots. She loved the tranquillity of going through the countryside even with the rain pouring down. I said to her, "Perhaps we can go home now." She said, "We're wet already. And who knows, something wonderful might happen!"
> —CHARLES WHITEHOUSE

Maurice would come down when she was in a competition, right there backing her up. John came down when she had a spill. We had her over to our house, she had friends over to eat at her house. She rented movies and did whatever was easy. But really, down here this was her place, her own time for herself, in

Cottage used each autumn and spring by Jackie Kennedy Onassis from mid–1980s to 1993, Middleburg, Virginia.

that little place on a private farm, down a winding, dirt road, behind trees. It was really just Jackie, at Jackie's Cottage.

—EVE FOUT

AN OFFICE WITH A WINDOW

JACKIE WAS PROMOTED TO SENIOR EDITOR IN 1984, GIVEN AN OUTSIDE OFFICE with a window, first at Doubleday's Fifth Avenue office, then in the new Bertelsmann tower, built by their German parent company, when Doubleday moved to Broadway in Times Square. By now, *she* was a Doubleday institution.

She approached me directly with projects. She was accessible to agents who submitted to her, and the many people she knew over the years often came to her directly with their ideas. On infrequent occasions, if something did pass my desk, I'd ask, "Jackie, what do you think about this?" or "Jackie, do you know so-and-so, because I need to get a hold of them." And she was very direct—yes or no. Her humor at work is hard to convey, since much of it was her voice and timing. We were talking about an allegedly literary person as a potential author. I said, "His favorite book is *The Prince* by Machiavelli." Without missing a beat, she looked at me, and in a delivery that only she could do said, "As well it should. It's probably the one book he has read."

—STEPHEN RUBIN, PRESIDENT, DOUBLEDAY

She knew that if she really wanted to sign up a book, she could walk in to see Steve Rubin and he'd acquiesce, but she was careful. If nobody felt the book was going to be profitable or believed in it, she wouldn't insist. She was a team player. She did take on some books nobody believed in that turned out phenomenally successful, like *The Last Czar*. She convinced everyone, they began to see her viewpoint, and went with it. She had known about Joseph Campbell having been a Svengali figure at Sarah Lawrence College, and Doubleday took a chance on *The Power of Myth* and boom—it sold millions.

There was a new Doubleday after the Bertelsmann takeover, more bottom-line oriented. Jackie stopped doing the expensive illustrated photo books. When she did Marc Riboud's *Capital of Heaven*, it was a stunning visual achievement and best-seller in France, but not in America. Her reaction was telling. She was mortified, feeling she had done Riboud a disservice.

—SCOTT MOYERS

Jackie only did books that interested her. She once told me, "I never think in terms of best-sellers. I think in terms of books." Luckily, so much of what interested her was of interest to a lot of other people. The irony of it is, here's someone who produced a large number of best-sellers simply by, in essence, opening up her own sensibility, and, in turn, finding that it was somehow a universal one among readers. She was a formidable sponsor of projects, representing her books within the process, unselfish and funny when presenting books at editorial meetings.

—STEVE RUBIN

In describing the success, for example, of her acquisition of the *Cairo Trilogy*, she said:

When I read in the paper that this Egyptian had won the Nobel Prize, I thought, We've got to have that. I've always loved the cultures of the Mediterranean, and I'd lived in Greece, and it clicked with some other Mediterranean writers I very much admired—Kazantzakis, for instance.

In addition to focusing on content, Jackie paid great attention to the marketing value of design.

> She had a taste that made you strive to keep up. The product always had to be absolutely correct. She was always tuned in to the overall visual impact. She had a classical point of view, but it was always couched in terms of the new and different.
>
> —PETER KRUZAN,
> ART DIRECTOR, DOUBLEDAY

> She was involved with every single aspect of her books—from the typeface to the jacket. Jackie brought that impeccable taste, which just came innately. She infused everything she touched. You can't learn that. You've either got that or you ain't. Her books were particularly beautiful and had a timelessness to them. The book I think that best expresses that is *Healing and the Mind*. If you look at that jacket, it will never date in any way. It's magnificent. She was a stickler for detail, and that's a very odd-size book. The jacket is magnificent. The inside is magnificent. The case is magnificent. Everything was like Jackie, herself. It wasn't well done. It was perfect. The *Cairo Trilogy* is another example—the covers evoke a mysticism of Egypt, not ancient but timeless. She was heavily involved and they have an extraordinary look.
>
> —STEVE RUBIN

Jackie worked closely with proofreaders, designers, marketers, and even booksellers, to whom she would write personal notes, promoting her titles. She collaborated easily.

> My image of Jackie in the office is sitting cross-legged on the floor with amazing flexibility, with three versions of a manuscript she's pulling together or two hundred photocopies of photos. Martha Graham died before her autobiography was scheduled for publication, and we had to rush it into print. Jackie said, "When this is all done, we are all going to lunch to celebrate." She made sure that we all went to the garden of Barbetta's and had a great time.
>
> She always had an amazing ability to see the big picture, in both a literary sense and a general sense. She saw the forest, not the trees. You bring your whole personality and style to editing. Although many editors no longer do this, she always put pencil to paper in her particular process of editing, with a

sense of what the elements meant to the whole. Jackie could be sitting here with you and me, and if a specific turn of phrase struck her, she would whip out her book and write it down. She enjoyed language. If you see her edited manuscripts, you realize she was like a conductor. She was a coach, instilling people with confidence and enthusiasm for what she knew they could do. If anything nice was said about her projects, Jackie would say who did what, always giving credit where credit was due—to assistants, designers, whoever.

—Bruce Tracy

While traveling, Jackie kept in touch by postcard with colleagues—often making herself the butt of a joke in relation to the picture on the other side and ending with a witty message—like pointing out the nudist beach on Martha's Vineyard.

She made herself directly accessible. I called her in the country, at home. She was always available for the publication party of one of her books—the first one there, the last one to leave.

—Steve Rubin

At a small dinner in the Greenwich Village apartment of former mayor Ed Koch, the guests introduced themselves around the table. She said, "My name is Jacqueline Kennedy Onassis. I am an editor, and I am now working on a book." It was simply how she now saw herself. In her last interview, with *Publishers Weekly* editor John F. Baker, her satisfaction was evident.

I'm drawn to books that are out of our regular experiences. Books of other cultures, ancient histories. I'm interested in the arts in general, especially the creative process. I'm fascinated by hearing artists talk of their craft. To me, a wonderful book is one that takes me on a journey into something I didn't know before. If you live through a time, it crystallizes later for you, and you want to know more about it. . . . I don't work with agents as much as some editors, perhaps, though sometimes, when something crosses their desk, I hope they think of me, and say, "Oh, she might like that."

One of the things I like about publishing is that you don't promote the editor—you promote the book and author.

I'm always optimistic that people will buy good books. There's nothing to complain about; I love my colleagues here. I love Doubleday.

LOBBYIST

DESPITE HER INCREASED WITHDRAWAL INTO HER LIFE AS AN EDITOR, JACKIE'S genuine commitment to preservation, paradoxically, only elevated her public visibility. Throughout the 1980s, she quite willingly became a more vocal lobbyist. After she had successfully lobbied the Supreme Court in the 1970s, her next major battle was fought with New York State—the news came that St. Bartholomew's Church was going to destroy its community house and construct a forty-seven-story office building above it, claiming that churches were exempt from landmark law. In February 1984, Jackie went to Albany, lobbying for landmark status for houses of worship and testifying before gathered legislators. She stated, in part:

> The future of New York City is bleak if the landmarks that mean so much to us and our children are stripped of their status. If you cut people off from what nourishes them spiritually and historically, something within them dies.

The effort in Albany involved delicate religious questions, as well as the kind of political glad-handing she liked least.

> A group of religious leaders from around the state had gotten together to oppose the designation of religious property as a landmark and succeeded in getting two significant people in Albany to introduce this bill. One was from Yonkers who was very responsive to the Catholic church; the other, Dan Walsh. Our chances were not considered good. Jackie agreed to go. On the train, she went around and talked to various state officials who got on at different points. As soon as we got to Albany, we stopped in Warren Davis's office, a proud, vocal Republican who was noncommittal on the issue. She was good at these things, always animated, they had a nice conversation. She didn't push. From his office she went to testify.
>
> After that, she walked into the corridor of the state capitol and greeted all the office workers who came out to cheer her. Dan Walsh asked her if she wouldn't mind having her picture taken. She said yes and went into his office. And there were about fifty people crammed in there, all waiting to have their picture taken. She talked to, and had her picture taken with, every living member of the senate. Meeting Jackie Onassis was a significant moment in many people's lives, but she treated everyone as if they were Winston Churchill.

Walsh was touched by this beyond the practical politics. I think he was changed by it. It wasn't just because he had his picture taken. It made him stop and think about the issue.

We then had a press conference, where Jackie spoke along with religious leaders and elected officials on our side. She spoke about how in other cultures houses of worship were revered and that the essential monuments of other countries included St. Paul's Cathedral and Notre Dame, places that were unthinkable to destroy. She also particularly mentioned Catholic countries, which may or may not have been because they have the greatest churches, but I think she was also playing her cards. In New York, it was very powerful to have the support of the Catholic church. She was one of the very few people imaginable who could lead the way for our side of the case as a Catholic. And we won. She never took a break all day—grace, and stamina.

—KENT BARWICK

In July 1987, Jackie headed another highly visible fight, this time to block construction of two proposed skyscrapers at Columbus Circle, because they would cast permanent shadows over Central Park and cause traffic congestion. Although her opponents were powerful, wealthy developers, she chaired a coalition of urban organizations. "It's time to stop the overbuilding in New York City by drawing the line at Columbus Circle," she angrily said at a press conference.

In the Columbus Circle fight, Jackie spoke directly to the point of the everyday person. She just looked me directly in the eye, and with visceral reaction said, "They're stealing our sky." Initially, we had had a tough argument to crystallize, but Jackie's statement was a guide. As we prepared for the first press conference, we had a blowup picture of what the buildings would look like. And it was Jackie who then and there figured out that these buildings were going to be so tall that they would cast a black shadow, at certain times a mile long, all the way across Central Park. Nobody had thought about the shadow. It led us to make a picture of what the shadowed park would look like—and that was what really gripped people's imaginations. When this was seen and heard, the instinctive reaction followed Jackie's initial reaction. And we won.

—KENT BARWICK

During her impassioned preservation battles, Jackie still avoided any politically partisan fights. Her frustrations with government—she strongly

Jackie Kennedy Onassis testifying on behalf of historic preservation at the state capitol, Albany, New York, 1984.

opposed the threat of dismantling the National Endowments of the Arts and Humanities—were expressed in conversation, not activism. As an editor, however, she chose books on subjects that she believed were politically important to disseminate—*The Cost of Courage: A Journey of an American Congressman* by Carl Elliot Sr., and *Taming the Storm: The Life and Times of Frank M. Johnson, Jr. and the South's Fight for Civil Rights*, by Jack Bass. Elliot, who was instrumental in local southern politics during the civil rights movement, was the first winner of the Profile in Courage Award, given out by the Kennedy Library, and Jackie attended the ceremony. It was at the library that Jackie was perhaps her most political, but only as a participant in events. When Nelson Mandela and Mikhail and Raisa Gorbachev made their respective American tours, Jackie greeted them there. During Russia's 1990 attempted coup by hard-line Communists, and the triumph of prodemocracy forces, Jackie was completely gripped by the human drama, watching the events unfold on television.

Isn't it fascinating, the whole struggle of men and power? The whole situation with Gorbachev making these strides and now he's toppled? Even though he was making progress, the march forward just overtook him.

Jackie was very much her own person. She was able to maintain her own unique identity and at the same time be very much a close and loyal member of our family. She showed her love and support by giving us her imaginative and creative gifts that she knew would have special meaning. She once had framed and gave me notes my brother made during the Cuban missile crisis. They are a real treasure and I have them hanging in my house.

—SENATOR EDWARD M. KENNEDY

Annually, Jackie hosted a Labor Day weekend barbecue on the beach near Red Gate Farm for Kennedy family members, one year entering the fray dressed in scuba gear and rushing into the ocean. Despite her physical distance from the maturing clan, Jackie privately worried about those of them going through personal turmoil.

She never said anything bad about someone else. Never even suggested things in a subtle or snide way. When several of the Kennedy children went through a bad time, she would say, "I feel so badly that so-and-so is going through this" and "Isn't it a shame." But she was completely unjudgmental when discussing

Jackie Kennedy Onassis meets with South African independence leader and later president Nelson Mandela, 1991, John F. Kennedy Library.

other humans and their difficulties. It was clear when she disapproved of an action, but she sympathized with people with problems.

—CHARLES WHITEHOUSE

Jackie felt a particular connection to one in-law, even after her divorce:

Jackie had encouraged my friendship with Leonard Bernstein, because of my work in classical music and as a concert pianist. The result was my book, *The Joy of Classical Music: A Guide for You and Your Family,* and it was published by Doubleday. I was frequently in New York to confer with my editor there, and Jackie and I began seeing each other again. We visited in her office, on and off for the two years before publication. We talked not only about the book—but about everything. We congratulated ourselves on how well our children turned out—and said we hoped we had something to do with it! Here we were, things so different, but through all the changes, we were still sisters-in-law.

—JOAN BENNETT KENNEDY

At weddings of some of the nieces and nephews of President Kennedy, "Aunt Jackie" was a familiar face, but as Rose Kennedy neared the one-century mark, she was too frail to attend. Her influence, however, had not been lost on Jackie, who became the matriarch of her own family.

I remember a couple of summers when Jackie just came down for the day to Hyannis Port to see my mother. She kept a very active interest in her. In earlier years, Jackie would always take her for a walk. She wanted to visit her in an unassuming way, and tried in every way to let my mother know how much she cared for her.

—SENATOR EDWARD M. KENNEDY

Jackie helped her grown children in handling the legacy of their father, and at Kennedy Library events, she made them, not herself, take center stage. Similarly, she deferred to Caroline in commissioning a JFK statue for Boston's State House.

Her love for Caroline and John was deep and unqualified. She reveled in their accomplishments, she hurt with their sorrows. At the mere mention of one of

Jackie Kennedy Onassis with members of the Kennedy family at summer picnic, Hyannis Port, Massachusetts, 1975.

their names, Jackie's eyes would shine brighter and her smile would grow bigger.

—SENATOR EDWARD M. KENNEDY

She raised her kids in a way that all three locked onto each other in a way that families almost never do. They all came through for one another. She really liked them as friends.

—FRED PAPERT

Jackie did all she could to encourage Caroline as she wrote her first book, *In Our Defense: The Bill of Rights in Action,* coauthored with Ellen Alderman, and developed a close relationship with her daughter's fiancé, artist Edwin Schlossberg.

[She] did not interfere with Caroline's wedding dress—"I am not going to get involved because Caroline is the one who will wear it. I want her to be the happiest girl in the world."

—CAROLINA HERRERA, DESIGNER AND FRIEND

At the reception following Caroline's July 1986 wedding at the Kennedy compound, Ted Kennedy raised his glass in toast to Jackie as "that extraordinary, gallant woman, Jack's only love." After the newlyweds were off, she wrote an emotional letter to Ted Kennedy from Red Gate Farm, thanking him for acting as a father in Jack Kennedy's stead, and wistfully wishing she were at the family party at the compound. Caroline made Jackie a grandmother with the birth of Rose in 1988, Tatiana in 1990, and John in 1993. They called her "Grand Jackie."

> Jackie loved being with her grandchildren, eagerly awaiting their weekly visits. With her . . . imagination, she was able to hold their attention for hours on end. There was this enormous red wooden chest in which she kept all sorts of hidden treasures for them: pirate loot, gypsy trinkets, beaded necklaces, rings with colored stones. As soon as they arrived, everything from the chest was dumped out on the bedroom floor and the children would dig in. They'd deck themselves out with jewelry, and put on costumes they'd make from old scarves and bits of material. Jackie would then take them on a so-called fantasy adventure. She'd weave a spellbinding tale while leading them through the darkened apartment, opening closet doors in search of ghosts and mysterious creatures. Once they were finished playing, they'd have their traditional afternoon tea party, sitting on the living room floor. The children loved these visits, but no more so than Jackie.
>
> —NANCY TUCKERMAN

When Jackie's sister Janet was diagnosed with cancer, Jackie went to every end to help—sitting in the hospital with her, donating her own blood through a transfusion. She was at her side when she died, and then she arranged the funeral. She was there, too, at the end for older relatives like her Aunt Edith Beale.

> When Big Edie had to go to the hospital, I called Jacqueline. Immediately she said get the best room possible for Aunt Edie! She would cover everything. At Edie's funeral, she arranged to have some of Edie's songs played on an old phonograph. And Edie's beautiful voice echoed through the church. As we were going to the cemetery, Jacqueline said she just had to have a tape of those old records. These were the songs she remembered and loved from her childhood, the songs Big Edie used to sing to her and make her laugh. When we discussed family troubles she simply said, "Oh, Doris, it's so much more complicated than you realize."
>
> —DORIS FRANCISCO, BOUVIER FAMILY FRIEND

Jackie Kennedy Onassis with granddaughters Rose and Tatiana, Martha's Vineyard, 1993.

Although she was now quite elderly, Janet Auchincloss still took great pride in her daughter's accomplishments. When a friend of Janet's wanted to publish an ill-conceived travel book, Jackie received a directive from her mother: "Dearest Jackie, Here is the information on the travel book I told you about. Will you please give this to Lisa Drew, and tell her I asked you to." Dryly, like a dutiful schoolgirl, Jackie told Lisa, "My mother told me to make certain that I get this to you. So, you see, I still do what my mother tells me to do."

By the mid–1980s, it became clear that Janet was suffering from Alzheimer's disease. On special occasions, Jackie gathered her family to make videotape greetings for Janet, as a tangible reminder. She also made a great effort to have Janet meet her great-granddaughter, Rose.

> Jackie arranged for Mummy to fly for the day from Newport to her house on Martha's Vineyard, along with Sally Ewall, who looked after her. A picture was taken of the four generations, and Mummy's memory wasn't there much, but at one point suddenly there was recognition. I think everyone felt very happy that there was that moment.
>
> —JAMIE AUCHINCLOSS

Toward the end of my stepmother's Alzheimer's she would often mistake me for my father. One day, I was driving her back from Boston and Jackie was sitting in the backseat. My stepmother was carrying on a complete conversation with me as if I were my father—who died in 1975. "Now, Hugh D., don't drive too fast," or "You mustn't do that." Jackie was taking this all in with great wonder. "Yusha, this is amazing." I thought she meant the illness. "No. You're not only my brother. Now you're my stepfather too."

—Yusha Auchincloss

Jackie was planning on being in Hyannis Port to help celebrate Rose Kennedy's ninety-ninth birthday in July 1989. But our mother was dying in Newport that day, so she chose to spend the last few hours of Mummy's life by her bedside. That night of Rose Kennedy's birthday, our own mother died. The day before the funeral, when she learned that our aunt was starting to suffer from Alzheimer's, she arranged for the same specialist to see her.

—Jamie Auchincloss

Jackie Kennedy Onassis with (left to right): brother Jamie, niece Tina, sister Lee, son John, mother in back, Jackie holding nephew Tony, sister Janet, and daughter Caroline, 1967.

THE FRIEND

I once wrote a piece about being at the beach with the president and Caroline and John. *Harper's* magazine was enthralled, but I had to get Jackie's permission. She said, "I know you'll hate me for this, but you can't publish that. I have to protect the children." She was my friend, I didn't mind. In 1992, I was doing a collection of my work and asked Jackie what her feelings were about that piece. She said, "Oh, I was so silly back then. It was such a lovely piece, like a portrait. You must do it. Please do it." And I did. That was what it meant to be friends with her.

—GEORGE PLIMPTON

For someone who could easily slip into full-time solitude, Jackie was attentive to her closest friends, who had earned her trust. She gave an annual Christmas party for them—and had no patience with snobs.

She was loyal to those who were also loyal, regardless of what role they played in her life. She was loved by Marta Sgubin. Marta was indispensable in her life—first as a friend, then as a governess, housekeeper, everything. She ran things. She had come to work for Jackie through Mrs. Auchincloss and she stayed on until the end. Jackie also remembered friends now gone. When I told her I was having a tree planted in memory of Luigi Barzini, our mutual friend, she sent me a check and said, "Plant a tree for me too. A big one."

—VIVIAN CRESPI

She never discriminated among her friends and that included economic status as well. One of her most enduring relationships was with her former maid Provy, Providencia Parades. For as long as I can remember she gave Provy and her family the use of her house at the compound for the month of August. Provy's son, Gustavo, was, and still is, among John's closest friends. Jackie set an example for her children that there should be no place for racism or anti-Semitism in our lives.

—SENATOR EDWARD M. KENNEDY

Because she was a member of a minority, one young woman in the company was having trouble getting into an apartment building where she desperately wanted to live. She asked if there was a chance that since Mrs. Onassis had worked with her on the book projects, she could write a nice word to the building. I called Jackie and she said, "I understand the situation completely, and the letter will be in your office in the next thirty minutes." Thirty minutes later the letter was in the office and the young woman got into the building.

—JOHN LORING, FRIEND AND AUTHOR

One of the most thoughtful things she did in sending a book proposal to me was the way she handled a sad situation. She wrote me a letter about this person on Doubleday stationery and went on about what a remarkable person he was, and loved by everyone who knew him and that his story would prove to be inspiring. She sent a copy of the letter to him, but sent me a cover note saying that, in fact, he was quite ill, but that she wanted to lift his spirits with as much hope as she could, and that she hoped I would please understand.

On another occasion, a friend of ours who'd been an editor at Doubleday was fired during one of the reorganizations. This person was unemployed for almost a year and then applied for a fairly high-profile job. There were something like one hundred other applicants for the position. Jackie heard about this and wrote an unsolicited note as a recommendation for this person to be taken seriously. And the person got the job.

—LISA DREW

There was a young man who was working his way through college as a doorman at 1040. He wanted to move on, and he asked me if I thought Jackie might write him a letter of recommendation. I asked her, and she said for me to draft something and she would sign it. While I wrote what I thought was a good letter, she read it over carefully adding her own words to improve it and make it more personal.

—NANCY TUCKERMAN

When she could step in to help, Jackie also aided immigration efforts for friends who wanted to live in America.

The man who ran the speedboat for Jackie on Skorpios, a small, wiry fellow, was wonderful to her. And she was very kind to him. He ultimately wanted to immigrate to America. Jackie wanted to help fulfill his dream, so we found him a job at a restaurant called Seafare of the Aegean. He started as a busboy, and later became wealthy enough to buy a restaurant in Greece.

—KARL KATZ

She made it very clear the first instant that we landed on Soviet soil that she was absolutely determined to get Jewish dissident Leonid Tarrassuk—on the Hermitage's curatorial staff—out of the Soviet Union, and as many members of his family as she could. She was willing to make a real front-page story out of it. We had a serious discussion with the undersecretary of culture. He said, "If you make this public, it will stiffen the people here. If you have a job for this guy that will make the case stronger." I said, "The Met can find a place for him." Jackie was an adept politician. She could tell when somebody was giving her the runaround, but she worked with them, and they let it happen.

—Tom Hoving

When close friends of Jackie's were in the hospital, she dispatched soups and other foods to them and sometimes even tried to get them into experimental drug therapies if they were suffering. As Diana Vreeland's eyesight, then health, failed, her museum pension was discreetly supplemented with money from Jackie. When Jackie's friend Rudolf Nureyev was dying of AIDS, Jackie checked in regularly with him, supportive to the end. During the latter part of his life, Jackie and Maurice Tempelsman often joined Nureyev and his longtime companion, Robert Tracy, for evenings of dinner and theater. Through Nureyev's final illness, she kept in close contact with Tracy.

I saw her sometimes in Paris, more often in New York. Amazing, through all the changes, we had still stayed friends with each other for almost half a century.

—Claude de Renty du Granrut

HER LITTLE FAMILY

WITH HER DEVOTION TO HER WORK, JACKIE DEVELOPED SOME CLOSE FRIENDSHIPS with fellow employees, literary agents, and booksellers. In cultivating the talents of her authors and young people who came to work for her, the mothering instinct that Jackie had carefully reserved only for her children and closest intimates began to display itself rather openly.

When manuscripts came in you couldn't just drop it right on her. Like any assistant editor, you read it yourself and then passed along your assessment. I hadn't realized that she had already published Jonathan Cott, but he sent in a proposal for two books—one on the priestess Isis, another on the history and

Jackie Kennedy Onassis, Nancy Tuckerman, and Lisa Drew at Doubleday company picnic in Central Park, early 1980s.

mystique of the number thirteen. I thought they were pretty wacky. I first had made the same presumption that the rest of the world made about Jackie, that she was purely interested in the fussy fine arts and French history. So I wrote that these proposals were not right for us. Two weeks later, Jackie had both books under contract.

That was the first big lesson I learned about her. I could never second-guess Jackie because—although it sounds like a cliché, or exaggeration—she really was interested in everything. She was interested in science, from the botany involved in *The Garden of Life,* or the book by Miriam Rothschild on the nature of bees, birds, and butterflies. For Jackie, more so even than most editors, adventure was a big part of editing. Jackie never categorically dismissed an idea because the subject matter was errant or foreign to her.

—BRUCE TRACY

Sometimes you had to filter out what she said, because she gave you so much encouraging, positive feedback it would swell your ego. She could even be flirtatious in the way she phrased her rejection letters. After I had been working a year, she really fought to get me a promotion. She went into the editor in chief's office and waved her magic wand. And it happened. Her caring came out in all kinds of random ways. One summer, I was going to be visiting a friend whose grandparents were on Martha's Vineyard. Jackie said, "You have to come see me and Maurice." And she took us out on Maurice's boat for this great day around the Vineyard.

—SCOTT MOYERS

In preparation for the illustrations of *The Garden of Life,* Naveen Patnaik came from his studio in Delhi to carry these priceless watercolors done by the descendants of the royal court painters of India. After the transparencies were taken, the originals had to be brought back to him, at the home of his sister, Gita Mehta. These paintings were in a box, and they didn't weigh anything. Jackie called over there, and then she came back and said, "Well, Bruce, you and Scott should take this box over there." I said, "Sure. I don't want to trust it to a messenger, but I don't think it takes two to go. I mean, Scott could go." She said, "No, no, no. You must both go."

I couldn't figure out why she needed the two of us to take this box. Anyway, we got there and here were the most fascinating people in the world! Brilliant! They had us sit down, gave us some coffee, and we just talked and talked about India. Jackie had tremendous affection for India, and she knew how into this book Scott and I both were. She knew that spending a couple of hours with Gita and Naveen was going to be infinitely more mind expanding and open more doors of thought than just working on the book. I didn't know, until we later returned to the office, that she had known all along that they were both there. It was important to her that we had the experience.

—BRUCE TRACY

She was a profoundly generous woman, a sort of mother figure to us all, with a lot of empathy. She put out a sense of family concern. When I got hit by a drunk driver, my knee got shredded. She said to me gently, "Now listen, Scott, if you need to borrow a few bucks, I don't want you to hesitate to ask. Your family isn't in New York—" And I said, "I'm okay. I'm okay."

It bothered her that I would wake up in the morning in a hurry, shower, and come to work in the winter with my hair wet. She snapped at me, "Scott, you're going to get a cold with your hair wet!" I ignored this, and then one day, she bought me a blue wool hat to wear to work. She had her little pet theories that changed from month to month on how to cure a cold or flu. At one point, she hit upon TheraFlu. I remember being really sick and Jackie threw a bunch of TheraFlu down on my desk and said, "Take that TheraFlu!" It was really bad flu and I was at work totally zoned out. She picked up on it, and without telling me, she called her doctor and asked him to see me. She shoved cab money in my hand, and she made me go to her doctor. I found out that she had also sent a previous assistant, Shaye Areheart, to her doctor.

—SCOTT MOYERS

Jackie's sensitivity to her colleagues became apparent in unpredictable, often humorous ways. When once, for example, a team was working under tedious conditions on a deadline, sorting through thousands of photographs in the Library of Congress, she slipped away, picked up a colleague's camera—and began snapping pictures of the frazzled group.

In the summer of 1992, *The Last Czar* was about to come out, and suddenly I had this great opportunity to go to London for a week, basically for the cost of airfare. If I went, however, I would miss this big book party at the Russian Tea Room. I had been working with Jackie on this book, and I didn't want to seem cavalier. So I went in to talk to her, apologetically saying, "I just got this chance to go to Europe, and I've never been." She looked at me like I had two heads. "Of course you go," she said, "life comes first."

—BRUCE TRACY

It had been three decades since Jackie Bouvier had given thought to becoming a writer herself, and she remained "always tolerant" of writers "who had that artistic sensibility of being neurotic," recalled Scott Moyers. Of the seventy-four books she edited at Doubleday, Jackie achieved with several authors a deep level of understanding. Olivier Bernier, for example, felt that she not only focused intently on the writer's needs and perspective, as opposed to her own, but also took on his viewpoint when it was attacked. Ruth Prawer Jhabvala said Jackie adopted people with such a complete empathy that she seemed to suffer the author's predictable pains of publishing.

I first worked with Jackie in 1986 on a book entitled *The Search for Omm Sety,* the story of a remarkable twentieth-century English-Egyptian priestess of Isis. Jackie informed me that she had met Omm Sety, who had lived in a mud hut in the Upper Egyptian village of Abydos . . . on a trip Jackie had taken down the Nile in the 1970s. Ever since then, Jackie said, she had been fascinated by this woman, and she talked to me with such intensity and passion about the book I was in the process of writing that it seemed as if she were dreaming it herself.

When I had completed the first draft of my manuscript, Jackie asked me to come to her office, where she had brought from her home a score of books on ancient Egyptian history, art, and religion, including one of the enormous twenty-four volumes of the *Description de l'Egypte* commissioned by Napoleon. . . . Listening to my editor's wonderfully knowledgeable ideas about ancient Egypt and to her enthusiastic but specific comments about my manuscript, I soon began to imagine that like Omm Sety, I, too, was entering the world of ancient Egypt, conversing with an Egyptian queen who was as beautiful as Nefertiti. . . .

And then I came out of my little trance . . . and Jackie was pointing to a page of my manuscript, saying, "A diminishing sentence. Pull out the stops. Make this passage more dramatic. . . . Let us understand what it meant for . . . Omm Sety . . . to come to know the meaning and purpose of her life. . . . Dottiness was her cover-up. Say she was a witch!". . . [Jackie was] my inspiring and magical editor, who took me on a journey I will never forget.

—Jonathan Cott

Consuming herself with the smallest detail, Jackie became thoroughly absorbed in a manuscript. In her cover note to Louis Auchincloss, the author of *False Dawn* and a step-cousin, she apologized:

Please realize that one gets obsessive and nitpicking when editing a manuscript filled with facts, in a concentrated session. I did yours in a day and a night in Martha's Vineyard. It isn't at all like reading a book for pleasure and I may have been overzealous.

When a proposed book subject so moved Jackie, she was literally willing to cross the ocean for it. The book idea of one of her authors so captivated Jackie that she made her first trip to liberated Eastern Europe in the dead of winter, 1993, with Maurice, to better understand it.

Peter Sis is a Czech artist, a well-known children's book illustrator who grew up in Prague and defected in the 1980s. He had always wanted to do a book about his childhood for his little daughter Madeleine, who was growing up in the new world, so she could know about her father's old world past. *The Three*

Golden Keys is about a balloonist who comes into this ancient city of his child-hood and goes home. It's dark. All the city is dark. No one is in the streets. He follows a cat from a locked door, and is led to these three landmarks, and at each one, something comes to life and tells a Czech fairy tale, and gives him a golden key. It's an allegory for the reclamation of a Czech identity after communism.

—SCOTT MOYERS

There was always something not quite right until she visited Prague. . . . She spent only four days there, but she knew the names of more of the Baroque architects than I ever did. I had tried before to propose a story about Prague to other publishers, but they were not interested, and I gave up. All of a sudden, I was asked by Jackie to do just that.

—PETER SIS

Jackie specifically insisted that she must do this children's book. The typical children's book is thirty-two pages long. Sis said that he had done sixty-four illustrations. Jackie said, "Let's use them all because this is your life's book." She did not like books dedicated to her, but Peter just insisted on getting this in—"Thank you for a dream, JO." She saw the original illustrations, and she edited the text, but she never saw the finished book.

—SCOTT MOYERS

BALLETOMANE

DANCE WAS AMONG THE BOOK SUBJECTS JACKIE AVIDLY PURSUED. SUCCESSFUL in signing Judith Jamison of the Alvin Ailey Dance Company to do her autobiography, she had to patiently pursue ballerina Gelsey Kirkland, who was then addicted to cocaine. As Kirkland sought recovery and met Greg Lawrence, who became her coauthor and husband, Jackie helped *Dancing on My Grave* become a best-seller.

When Jackie gave me the opportunity to write my autobiography, she helped me recover my life and my career. This was no small gift, and she gave it over and over through the years. As my husband and I finished each chapter . . . we were constantly spurred on by her unbridled enthusiasm. Her encouragement kept us going. Jackie believed in us when few others did. She was both an editor and a friend, and whenever the two roles came into conflict, the friendship and affection won out. She was protective of us and steadfastly loyal.

—GELSEY KIRKLAND AND GREG LAWRENCE

For Jackie, ballet had remained a secret world to which she was deeply drawn.

Perhaps she found a sense of escape in a private world on stage that was so hard for her to find personally. Whether you escaped into it or simply enjoyed it, a lot of direct emotional engagement happens. I do know, from one conversation and from watching what she attended, that she was genuinely interested in young and developing artists. . . . She felt that eventually education for young people in ballet should be part of our mission.

—GARY DUNNING, DIRECTOR, AMERICAN BALLET THEATER

In 1979, Jackie chaired a benefit performance of the American Ballet Theater of skating champion John Curry's dancing debut. The company was also celebrating its recent award of a $1 million NEA grant. A dozen years later, however, ABT was in dire financial straits.

In 1992, when Kevin Mackenzie and I were appointed directors, ABT was in financial turmoil and close to closing and we had to try to save the company. Oliver Smith, one of our first directors, had remained involved, and Jackie had always been supportive since she became a trustee in the late 1960s. She expressed a desire to help in this turmoil. Oliver asked us to join him at her apartment. We sat in her smaller room right off the hallway, beautiful books everywhere, and just talked about what ideas we had for ABT, why it was important and how it could be saved. Our specific agenda was to try and gather a sort of ad-hoc help commission, and I had Mrs. Onassis in mind as an honorary chair, and to perhaps host a luncheon for people who could make large donations, but the discussion wandered into the value of the arts. I found her to be quite practical in dealing with the funding problem—how and why people are motivated to give. She spoke easily and from the heart about the value of art on a daily basis, and how humans can change if they were introduced and exposed to it, and how ballet was important to her as an art that expressed emotion on a basic level. Because it was so light, her voice was very misleading. When you spoke with her, you heard these remarkable comments that indicated serious reflection, never something off-the-cuff. She talked about the sense of responsibility she felt that she owed to Americans to make this company's art survive and flourish because it had merit and value. I finally made my pitch—"I'd really like you to help us identify friends who you might think would be of great help. Your name would open a lot of doors, but we're not asking you to go out and ask for money." And she said, "Gary, I'd love to help, but I don't really know anyone." Oliver stepped in—they were refreshingly candid with each other—and said, "Oh, Jackie, be quiet. Everyone knows you and that's all that matters!"

—GARY DUNNING

THE CLINTONS

*J*ACKIE CLOSELY FOLLOWED THE EMERGENCE OF ARKANSAS GOVERNOR BILL Clinton as a presidential candidate. As the 1992 primaries ensued, she even badgered a friend out of supporting Paul Tsongas and into supporting Clinton. When the friend capitulated, Jackie sighed, "It's about time."

In the late summer of 1991, my husband received word that both Jackie and her son had been talking about him and were very interested about whether or not he was actually going to throw his hat in the ring. They were among two of the earliest contributors to his presidential campaign. She was very interested in the positions he took, and found what he had to say to be very much in line with her beliefs. I never got a chance to speak with her until June of 1992, when she invited me to lunch. When I met her in that marvelous apartment with books everywhere, she made me feel like we were old friends. What could have been a short, courtesy lunch turned into a several-hour conversation. She had out a lot of her latest projects and the books that she had edited, and other books that she was interested in. We talked a lot about our mutual interest in writing and kicked around ideas for other books she might do in the future. Mostly, we talked about children, what it's like to live in the White House. She was convinced that my husband was going to win, and she wanted to give me advice. We saw each other during convention week. It was a big decision for her to come into Madison Square Garden.

—HILLARY RODHAM CLINTON

Jackie Kennedy Onassis visiting Margot Fonteyn backstage at the ballet, actress Elizabeth Taylor at far left, 1978.

Attending her third convention, Jackie watched the nomination from a viewing box.

> She was so excited about going. She said, "Can you believe it, Maurice has managed to get tickets to everything—just everything!" It was very funny because it was as if she didn't realize that as Jacqueline Kennedy Onassis she could have asked to go to anything!
>
> —LISA DREW

> She was early on aware that as a young person Bill Clinton had met President Kennedy in the rose garden she created. I think that meeting established an emotional link for her. She talked with the president [Clinton] about the history of the South, and the issues of integration. One of the things that Jackie was very interested in—which the president knew a great deal about—were the basic judgments that were made in the 1950s by the conservative fifth circuit court, which opened up the opportunities for equality of race. . . . [The judges] had all been appointed by Republicans, principally Eisenhower. And she talked of the enlightened views that they had as real leaders of the bar and as judges, and why they had all had this open, progressive view on race. The president [Clinton] explained the real latent tradition of the Republican party in the South as a progressive party on issues

of race, tracing itself back to the Lincoln tradition, and that it was only in recent years that there was a different kind of tradition. Jackie was quite fascinated by this. She had read a great deal about the South—histories, novels, studies.

—SENATOR EDWARD M. KENNEDY

We were [also] talking then about how the Democratic Party had changed and how hard it was in the fifties; how most of the Republicans in the South, like those Eisenhower would appoint, were people whose families had been Republicans coming out of the Civil War. So they tended to be more progressive on race. And the Democrats that President Kennedy was trying to appoint—he wanted to appoint people who would basically be sympathetic on civil rights, but you had to get them through the southern senators, and the Democratic Party in the South was still largely in the control of the conservatives, so it was kind of a constant struggle. And we were talking about how it completely had flipped now . . . about how one of the dilemmas that the president has is trying to honor his political obligations and still make sure things come out the way he believes they should.

—PRESIDENT WILLIAM JEFFERSON CLINTON

"She loved that the Clintons love the Kennedys," said one friend. "And she was intrigued with the continuity, the idea that her husband in some way launched Bill Clinton's political career." It was Hillary Clinton that she became most defensive of, particularly after attacks on the new first lady began in the spring of 1993. At work, Jackie said, "America is getting a bargain with her. She's worth two Helen of Troys." She even discussed the possibility of making a return visit to the White House.

I told her she had a standing invitation to come here. It was something she was working herself up to, and [she] gave me every reason to believe that she would visit. She said she had no real desire before Bill became president to come back. She went, however, every year to Virginia to ride, and she laughed about how we would sneak her in, wearing a kerchief and old, baggy riding clothes through a side entrance so nobody would know she was coming in. And I think that's the way she would have really wanted to come in!

—HILLARY RODHAM CLINTON

When you get written about a lot, you just think of it as a little cartoon that runs along at the bottom of your life—but one that doesn't have much to do with your life.

—JACQUELINE KENNEDY ONASSIS

When it came to the projects that she supported over the years, Jackie sought publicity. When it came to her personally, being famous was the last thing she wanted out of life.

That Andy Warhol did a portrait, that there was iconography—she was dismayed by it and I'm not sure that that was something she would respond to. I can't fully convey this enough: she did not want a part of anything like that. Some famous people just glory in it, walking along the street, hoping to be recognized. Bob Hope, for example, went to Moscow where nobody knew him and he was struck by such waves of insecurity. There was nothing less a part of Jackie.

—GEORGE PLIMPTON

She didn't really think of herself as being famous. She thought that people who accomplished things in their own right—they were the ones who should be famous. Not her.

—NANCY TUCKERMAN

I'm sixty-two now, and I've been in the public eye for more than thirty years. I can't believe that anybody still cares about me or is still interested in what I do. . . . I don't have any desire to force myself into people's minds. It makes me uncomfortable to read about myself in the newspaper.

—JACQUELINE KENNEDY ONASSIS

Wherever she went, however, whatever she did, Jackie understood the reality that the media followed her every move in the hope of creating a news item. Since Doubleday was the only contact the public had for her, it was where she was most often sought out.

Her direct real phone line was 9747, and 9728 was the line to which the switchboard would transfer all incoming calls asking for Mrs. Onassis. I called that the kook line. You had to steel yourself for anything when it rang—UFO reports, conspiracy theorists, troubled people spewing out surrealism. And you'd get weird things in the mail—adult videos, women from Brazil proposing marriage to her son. It wasn't always funny. Someone once sent a gun. But she never had to take those calls, or open those letters. We all tried to protect her in just a daily normal office setting. By her being herself and you just treating her as a regular person, it was as if she was asking you to join in this conspiracy to fight all the celebrity garbage.

—SCOTT MOYERS

I used to worry about her going into town as the most famous woman in the world or at the races in Middleburg where people might have had a beer or two and bother her. She was quite capable of giving people the most polite slip. She would avoid people by saying thank you or something, and if they tried to get a picture or autograph, she simply said, "Oh, we're about to walk over there," or "I'm with some friends now." Always just right. Never, never rude.

—CHARLES WHITEHOUSE

Jackie never lent herself to any commercial venture, and if there was a suggestion that she was sponsoring a product—as when she was portrayed in a Christian Dior magazine ad—she took legal action. When exploitative books and articles appeared, however, she simply ignored them.

The sensational pieces will continue to appear as long as there is a market for them. One's real life is lived on another private level.

—JACQUELINE KENNEDY ONASSIS

Jackie never aimed for anything she wasn't. She wanted to express herself as a person as she felt she should, but she had no personal ambition. Her ambition was not in relation to her self-esteem or pride. She took herself as she was. She was not given to self-promotion, and if anything, she was a little bit suspicious of people who were.

—JOHN KENNETH GALBRAITH

In sending a friend a story about actor Steve Martin, she marked a part where he discussed fame: "There is nothing good about it. What's so demoralizing is that it has nothing to do with me. . . . It has nothing to do with my work. . . . It has to do with recognition. . . . It's not that your presence lets them get in touch with their fantasies. It's that your presence lets them get in touch with reality." Jackie scribbled, "That's the truth." If she was human enough to at times fall prey to the privileges of fame, she never fell prey to fame itself or indulged in the reality that she had become part of the consciousness of millions of strangers for some three generations.

I asked her how she managed to deal with the tabloid trash that was constantly being written about her. "The river of sludge will go on and on," she said. "It isn't about me."

—DAVID WISE, WRITER AND JOURNALIST

By the time I was being written about, I asked her how she handled it. She said, "I just don't read it." I believe that. It took willpower, and division between the public and the private.

—GLORIA STEINEM

In later life, however, Jackie learned to turn the tables on fame, deflating the attention with her droll humor. When once she and Carly Simon were swimming at the Vineyard, some helicopters with photographers circled up above them. Shrugging with resignation, Jackie stood in the water and said, "They must know you're here!" When she and a Doubleday executive rushed down the aisle of a plane to get seats at the back, all the other passengers stared in shocked curiosity, some continuing to look back throughout the flight. She stage-whispered to him, "They all know you!"

Once she was in my showroom, and I had some buyers from Neiman Marcus. She was trying on a suit. She came out and she saw all these people sitting there and she turned to them and said, "Don't you think this is lovely." And they almost fainted when they saw who was modeling. We used to laugh about it a lot.

—CAROLINA HERRERA, FRIEND AND DESIGNER

Once, over lunch, I asked her whether it ever bothered her that every pair of eyes was trained upon her. "That's why I always wear my dark glasses," she said. "It may be that they're looking at me, but none of them can ever tell which ones I'm looking back at. That way I can have fun with it!" A smile of almost pure glee illuminated her face.

—ANDRÉ PREVIN, AUTHOR AND CONDUCTOR

Once, she joined me while I was photographing at the University of Beijing. I introduced her as my assistant. She took notes, I took pictures. For an entire day, among students at the cafeteria and in dormitories, with professors and even the rector, she went completely unrecognized. This greatly delighted her.

—MARC RIBOUD

She was irreverent about herself, recalling silly situations and then impersonating herself and her reaction. Once, as she had tea with a friend of ours, the woman's daughter came in, stared at Jackie, and asked her, "Don't I know you from somewhere?" She was amused by that.

—CHARLES WHITEHOUSE

When she'd visit her mother, I'd meet and send her off at the airport. We would hug hello and good-bye, and when a crowd gathered to see her, she'd throw her arms around me, causing me to blush. "Now they'll be calling you the mysterious lover of Jackie O." She really ridiculed the silly attention given her by those inane magazines and television stories.

—YUSHA AUCHINCLOSS

Jackie could not have known on that day three decades earlier when she married John F. Kennedy that from then on she would have no anonymity, but by the 1990s, she had reached a certain degree of peace with it. At a press reception for a book Jackie edited on the private life of Catherine the Great, reporter Judith Martin asked if her "point of view had changed about the propriety of examining the private lives of public figures." Jackie responded, "When it's past, it becomes history." And if an historian someday used her letters? "I won't be here to mind."

HISTORY

One day at lunch, over scallop salads, we talked shop. But, as was usually the case with any conversation with Jackie, one thing inevitably led to another, and we found ourselves plunged deeply into a dissection of the country's propensity toward violence, the fracturing of the social consensus, the erosion of citizenship. Suddenly, she turned to me, and putting a slender hand upon my arm, she said, "Tell me, Steve, where did it all go wrong?" She was silent for a moment and then answered her own question. "It was Vietnam, wasn't it?" I didn't disagree. And then we traced the slippery slope that somehow had led from Vietnam to the films of Arnold Schwarzenegger—movies she refused to see. "I loathe," she said, "everything he stands for."

—STEVE WASSERMAN,
FORMER EXECUTIVE EDITOR, DOUBLEDAY

Jackie was understandably ambivalent about history. She read history, and she was conscious of the cause and effect of turning points in history. She had lived and made history herself. She realized that she was to most people a living symbol of an earlier point in history. Yet she never would permit herself to live in the past. "I want to savor it," she said of life, "I'd rather spend my time feeling a galloping horse, or the mist of the ocean up at Martha's Vineyard."

She was not unmindful of her obligations to history. It was untrue that she never gave an interview after leaving the White House. Besides the Teddy White interview and the Manchester tapes she did in 1964, she spoke often extensively with reporters at important points in her life: in 1967 about her life with her children; in 1968 about her remarriage; in 1972, she addressed personal misconceptions about herself; in 1977, she talked about returning to work; in 1978, she talked to Gloria Steinem at *Ms.* magazine about what working was doing for her; and in 1993 she discussed her achievements at Doubleday. She also granted two extensive oral histories in 1973 and 1981. In fact, she gave more interviews than many other former first ladies, such as Edith Wilson, Mamie Eisenhower, Bess Truman, and Pat Nixon. It was just that the public always wanted more from Jackie.

When her half-brother sent her a postcard of all six of the other first ladies gathered together, he humorously penned on the back, "Wish You Were Here!" Despite everyone else's perception of her, however, by 1980 Jackie rarely viewed herself as a former first lady. When it came to those of long acquaintance, she fondly remembered them as people—not as first ladies. She wrote and permitted publication of a letter to Lady Bird Johnson on her eightieth birthday, for example, and wrote a private letter to Pat Nixon in 1993, on her eighty-first birthday, with the knowledge that Mrs. Nixon was extremely ill. Her friendship with Hillary Clinton had more to do with enjoying her as a person, rather than sharing the same status.

It was also untrue that she refused to cooperate with authors and historians. She proofread Arthur Schlesinger's book on the Kennedy administration, gave extensive interviews for Rose Kennedy's autobiography, verified material for Richard Reeves in his book manuscript on President Kennedy, spoke freely to Doris Goodwin for her Kennedy family history, and responded to questions for a White House music history project. She made large contributions to the two-volume *First Ladies,* submitting handwritten responses to questions on long yellow lined paper, her writing reflecting that she wanted to set the record straight. In 1993, when a newspaper piece placing Hillary Clinton's role in health care legislation in an historical context was being researched, Jackie not only responded about her lobbying efforts for preservation but also wanted to be directly quoted.

And yet there were many contradictions in the highly complex Jacqueline Onassis. Her oral history with William Manchester, for example, was not to be released until fifty years after the deaths of her children, a situation comparable to releasing a Mary Lincoln oral history in 1995. Nor did Jackie want her previously unpublished letters to be printed. In fairness, it was as much a matter of Jackie's modest view of her own historical value as it was of her personal privacy. When Pat Nixon told her of the tremendous anticipation there was about the unveiling of her official portrait at the White House, Jackie was flattered but truly shocked. President Kennedy, she told Pat, was "the one who warrants consideration—not me. I could never think otherwise."

For much of her life, Jackie had defined her personal value as the wife of her husbands. It was not until after she found her niche as an editor that many of her insecurities fell away and she came to see her own place in history. By the time she was sixty, Jacqueline Onassis was capable of dispassionately, objectively viewing the self that she was as the thirty-one-year-old Mrs. John F. Kennedy. Pleased with results of *First Ladies,* for example, she told the book's editor, "Maybe now people will realize that there was something under that pillbox hat." On occasion, topics arose at work prompting White House anecdotes from her.

Once she was talking about *To the Inland Empire,* which she did with Stewart Udall, and she unself-consciously remarked, "He was secretary of the interior under Jack." It wasn't frequently that she talked about being first lady, but she wasn't obsessed with not talking about it. She was once talking about her interest in Hinduism and remembered this particular temple that she saw as first lady with her sister, and this shrine of a long stone in the temple. The big joke for the Indians was to get western tourists, especially girls, to take the grand tour and rub the stone for luck. She did. Only later did she find out it was actually the phallus of the Bathsheba.

—SCOTT MOYERS

Would Jacqueline Onassis have someday written her memoirs? She made it clear that she would not. In 1967, she worked closely with Molly Thayer in putting together an informal history of her years as first lady. This was the only period of her life that Jackie felt qualified as public domain. Still, in 1981, she expressed some ambivalence about not having written her memoirs:

> It's really a shame [that] I sort of never wanted to. So many people, you know, hit the White House with their dictaphone running! I never even kept a journal. I thought, I want to live my life, not record it. And I'm still glad I did that. I think there's so many things that I've forgotten.

In 1992, Jackie lunched with one of her authors, who had covered Kennedy in the White House. He pressed the memoir question, as did other friends and her family.

> I reminded her that several years before, in her mother's house in Georgetown, I had asked her when she would write her own book. She had laughed and replied, "Maybe when I'm ninety." This time, she said more. People change, she said. The person she might have written about thirty years ago "is not the same person today. The imagination takes over. When Isak Dinesen wrote *Out of Africa*, she left out how badly her husband had treated her. She created a new past, in effect. And why sit indoors with a yellow pad writing a memoir when you could be outdoors?"
> —DAVID WISE, WRITER AND JOURNALIST

> I once brought it up, that she had seen so much history and that it would be a shame not to record it. She didn't really say anything.
> —LISA DREW

> Our mother used to say to her, "Of course, Jackie, someday you must write your memoirs." She didn't respond to that.
> —JAMIE AUCHINCLOSS

> My great regret is that she never did this book that I think she could have done. I once wrote her a long letter about it, because she had told me this wonderful story about the president sitting next to Mrs. de Gaulle at the state dinner in Paris—while she and de Gaulle were speaking French together—and

the president couldn't think of anything to say. Finally in his desperate attempt to open things up in conversation, he said something about the centerpiece, and Mrs. de Gaulle responded flatly, if I recall, "We had a much better one yesterday." Little vignettes like that were so charming. I wrote Jackie this long letter and said, "Look, these stories must not be lost. You really must get them down, and I'll tell you what we'll do. Why don't we just sit down and record some of this and it won't be for publication. We won't tell anybody we're doing it. It can be for your children, but you must not let these stories go, because they're important." I thought that there might be a chance because it wasn't going to be for publication. She said, "Well, you know, I don't really want to sit at a window looking out at a field, and feel that life is going by."

—George Plimpton

And yet, as the years passed into decades, Jackie began to recall her White House years with people besides friends and family. At one event, she introduced a *New York Times* op-ed editor to the person "who first danced the twist" in the White House. When she edited a book on ballet impresario George Balanchine she freely talked to reporters about his advice on her cultural role as first lady. She also seemed eager to have her legacy accurately recorded.

In 1993, proposals were advanced for giving others recognition for saving Lafayette Square—including placing a bronze plaque. Jackie was most upset. She had, for good reason, avoided Texas all these years, but at last she said she was ready to come west and participate in studies related to the importance of the role of the client in architecture in which I proposed using her as the client and Lafayette Square as an example. She loved that.

—John Carl Warnecke

In later years, during a routine conversation, she was apt to mention "Jack," as if he were nearby—his favorite authors, places he'd visited, people he liked. She did likewise with Onassis.

She would talk about a person and say, "That was one of Jack's friends." I would stop short—"Jack"—the president. It was remarkable how easily she made me forget who I was speaking with.

—Gary Dunning

I told her how much it had meant to me [to meet President Kennedy] and how important I realized it was for presidents to try to inspire young people. And she just said that that's one of the things that he liked best about the job, that he observed that even when things were going terribly in Washington and nothing good seemed to happen, that if you kept trying to inspire young people and touch young people that it was something you could always do—even when the bills wouldn't pass Congress.

—President William Jefferson Clinton

She discussed Ari in casual conversation, in the context of some beautiful antiquity they might have seen together, or of some exotic part of the globe that they had traveled [to] together on the yacht. She mentioned him in a general fashion as being part of her life. But she never reminisced, she never looked back or pored over the past. She was part of the philosophy of being a "now" person; she lived completely in the "now." Which is not to say she didn't plan or look forward to things, but I don't think she had any expectations or apprehension of future events.

—Charles Whitehouse

Realistic, practical, Jackie moved ahead with life. Yet she still remembered. When a friend lost her husband in 1993, Jackie wrote movingly to her, reflecting her own effort to find comfort after loss. She said that there were no words that could help when a partner in life was lost, but that "love and time" could sustain her. "And later, memory."

TEN

A Full Year

1993–1994

But even if I have only five years left, so what, I've had a great run.

—Jacqueline Kennedy Onassis

Jackie Kennedy Onassis attending American Ballet Theater Gala with companion Maurice Tempelsman, May 1993.

SUMMER AT THE SHORE

BEFORE OPENING RED GATE FARM ON MEMORIAL DAY FOR THE SUMMER OF 1993, Jackie made one of her rare public appearances.

We hadn't had a big, successful gala for some time, but we thought of having one, and she agreed to be honorary chair. Held in May of 1993, it was extremely successful. My wife and I sat at her table and were a bit nervous, but she was bright, gentle, and very kind. It was my first experience watching the paparazzi go after her, and even the socialites. A funny thing, a couple of our dancers were invited for the first time to attend the gala, and a girl of about eighteen just walked up and tapped Mrs. Onassis on the shoulder and said, "Can I have my picture taken with you?" And a couple of the company members were appalled. But Jackie enjoyed it and posed because the dancer was a real person, not a hanger-on.

—GARY DUNNING

In June, Jackie returned one more time to Europe, voyaging with Maurice on the Rhone River, to France's Provence region, where the Bouviers had originated. Her attachment to France had remained strong. Four summers earlier, during that nation's Bicentennial celebration in 1989, she was right there in Paris on the Champs-Élysées to take in the fireworks and parade. In July, Jackie marked her sixty-fourth birthday—with no sign of slowing down.

Even though she was in her midsixties, there was never any inkling of her work load lessening. I had no notion of Jackie thinking about retiring. She carried on as if she was going to go on for twenty years.

—BRUCE TRACY

On Martha's Vineyard full-time by August, Jackie had a standing appointment in Oak Bluffs, a section of the island long occupied by generations of African Americans. Here, she met weekly with Dorothy West, a writer who had earlier enjoyed recognition during the Harlem Renaissance. Jackie had been reading West's short stories every week in the island newspaper, *Vineyard Gazette,* and was encouraging her to complete her second novel, *The Wedding,* begun years before, which Jackie would edit. West said she and Jackie were "mismatched in appearance" but "perfect partners."

I was without self-consciousness and so was she. Neither of us felt that we had to apologize to the other for being . . . different from the other and indeed [we] were enchanted by the difference. . . . She came to see me every Monday to assess my progress, driving herself in her blue Jeep, losing her way fairly regularly in the Highlands.

—DOROTHY WEST

At the end of August, when Maurice headed down to welcome the president and Mrs. Clinton and their daughter on board his boat for an afternoon cruise with members of the Kennedy family, Jackie's political instincts emerged as she turned to her brother-in-law. "Teddy, you go down and greet the president. . . . Maurice isn't running for re-election."

It was a glorious day. When word got out that we were going to the Vineyard, we heard from her that she hoped to get together. We spent the whole day together, starting out on Maurice's boat. We went out and traveled to all those little islands around the coast there, ending up anchored off a deserted island, and everyone went down to change for a swim. I came up to see Caroline and Chelsea standing on the highest diving board of this yacht—a good fifty feet, and they just jumped! On their way up to jump again, Chelsea said, "Come on, Mom, it was really fun." I said, "No, no I don't think so." Then my husband and some of the others were saying, Come on, jump. I went up. It was very high. And Jackie was down in the water, yelling, "Don't do it, Hillary! Don't do it! Just because they're daring you, you don't have to do it!" I went down a little lower before I jumped in.

Then we swam for hours. She was a great swimmer. She didn't just hang around in the water, she swam toward the island, then got out and walked on the rocky shore. Then we had lunch up on the deck while anchored there. The sun was shining, there was a breeze, it was cool, and we just sat and talked for hours. We motored around some more. We got back to the dock and went over to Jackie's house. It was such a refuge, so private, beautifully done, simple, not at all elaborate, just perfectly in tune with the surroundings. We took four-wheel vehicles to her private beach and walked down the shore. Caroline and Chelsea walked up ahead together. Jackie and I kind of lagged behind, talking on the beach. Then we came back, and Bill and I took everyone to dinner at a little inn run by James Taylor's family. We had a great night just talking about everything, and laughing, and it went late into the night.

—HILLARY RODHAM CLINTON

The most vivid memories I have of her are of the times we spent together on Martha's Vineyard. . . . We spent the day talking mostly about her life, the things they had done on their vacations, and things she had done with the children. And then at dinner . . . I sat with her, and we just talked for a long time. And she talked about President Kennedy and the White House, but it was all, it was always very personal. It was more like what their private life had been like. . . . It was very moving. . .

—PRESIDENT WILLIAM JEFFERSON CLINTON

There was also another special guest for Jackie as summer faded, one of the "sorority," a friend who had once shared the saddest moment of their history together.

That last summer, we saw each other again. She invited me for Sunday lunch. The house was down off of the main, winding road, a countryside type of world, where people are inclined to get into white slacks and bright tops, and live in them. Her house there spoke of her eloquently—casual, comfortable, in tune with the ocean so close by, but yet with elegance. The first thing you saw when you walked in the door was an Audubon painting of a waterbird. We ate out under an arbor of vines, with the sea, across the sand dunes and grasses, murmuring out beyond. It had the lulling qualities one wants in a vacation home. We talked about authors and the books coming across her desk and into her life, and the children, now grown of course. We did not reminisce about the past. In all of that, in looking back and remembering now, I have a feeling of ineffable sadness. She had just reached this quiet harbor of doing things she wanted to do, and being with people she wanted to do them with, and then, life came to an end.

—LADY BIRD JOHNSON

As summer faded, Jackie's growing family joined friends in a last picnic at the shore.

We were all enjoying ourselves at her annual Labor Day beach picnic. And there's a picture of Carly Simon and Jackie smiling, singing "Insy, Weensy Spider" for little Jack, her grandson, who was being held by his father, and he was happy, giggling. And Jackie was so happy, even though it was the end of a glorious summer. She had told me that year, "Come on up and I'll give you a kayaking lesson!" She was generous about including people in her activities, but I would never have presumed to ask, because she was so private and was busy and didn't get a chance—but I wanted to go kayaking with her. When we separated in September, I regretted that I had never gone. She said, "Don't worry, we'll do it first thing when I arrive next spring."

—ROSE STYRON

AUTUMN IN THE COUNTRY

BACK IN NEW YORK, JACKIE MADE HER FIRST PUBLIC APPEARANCE AT A DAYTIME event in Brooklyn, at a dance performance celebrating the 500th anniversary of Columbus's discovery of America. There, she unexpectedly came across an old familiar face, from college days at George Washington University.

She sat there very quietly at the Brooklyn Academy for a Jacques D'Amboise performance of a thousand New York City schoolchildren performing dances and music from the time of Columbus until the hip-hop era—a whole kind of panorama—and we had a chance to speak. She enjoyed it, she said, not only because of the choreography and the music, but also because she was watching a thousand children of all backgrounds together creating. She gave support to so many artistic events that did not bear her name, not only financially, but with her spirit.

—DAVID AMRAM

A few weeks later, on October 27, Jackie went with two friends to the Children's Storefront School in Harlem.

I started working in Harlem thirty years ago at a little storefront school, and it grew into an established tuition-free school for children from about the ages of two until the eighth grade. There are about fifty students. Jackie met a bunch of them, came on our committee, and donated several thousand dollars. She came up not only to talk to me about my autobiography, but also because she was interested in children. She arrived around nine o'clock and spent two hours at the school. We were talking in my little office. A very nice guy who lived on the street knew she was there, came in, and said, "Hi, Jackie." And she turned around and gave him a warm smile. She looked immensely fragile, almost transparent. She was exquisitely responsive, curious about the school and children. She was wonderful with the kids. She just sat quietly, and watched them, as she went to all the classes. The children responded—but they didn't know who she was—to the sweetness in her way with the little ones. More than polite. Truly interested.

—FRED O'GORMAN, FOUNDER, CHILDREN'S STOREFRONT SCHOOL

That night, Jackie cochaired the black-tie Centennial Celebration of the Municipal Arts Society, with 1,200 guests gathered in the newly restored Waiting Room of Grand Central Station. There, she presented an award in the shape of a crystal star to the Metropolitan Transit Authority chairman for its underwriting part of the restoration.

That fall, Jackie and I were seated together at a dinner. I was going through a tough time just then, being criticized for the book I was writing about the mistake of our Vietnam policy. I was feeling low and Jackie turned to me and said, "Just remember what Eleanor Roosevelt said—nobody can make you feel bad about yourself unless you give them permission."

—ROBERT MCNAMARA

In October, Jackie was once again before the eyes of the world at the rededication of the Kennedy Library. Ed Schlossberg had reconceptualized the museum exhibit halls, which now not only displayed objects and pictures but also conveyed an ambience of the times in which President Kennedy lived.

Jackie felt very strongly that the library museum should not just be a depository of political memorabilia. She felt it should give a sense of the values that permitted President Kennedy to have his extraordinary political opportunities. That was something she always wanted emphasized and stressed. Not just politics, but values.

—Senator Edward M. Kennedy

On the podium that day, Jackie was joined not only by her family and in-laws but also by President Clinton. Hillary Clinton was not there, but she spoke often with Jackie.

We talked on the phone a couple of times, and had a wonderful, long lunch again in her apartment. She gave me good pieces of advice on trying to get the White House to be a home. She was conscious of how, in her own time, it was a real challenge to fulfill her roles and responsibilities in a way that not only bore her own stamp, but also fit who she was. "You've got to do things that are right for you. Don't model yourself on anybody else. There are certain things other people may have done that are of interest to you, that you should learn about, but you have to be yourself."

—Hillary Rodham Clinton

November came around again. This year was the thirtieth anniversary of the president's assassination. While the annual media glare of television and magazine specials and newspaper coverage focused on her past, Jackie was in Middleburg enjoying life.

We teased each other about being fit. I said to her, "I get fairly out of breath, going around this course." And she said, "Well, I never get out of breath. I jog around the reservoir as you know." But when we finished, there she was at the finish line, her tongue hanging out, and I joked, "Jackie, I don't think you're doing as much jogging as you pretend!" During one of our team point-to-

Jackie Kennedy Onassis, Caroline Kennedy Schlossberg, John Kennedy, and President Bill Clinton at rededication of John F. Kennedy Library, October 1993.

point races, I entered our group for the "best older team." She pretended to be outraged! And I said, "But, Jackie, we weren't born yesterday you know." In fact, she didn't think of herself as "older," and it was hard to believe that she had been first lady thirty years before!

—CHARLES WHITEHOUSE

That month, when Jackie had an uncharacteristically bad tumble from her horse, and was knocked unconscious and had to be hospitalized for several days in Middleburg, she found that her usual strength had somewhat diminished. In the holiday season, however, she was back in full force. At a dinner, she was typically engaged in literary conversation.

We talked a lot about books, and a lot about Paris, and then we talked about the differences between the *Paris Review* crowd of the 1950s, and their attitude toward Paris, and the Hemingway crowd of the 1920s, and their attitude toward it.

—ADAM GOPNIK, ART CRITIC

During the Christmas season, Jackie went to the country again, to her home in New Jersey, with all three of her grandchildren. She took them across the road to Peggy McDonnell for cookies and hot chocolate. Jackie's grandson, not quite a year old, began to cry in her arms. McDonnell tried to calm the child, but he wailed louder. Finally, someone else had to be called in to soothe him. The two old friends, with many children and grandchildren between them, began to laugh about their reputedly great mothering skills.

> I remember her talking about how exciting it was for her to watch her grandchildren around the Christmas tree in her apartment, and how animated it made the moment. She took her granddaughter to the ballet, I believe *The Nutcracker*. She talked about how having grandchildren was reconnecting her to things like ballet that had been part of her earlier life.
>
> —GARY DUNNING

After Christmas, Jackie and Maurice flew to the Caribbean and began a cruise. Gradually, however, she became extremely ill, noticing pains in her stomach and back. After consulting by phone with her doctor in New York, she decided to fly back to enter the hospital for tests.

> At the very end of the year, Jackie and I spoke by phone, and she agreed to be chairman of our gala for that spring, in May 1994. She quite deliberately accepted and said she was especially looking forward to it. I know now that she knew she was ill.
>
> —GARY DUNNING

WINTER IN THE CITY

> It was right after Christmas vacation. She said, "Scott, do you want to come into my office?" And then she told me that she had been diagnosed with this thing. Yet she was very upbeat about it, said she felt great, and there was a good chance that she was going to beat it.
>
> —SCOTT MOYERS

For thirty years, Nancy Tuckerman had been her best friend's liaison and buffer with the media and had helped create a peaceful compromise between Jackie's need for privacy and the public's interest. Now, on February 11, 1994, she announced that Jackie had non-Hodgkin's lymphoma, a form of cancer, but that she had good prospects for recovery because of early detection.

She said, "I feel it is a kind of hubris. I have always been proud of keeping so fit. I swim, and I jog, and I do my push-ups, and walk around the reservoir—and now this suddenly happens." She was laughing when she said it. She seemed cheery and hopeful, perhaps to keep up the spirits of her friends, and her own. Chemotherapy, she added, was not too bad; she could read a book while it was administered. The doctors said that in 50 percent of cases lymphoma could be stabilized. Maybe she knew it was fatal. Maybe she didn't know at all, but even if she did, she still had hope for some other future.

—ARTHUR SCHLESINGER

In the midst of the harsh January weather, despite her shocking discovery, Jackie slipped out of New York for a day in Hyannis Port. There, she visited Rose Kennedy, ailing at 103 years old, in the familiar old big house of the Kennedy compound. It would be her last glimpse of the shore. "I'm almost glad it happened," she told a friend of her illness, "because it's given me a second life. I laugh and enjoy things so much more." She decided to just keep going on with life.

She never once complained of any pain. She never once let anything show. She kept coming in. She was so indomitable. She was so upbeat. Sometimes, she had Band-Aids on, and bruises from the therapy, but she carried on with her projects until the end. And then there was the day when she was rushed to the hospital the first time. When she came to consciousness in the hospital, she realized that she had an appointment with Peter Sis, over whose work she had so lovingly labored, and the first thing she thought about and said was, "Please call Peter Sis and tell him I won't be able to make it."

—SCOTT MOYERS

The worst illness Jackie had previously faced was a nagging sinus infection in the winter of 1962. She had feared that she might genetically inherit alcoholism and Alzheimer's, according to Yusha Auchincloss, but never cancer. Still, she used all the knowledge available to help herself.

She had long been fascinated with eastern religions, particularly Buddhism, and she had edited books on the healing plants of India, physical healing through meditation, and the powers of the mind. Jackie augmented her own spiritual beliefs with these larger perspectives. She also sought a rigorous medical treatment. And when she lost her hair because of chemotherapy treatments and wore a turban, her humor even helped her cope, as she joked to friends that maybe she would set off another fashion trend.

Even during the bitter cold, Jackie wanted to be in the fresh air. She took many walks in Central Park with Maurice, and even had a snowball fight with her granddaughters. She took in the movie *Schindler's List,* which recalled with startling reality the story of a group of Jews who were saved from death in concentration camps by hope and work. It was the last film she saw.

As March began, Jackie held on with great hope, and while she clearly couldn't make her sojourn to Middleburg, she joined the community fight there against Disney's proposed American history theme park in the area, lending her name to the formal organization that ultimately stopped the development threat. "I pray every night against that park," she told Eve Fout.

> When we got word that she was sick, everyone in town was upset. Not just the people who rode in the hunt or took care of the horses. The townspeople and the shopkeepers all felt that she was part of the place. The local baker, Jim Stein, baked Jackie her favorite cookies and sent them up to her in New York. They had spent a time getting to know each other.
>
> —CHARLES WHITEHOUSE

Jackie Kennedy Onassis walking with her son, March 1994.

I had wanted to get together with her for some time. Then when I heard she had cancer I called her and she was so upbeat, in fact so much so that it sounded like everything was going to be fine. I invited her down [to North Carolina] and she said, yes, let's get together in the summer. I really thought we would.

—MIMI CECIL

I remember our last encounter at the reservoir. . . . We walked slowly around the track. It was a bright and sunny day, but cold, and in the distance you could see the majestic skyline of Manhattan. She kept talking about spring, which was still weeks away. As we neared the exit to Fifth Avenue, she said quietly, "Let's trot next time." She veered off to the east and waved.

—JASON P. RUSSO, JOGGER AND ACQUAINTANCE

SPRING

Isn't it something? One of the most glorious springs I can remember. And after such a terrible winter.

—JACQUELINE KENNEDY ONASSIS

The colorful spring Jackie had been anticipating all winter finally arrived in New York, with Central Park's trees and flowers in full bloom. It brought a sense of relief for Jackie as she busied herself with editing and responding to a particularly heavy load of correspondence.

I sent her a note telling her how much the way she had lived her life with such style, grace, and beauty meant to me. She wrote back in her humble way saying that she was surprised. She answered at a time when her own situation must have been clear to her, but it was joyful and warm. You could just see her smiling. In my note I had said I looked forward to seeing her on the Vineyard this summer. The last line in her note was, "Definitely, this summer."

—CHARLAYNE HUNTER-GAULT, FRIEND

I got a note from her saying, "Don't worry, everything's fine, and soon we'll be out having festive lunches." Instead of writing something sad or dramatic, she wanted you to feel good and didn't want anybody to worry.

—JOHN LORING

When she became sick, I wrote to her immediately. In early April, she told me there was nothing to worry about, that spring had finally arrived, and everything was now well.

—VIVIAN CRESPI

Only once, in April, would Jackie have to stay at New York Hospital for treatment of an ulcer, a result of medication. It was at the same time that former President Nixon, who soon died, was being treated there. Upon her release, there were more walks with Maurice and her family, now in the tepid spring air. When she ventured out once alone, sitting on a bench near the reservoir, an elderly jogging colleague, Alberto Arroyo, sat down with her, and they talked of all the cultures she had explored in her world travels. He asked her favorite. She smiled. "What's wrong with America?"

Spring also brought her and her family back to their New Jersey home for Easter Sunday.

As her kids grew up, Jackie came out on her own to read, rest, and ride in Peapack. Most Easter Sundays would find her here, creating a silly hat. And when she had grandchildren, she called to see if she could bring them over for the parade. The last Easter found her here again, with a gorgeous scarf wound into a turban for her Easter bonnet, doing what seemed to make her very happy, sharing a special holiday with her family, watching the next generation winding across the green grass, singing "Put on Your Easter Bonnet" on a cool spring day.

—PEGGY McDONNELL

HOME AGAIN

I was getting coffee on the corner and I saw her walking down the street with Mr. Tempelsman on [May 13]. . . . She looked just fine. Everyone loved her a lot here.

—JEAN RIGAL, MANAGER, CHILDREN'S SHOE STORE

On Sunday, May 15, Jackie went out with Maurice, her daughter, and her grandson for a final walk in the park so familiar since childhood, along the winding paths she had strolled as a child while living at her Grandpa Lee's Park Avenue apartment. Disoriented and weak, she returned to the hospital the next day, only to discover there was nothing more that could be done for her.

Nancy told me a few hours before the end that she wasn't going to make it. Really, I thought, naive as I must have been, the thought had not entered my mind, because she was so sure, she was so strong, and she was carrying on as if this were just a minor nuisance. She was just getting bombarded with unbelievable levels of toxins, and she was just not letting it get her down. That's just who she was. I remember clearly when Nancy told me that that was going to be it. She wasn't going to make it. All I could think was that this was a true tragedy because I got a strong sense that this woman, at this point, had life figured out. And that she had surrounded herself with this constellation of cultured, wonderful people, that she had interests that she cared deeply about, she was constantly immersed in new and stimulating ideas, that she had strong family ties, that her personal life was absolutely solid, that she had places she loved—Virginia, the Vineyard, Manhattan. God, this woman had finally figured it out, and then it was snatched away.

—SCOTT MOYERS

Jackie wanted to see her closest friends and family members in the familiarity of her room, and so they came to 1040. She slipped in and out of consciousness. Many others came, outside 1040, hundreds of people who never knew her personally but felt they did—along with the media.

I remember driving quickly to New York from Newport to hopefully visit Jackie in time to say good-bye. I had recently been in Italy and sent her postcards with pictures of the art she knew so well, and left many dripping candles with prayers for a miracle or at least for the end of her suffering. No matter how uncomfortable she might be, she wanted those around her to feel comfortable. I arrived at her apartment in time to spend the evening visiting her off and on. Nancy said that Jackie knew I was there. At first, I didn't go in right away, and as soon as I saw Nancy and Maurice—the three of us went into the outer room. I calmed down, realizing that Jackie didn't want to see me upset. She knew when it was time to go. She left without complaint or regret. I touched her hand, kissed her good-bye, and whispered some words about her that I knew she needed to carry her through the evening. When I sat by her bedside, before she passed away, all the many memories of happy days flashed by.

—YUSHA AUCHINCLOSS

Throughout the day, sunlight splashed the pale sashes in her room, the familiar treetops of Central Park within sight. After a full day with her children and Maurice at her side, with friends and family in the outer rooms, Jackie fell asleep that night, and died.

> In all these years, I never heard Jackie being nasty or bitter or mean or spiteful. And that imagination she had. Beauty, brains, courage, passion, artistic sensibility. One of the most unusual personages of these times. You'd think it impossible for her to avoid becoming self-centered and egotistical. But that never happened to her. She was just as beautiful when she died. Even illness hadn't ruined her beauty. I was lucky to see her. She was peaceful. Is there any better way to leave this life?
>
> —SARGENT SHRIVER

The next morning, the twentieth of May, John Kennedy spoke to the press.

> Last night, at around ten-fifteen, my mother passed on . . . surrounded by her friends and her family and her books and the people and the things that she loved. And she did it in her own way and in her own terms, and we all feel lucky for that, and now she's in God's hands.

The afternoon before the funeral, there was a private wake at 1040. Jackie's casket was closed, beneath a colorful satin quilt from her bed. On a sunny Monday morning, her funeral was held at the same church where she had been baptized and confirmed, St. Ignatius Loyola. John Kennedy told the gathered friends, family, and colleagues about the readings he and and his sister had chosen. "Three things come to mind over and over again and ultimately dictated our selections. They were her love of words, the bonds of home and family, and her spirit of adventure."

> Stupid people have asked me, "Who are you going to replace her with at Doubleday?" And, I think, What? You can't replace her with anybody. There's no one to replace her.
>
> —STEVE RUBIN

After the readings, the cortege proceeded through New York, to the airport. The casket was flown to Washington, and the mourners proceeded to Arlington National Cemetery, to the site she had first seen as a teenage girl, some fifty-two years before, the spot where she had ignited the eternal flame for her husband's burial, thirty-one years before. There, "Jacqueline Bouvier Kennedy Onassis"

IN MEMORIAM

JACQUELINE BOUVIER KENNEDY ONASSIS

1929 - 1994

ST. IGNATIUS LOYOLA

MAY 23, 1994

GIVE me my scallop-shell of quiet,
My staff of faith to walk upon,
My scrip of joy, immortal diet,
My bottle of salvation,
My gown of glory, hope's true gage;
And thus I'll take my pilgrimage.

SIR WALTER RALEIGH

was buried besides John F. Kennedy, and their two children Arabella and Patrick.

At the funeral, Maurice Tempelsman recited the poem "Ithaka" by C. P. Cavafy. It had been one of her favorites, but her love of the romantic mystery about that Greek island had come from Onassis; Ithaka had been his favorite island. The summer after Ari's death, Jackie had studied Cavafy's poetry. Now Maurice paused after he finished reading, then added his own lines, as if it were a forgotten stanza:

And now the journey is over.
Too short, alas, too short.
It was filled with adventure and wisdom
laughter and love, gallantry and grace.
So farewell, farewell.

Caroline Kennedy read from the book given to Jackie at her high school graduation as a prize for winning the literary award. It was one of her favorite poems, "Memory of Cape Cod," by Edna St. Vincent Millay.

The wind in the ash-tree sounds like surf on the shore at Truro.

I will shut my eyes.

Hush, be still with your silly bleating, sheep on Shillingstone Hill.

They said: Come along!

They said: Leave your pebbles on the sand and come along, it's long after sunset!

The mosquitoes will be thick in the pine woods along by Long Neck.

The wind's died down.

They said: Leave your pebbles on the sand, and your shells, too, and come along,

We'll find you another beach like the beach at Truro.

Let me listen to the wind in the ash.

It sounds like surf on the shore.

SOURCES

THE QUOTED MATERIAL THROUGHOUT THE BOOK IS TAKEN FROM SEVERAL primary resources. The largest resource is from author interviews. The second largest resource is the Kennedy Library oral history interviews. The third greatest resource was from assorted biographies, memoirs, and autobiographies of individuals who knew or worked with Jacqueline Kennedy Onassis. Finally, a wide assortment of newspaper and magazine clippings provided quoted material.

General background material was also derived from biographies of Jacqueline Kennedy Onassis, John F. Kennedy, and Aristotle Onassis, and other books on the Kennedy family.

For the sake of brevity and grammatical accuracy, only portions of lengthier quotes were often used. In the case of some of those individuals who were interviewed by the author, and who had also written or spoken in other publications, quoted material was consolidated into one passage, separated by ellipses.

AUTHOR INTERVIEWS

Most of the quotes in this book, as well as the narrative background material, come directly from interviews conducted by the author. The following individuals provided their personal recollections, assessments, and anecdotes by personal or telephone interviews and conversations, or in writing, in 1995: Hugh D. "Yusha" Auchincloss Jr., James Lee "Jamie" Auchincloss, Letitia Baldrige, Kent Barwick, Edith Beale, Bernard Boutin, Joan Braden, Mimi Cecil, Schuyler Chapin, Hillary Rodham Clinton, Vivian Stokes Crespi, Charles Daly, John Davis, John Doar, Lisa Drew, Gary Dunning, Eve Fout, Doris Francisco, John Kenneth Galbraith, Roswell Gilpatric, Senator John Glenn, Claude de Renty du Granrut, Pamela Harriman, Kitty Carlisle Hart, Thomas Hoving, Lady Bird Johnson, Karl Katz,

Senator Edward M. Kennedy, Joan Bennett Kennedy, James Ketchum, Peggy McDonnell, George McGovern, Robert McNamara, Melody Miller, Richard Moe, Scott Moyers, Richard Neustadt, Fred O'Gorman, Fred Papert, Senator Claiborne Pell, George Plimpton, Lucky Roosevelt, Stephen Rubin, Pierre Salinger, John Sargent, Arthur M. Schlesinger Jr., Eunice Kennedy Shriver, Ted Sorenson, Helen Bowdoin Spaulding, Gloria Steinem, Rose Styron, Bruce Tracy, Aileen Bowdoin Train, John Carl Warnecke, Frank C. Waldrop, Charles Whitehouse, Duke Zeller. Some provided pictorial and archival materials, others provided lunch and dinner—and even some chauffeuring about. My great thanks to them all.

Remarks of Dave Powers in regard to *Profiles in Courage*, the 1958 and 1960 campaigns, the White House years, and Dallas are from a July 1987 interview with him by the author; materials from Muriel McClanahan and David Amram are taken from remarks and conversation with the author at the May 8, 1995, dedication ceremony of Jacqueline Kennedy Onassis Hall, George Washington University as broadcast on GWTV. The remark by Sargent Shriver came from a brief author conversation with him in May 1994, for the *Town and Country* tribute to Mrs. Onassis. My great thanks and appreciation to all of these individuals for their trust, time, and effort.

There were quite literally hundreds of people who might have been interviewed, but given the time and space limitations, I attempted rather to speak with people representative of particular aspects and periods of Mrs. Onassis's life. There were many other close friends, family members, and colleagues whose recollections could be illuminating, and no persons were studiously ignored.

ORAL HISTORIES

Oral histories from the John F. Kennedy Library included: Dean Acheson, Anthony Akers, Herve Alphand, Larry Arata, Janet Lee Auchincloss, Letitia Baldrige, Charles Bartlett, Howard Beale, Edward Berube, Bernard Boutin, Henry Brandon, Dinah Bridge, Jerry Bruno, Charles Burrows, Arthur Chapin, Alfred Chapman, Joseph Cerrell, Charles Cole, Maurice Couve de Murville, Richard Cardinal Cushing, William deMarco, Grace de Monaco, Michael DeSalle, William Douglas-Home, Angier Biddle Duke, Peter Edelman, William Fraleigh, Lawrence Fuchs, Elizabeth Gatov, Lincoln Gordon, Josephine Grennan, Kay Halle, Walter Hart, August Heckscher, Jacqueline Hirsh, John

Horne, Charles Horsky, Barbara Ward Jackson, Ira Kapenstein, Joseph Karitas, Mary Kelly, Carroll Kilpatrick, Laura Berquist Knebel, Theodore Kupferman, Belford Lawson, Peter Lisagor, Katie Louchheim, John Macy, Norman Manley, Thomas Mann, Jean Mannix, David McDonald, Godfrey McHugh, James McShane, Thurston Morton, Esther Peters, Nelson Pierce, James A. Reed, Leonard Reinsch, Charles Roberts, Leverett Saltonstall, Leopold Senghar, Maude Shaw, Hugh Sidey, Charles Spalding, Cordelia Thaxton, Stanley Tretick, Dorothy Tubridy, Nancy Tuckerman, Pamela Turnure, William Walton, Thomas Watson, George Weaver, Roy Wilkins, G. Mennen Williams, Harris Wofford, Clement Zablocki, Eugene Zuchert.

BOOKS

The third largest source of quotations was material from biographies, memoirs and autobiographies of the following:

Adams, William Howard. *Atget's Gardens.* Garden City, New York: Doubleday, 1979.

Baldwin, Billy. *Billy Baldwin Remembers.* New York: Harcourt Brace Jovanovich, 1974.

Buck, Pearl S. *The Kennedy Women: A Personal Appraisal.* New York: Cowles Book, 1970.

Cassini, Oleg. *In My Own Fashion.* New York: Simon & Schuster, 1987.

Clifford, Clark. *Counsel to the President.* New York: Random House, 1991.

Duchin, Peter. *Ghost of a Chance: A Memoir.* New York: Random House, 1996.

Kamante. *Longing for Darkness: Kamante's Tales from Out of Africa.* Collected by Peter Beard. New York: Harcourt Brace Jovanovich, 1975.

Kennedy, Rose Fitzgerald. *Times to Remember.* Garden City, New York: Doubleday, 1974.

Krock, Arthur. *The Consent of the Governed.* Boston: Little Brown, 1971.

———. *Memoirs: Sixty Years on the Firing Line.* New York: Funk and Wagnalls, 1968.

Lawrence, Bill. *Six Presidents, Too Many Wars.* New York: Saturday Review Press, 1972.

Louchheim, Katie. *By the Political Sea.* Garden City, New York: Doubleday, 1970.

Lowe, Jacques. *Jacqueline Kennedy, First Lady.* New York: Wykagyl, 1961.

Nixon, Richard. *RN.* New York: Grosset & Dunlap, 1978.

O'Donnell, Kenny P., and David F. Powers. *Johnny, We Hardly Knew Ye.* Boston: Little Brown, 1972.

Porter, Katherine Anne. *The Collected Essays and Occasional Writings.* New York: Delacorte Press, 1970.

Potter, Jeffrey. *Men, Money & Magic: The Story of Dorothy Schiff.* New York: Coward, McCann, Geoghegan, 1976.

Radziwill, Lee Bouvier, and Jacqueline Bouvier Onassis. *One Special Summer.* New York: Delacorte Press, 1974.

Reeves, Richard. *Convention.* New York: Harcourt Brace Jovanovich, 1977.

———. *President Kennedy.* New York: Touchstone, 1994.

Rhea, Mini. *I Was Jacqueline Kennedy's Dressmaker.* New York: Fleet Publishing Corp., 1962.

Sidey, Hugh, Chester V. Clifton, and Cecil Stoughton. *JFK: The Memories, 1961–1963.* New York: W. W. Norton, 1973.

Sidey, Hugh. *John F. Kennedy, President.* New York: Antheneum, 1963.

Sulzberger, Cyrus Leo. *The Last of the Giants.* New York: Macmillan, 1970.

Sidey, Hugh. *John F. Kennedy, President.* New York: Antheneum, 1963.

Talbott, Strobe, ed. *Khrushchev Remembers.* Boston: Little Brown, 1970.

Travell, Janet. *Office Hours: Day and Night.* New York: World Publishing, 1968.

Walker, John. *Self-Portrait with Donors.* Boston: Little Brown, 1974.

Wiseman, Carter. *I. M. Pei: A Profile in American Architecture.* New York: Harry N. Abrams, 1990.

Narrative background information was gathered primarily from the above sources, as well as many biographies of Jacqueline Kennedy Onassis, President Kennedy, and other assorted secondary sources. The two most accurate accounts of Jacqueline's life remain *Jacqueline Bouvier Kennedy*, by Mary Van Rensaeler Thayer (New York: Doubleday, 1961), and *Jacqueline Kennedy: The White House Years* (Boston: Little Brown, 1971), also by Thayer. These books most closely reflect the former first lady's own recollections because they were authorized by her, and she assisted in drafting them. She did not write them, as has been suggested. While Thayer, a family friend and reporter, gives a highly affectionate account and writes in a romanticized manner, her books provide the most detailed record of Jacqueline's early years and public life. The family letters and White House correspondence and memos to staff written by Mrs. Onassis reproduced by Thayer are the most revealing of the former first lady's intelligence, creativity, sense of humor, and vision for the nation.

Surprisingly, two of the paperback biographies written about Mrs. Kennedy while she was in the White House are an excellent source of her interview materials during the 1960 campaign and the White House years. *First Lady* (New York: Pyramid Books, 1962), by Charlotte Curtis, the *New York Times* reporter and Vassar classmate of Jacqueline; and *Jacqueline Kennedy* (Derby, Connecticut: Monarch Books, 1961), by Deane David Heller.

Laurence Learner's *The Kennedy Women* (New York: Villard Books, 1994) is one of the most valuable sources of accurate information on Jacqueline Kennedy, and he finally places her in the context of her time and background. The quotes and writings of hers which he uses in his book are excellent. Certainly the one book on the Kennedy years that gave me the widest range of quotes and materials was Ralph G. Martin's *A Hero for Our Times: An Intimate Story of the Kennedy Years* (New York: Fawcett Crest Books, 1983). Martin had many conversations with Jacqueline during the 1960 campaign which he uses, and from which I drew. He also interviewed many invaluable sources, such as Chuck Spalding, Charles Bartlett, Bill Walton, Larry Newman, and David Ornsby-Gore, who focused in on Jacqueline Kennedy's artistic, historical, and political sensibilities in a way that greatly assisted this book.

The single best source on the Bouvier family was written by John H. Davis. *The Bouviers* (New York: Farrar, Straus & Giroux, 1969) is not a romantic family tale but rather a painstakingly researched and thorough history, based on thousands of family documents. No other work provides such a thorough history and background. Kathleen Bouvier, the wife of Jacqueline's favorite cousin, Michel Bouvier, wrote *To Jack, With Love* (New York: Zebra Books, 1970), a beautifully written book, providing quite personal recollections of Jacqueline's father and mother, and their daughter's relationship with each.

Of all the books done on the Kennedy administration, only *A Thousand Days* (New York: Fawcett Premier Books, 1965), by Arthur M. Schlesinger Jr., seeks to integrate Jacqueline Kennedy and her social and political roles as first lady into the larger context of the presidency. This was written at a time when practically no historian considered any first lady of much value to a full account of a president. It was not only Schlesinger's friendship with Jacqueline that provided this focus, but also his respect for her intelligence. Although Ted Sorenson did not work closely with her in the White House years, his two works, *Kennedy* (New York: Bantam Books, 1965) and *The Kennedy Legacy* (New York: Macmillan, 1969), also include and assess her role in the president's life. A third book, *With Kennedy* (New York: Doubleday, 1966), by Pierre Salinger, also incorporates Jackie into the context of the administration, rather than treating her as apart from it.

Two individuals who worked closely with Jacqueline Kennedy in the White House also wrote excellent memoirs, which provide valuable resources: former Chief Usher J. B. West's, *Upstairs at the White House* (New York: Coward, McCann, Geoghegan, 1973) and Letitia Baldrige's *Diamonds and Diplomats* (Boston: Houghton Mifflin, 1968).

Other works that provide background for the narrative:

Bair, Marjorie. *Jacqueline Kennedy in the White House.* New York: Paperback Library, 1963.

Birmingham, Stephen. *Jacqueline Bouvier Kennedy Onassis.* New York: Grosset & Dunlap, 1978.

Brown, Gene, ed. *The Kennedys: A* New York Times *Profile.* New York: Arno Press, 1980.

Carpozi, George. *The Hidden Side of Jacqueline Kennedy.* New York: Pyramid Books, 1967.

Carr, William H. A. *Jacqueline Kennedy: Beauty in the White House.* New York: Magnum, 1961.

Dareff, Hal. *Jacqueline Kennedy, a Portrait in Courage.* New York: Parents Magazine Press, 1963.

Goodwin, Doris Kearns. *The Fitzgeralds and the Kennedys.* New York: Simon & Schuster, 1987.

Guthrie, Lee. *Jackie: The Price of the Pedestal.* New York: Drake Publishers, 1978.

Gutin, Myra. *The President's Partner: The First Lady as Public Communicator, 1920–1976.* University of Michigan, 1983.

Hall, Gordon Langley. *Jacqueline Kennedy: A Biography.* New York: F. Fell, 1964.

Harding, Robert T. *Jacqueline Kennedy, A Woman for the World.* New York: Encyclopedia Enterprises, 1966.

Lester, David. *Jacqueline Kennedy Onassis.* New York: Birch Lane Press, 1994.

Lieberson, Goddard, ed. *John Fitzgerald Kennedy ... As We Remember Him*. New York: Macmillan, 1965.

Lincoln, Anne H. *The Kennedy White House Parties*. New York: Viking, 1967.

Manchester, William. *Portrait of a President: John F. Kennedy in Profile*. Boston: Little Brown, 1962.

McLendon, Winzola. *Don't Quote Me: Washington Newswomen and the Power Society*. New York: Dutton, 1970.

Means, Marianne. *The Woman in the White House*. New York: Putnam, 1963.

Peterson, Peter. *Jacqueline Kennedy, La Première Dame des États-Unis*. Paris: Centre European de Press et d'Édition, 1963.

Safram, Claire. *Jacqueline Kennedy, Woman of Valor*. New York: Macfadden-Bartell, 1964.

Shulman, Irving. *Jackie: The Exploitation of a First Lady*. New York: Trident Press, 1970.

Stevens, M. Metryl. *Jacqueline Bouvier Kennedy, First Lady of the United States*. New York: Lifetime Heritage, 1964.

Suares, J. C., and J. Spencer Beck. *Uncommon Grace*. Charlottesville, Virginia: Thomasson-Grant, 1994.

Time, editors. *Remembering Jackie*. New York: Warner Books, 1994.

U. S. President's Commission on the Assassination of President Kennedy. Washington, D.C.: U. S. Government Printing Office, 1964.

Wolff, Perry Sidney. *A Tour of the White House with Mrs. John F. Kennedy*. Garden City, New York: Doubleday, 1962.

Biographies of Aristotle Onassis that were used for background include:

Brady, Frank. *Onassis*. Englewood Cliffs, New Jersey: Prentice-Hall, 1977.

Fraser, Nicolas, Phillip Jacobson, Mark Ottaway, Lewis Chester. *Aristotle Onassis*. Philadelphia: Lippincott, 1977.

Evans, Peter. *Ari: The Life and Times of Aristotle Socrates Onassis*. New York: Summit Books, 1986.

Frischauer, Willi. *Onassis*. New York: Meredith Press, 1968.

Lilly, Doris. *Those Fabulous Greeks*. New York: Cowles Book Co., 1970.

The two most controversial biographies of Jackie—Kitty Kelley, *Jackie O* (New York: Lyle Stuart, 1978); and David Heymann, *A Woman Named Jackie* (New York: Lyle Stuart, 1989)—contain some original documentation, letters, and other materials directly from the hand of Jacqueline Onassis. They also contain several remarks by individuals which add greatly to the portrait of a person of political insight and perception. Heymann's interview with David Ornsby-Gore, for instance, is valuable in its political commentary, as are quotes from Charles Bartlett, Charles Spalding, and Godfrey McHugh.

OTHER RESOURCES OF THE JOHN F. KENNEDY LIBRARY

In addition to the oral history interview transcripts of the John F. Kennedy Library (JFKL), a variety of sources were used that are available there only.

Jacqueline Kennedy Onassis Newsclipping Files

The Kennedy Library has an extensive clipping collection of two boxes covering the life of Mrs. Onassis from the time of her marriage until her death, representing hundreds of printed articles and full-length stories. Some of the clippings, primarily newspaper pieces, are undated, however, and their publication of origin is not identified. There are also clippings from magazines, most of which are identified and dated.

The author conducted further research for material in publications not included in the JKO clipping files, most of which were dated from the time of her death in May 1994 and several weeks afterward. In general, publications from which attributed quotes derived included *Town & Country*, *Vanity Fair*, *People*, *Time*, *Newsweek*, *U.S. News & World Report*, *Ladies' Home Journal*, *Ms.*, *Paris Match*, *Good Housekeeping*, *McCall's*, *The New Yorker*, *New York Times*, *New York Post*, *New York Daily News*, *Washington Post*, *New York*, *New York Journal-American*, *New York Herald Tribune*, *Boston Globe*, *Boston Herald*, and *Washington Post*. The UPI wire service stories from May 19–23, 1994, were also included.

Manuscript Collections at John F. Kennedy Library

Items also used in research were taken from the following collection: John F. Kennedy, Pre-Presidential Papers; President Kennedy's office files; White House Central subject files; Personal Papers of John F. Kennedy; White House staff files of Chester Clifton Jr.; White House staff files of Pierre Salinger; Personal Papers of Theodore Sorenson; Democratic National Committee files; The Arthur M. Schlesinger Jr. Papers; August Heckscher Papers; Bernard Boutin Papers; White House press releases; the White House social files; Vogue magazine file; JBKO accessioned items, manuscripts 1964–1994, uncatalogued; Audio-Visual Archives, Still Photographs, Motion Picture Films and Sound Recordings of Jacqueline Kennedy Onassis; the Greek press on Mrs. Kennedy's visit to Greece, June 1961, clipping book; "The Kennedys in Mexico," reprinted from *Catholic Messenger*, Davenport, Iowa, July 12, 1962; H.S. *Mordia*, Welcome presented to Jacqueline Kennedy, during Indian visit, 1962; Theodore H. White, "Camelot Documents."

OTHER SOURCES

Southhampton Hospital; East Hampton Free Library, East Hampton Star microfilms, 1929–1940 and Jacqueline Onassis file; Miss Porter's School Archives including Jackie Bouvier's published work in *Salmagundy*; George Washington University TV; National Holocaust Museum; Office of the U. S. Senate historian; Martin Luther King Jr. Library, Washingtoniana Collection, *Washington Star* Collection, 1953–1981, and *Washington Times-Herald*, 1951–1953; Jacqueline Onassis oral histories, Lyndon B. Johnson Library, and John Sherman Cooper papers, University of Kentucky; manuscript material and notes from Jacqueline Onassis to author, 1987, 1989, in preparation for *First Ladies*, vols. 1 and 2 (New York: William Morrow, 1990, 1991); Municipal Arts Society Library, newsletters, 1984–1994; *A Tribute to Jacqueline Kennedy Onassis* (privately printed, New York: Doubleday, 1995); *Paris Review*, Twenty-fifth Anniversary, 1981; John F. Baker interview with Jacqueline Onassis, *Publishers Weekly*, April 10, 1993.

INDEX

Moyers, Scott, 286, 287, 307, 322-324, 325-326, 331–332, 349, 350, 354
Moynihan, Daniel Patrick, 147-148, 275
Ms. magazine, 273, 335
Municipal Arts Society, 265, 274-276, 346
Munro, Ronald, 95

National Archives, 213
National Endowments for the Arts and Humanities, 163, 170, 312
National Gallery of Art, 23, 139, 140, 168, 246
National Geographic magazine, 143
National Trust for Historic Preservation, 144
Nehru, Jawaharlal, 148, 153
Neustadt, Richard, 216, 133-134
Newsweek magazine, 99
New York Catholic Charities, 261
New York City Ballet, 163, 165
New Yorker, The magazine, 55, 126, 263
New York Journal-American, 16
New York Philharmonic, 165
New York Shakespeare Festival, 165-166
New York State Assembly, 310, 312
New York Times, 9, 14, 60, 81, 143, 156, 161, 274, 284, 338
Nichols, Mike, 229
Niebuhr, Reinhold, 115
Nixon, Patricia, 69, 120, 255-256, 336
Nixon, Richard M., 95, 205-206, 353
Nobel Prize, 167, 231, 307
Norton, Mary (great-grandmother), 12
Norton, Sue, 33
Nuclear Test Ban Treaty, 181-182, 195
Nureyev, Rudolf, 321

Octagon House, Washington, 64-65
O'Donnell, Kenny, 74, 107, 109, 113, 115, 150, 169-170, 180
O'Ferrall, Frank, 102
O'Gorman, Fred, 346
Old Executive Office Building, 147
Olympic Airlines, 250
Olympic Towers, 251
Onassis, Alexander, 239, 250, 258

Onassis, Aristotle: biography of, 239; death of, 259, 265-267; early relationship of with Kennedys, 97-98, 110, 194, 231, 237; marriage of to Jackie, 242-243, 248-250, 251-252, 258-261
Onassis, Artemis, 239, 240, 265, 266, 267
Onassis, Calirrohe, 239
Onassis, Christina, 239, 240, 250, 266-267
Onassis, Jacqueline Bouvier Kennedy:
-career of as editor, 270-274, 285-288, 306-309, 331, 355
-education of, 17-19, 32-37, 38-39, 28, 48-50
-family relationships of: born, 8-9; with father, 26, 27-28, 104-106; forebears of, 10-13; with grand-father, 12; with mother, 26, 29, 30, 202
-as First Lady: as activist for his-toric preservation, 139-144, 144-148; as diplomat, 148-156; political interests of, 170-182; running the White House, 125-126, 128-207, 130-132
-as icon, 2-3, 5, 132-135, 330-332
-interests of: animals, 14, 16; the arts, 162-170, 326-328; fashion, 120, 124, 187-188; foxhunting, 304-306; Francophilia, 112, 150; history, 42-43, 162; jog-ging, 295, 297, 351; languages, 29, 37-38, 93, 109-110; poetry, 20-21, 34, 85-86; reading, 17-18, 112, 114, 118, 137, 254, 261, 271; space program, 176. *See also* historic preservation
-as journalist, 60-64, 65-67, 67-69, 74, 75-76, 290
-last illness of, 349-353, 355-357
-as mother: 95, 100-101, 157-162, 193, 224-226, 314-316; and grandmother, 316, 348-349
-and John F. Kennedy: assassina-tion of, 196-207; courtship, 56, 70-75, 76-77; early marriage of, 85-89, 92, 184; later marriage of, 101-104, 182-189; wedding of, 79-82, 105
-marriage of to Ari Onassis, 2, 238-243, 250-252
-as New Yorker, 4, 221, 227-228, 276-278, 294-297. *See also* 1040 Fifth Avenue
-and politics: 67-69, 90-95; as

campaigner, 84, 109-119, 121-123; on gun control, 257; as lobbyist, 310; and Stevenson, 98-99, 112, 193
-and Robert F. Kennedy: after John Kennedy's death, 219, 231-232, 235-236, 237-238; before John Kennedy's death, 79, 86, 101, 137, 202
travels of: Europe, 37-44, 56-59, 149-152, 155, 343; Greece, 151, 194-196, India and Pakistan, 153-155; Israel, 281; Latin America, 152-153; Mexico, 83, 155, 235; New Mexico, 280; Russia, 278-280; Thailand and Cambodia, 232-233
Onassis, Metrope, 239, 266
Onassis, Socrates, 239
Onassis, Tina Livanos, 239
Ormsby-Gore, David, 178, 180, 181
Oswald, Lee Harvey, 202
Out of Africa, 263

paparazzi, 257, 293
Papert, Fred, 219, 274, 276-278, 282
Parades, Providencia, 189, 319
Parent, Fred, 315
Paris Review, 271, 348
Patnaik, Naveen, 280, 323
Peale, Rembrandt, 141
Peapack, New Jersey, 223, 224, 348–349, 353
Pearson, David, 203
Pei, I.M., 214-215, 281, 288
Pell, Claiborne, 163-164
Pennsylvania Avenue Redevelopment, 147-148, 204
Perse, St. John, 168
Peters, Charles, 115
Phillips, Carol, 55
Pierce, Nelson, 140, 202-203, 206
Plimpton, George, 231, 249, 271, 272, 319, 330-331, 337–338
Porter, Katherine Anne, 103
Powell, Adam Clayton, 123
Powell, Lewis, 276
Power of Myth, The, 2, 307
Powers, Dave, 79, 93, 96, 109, 115, 117, 198, 201, 215
Prendergast, Maurice, 135
presidential advisor on the arts, 163, 164-165
Presidents, The, 144
Previn, André, 333
Prix de Paris contest, 52-55

ILLUSTRATION CREDITS

Every good faith effort was made to determine the origin of each illustration.